IN
PUBLIC
SERVICE

IN PUBLIC SERVICE

A History of the Public Service Executive Union 1890-1990

GARRY SWEENEY

Public Service Executive Union
with assistance from the Institute
of Public Administration

© Garry Sweeney 1990

ISBN 1 872002 71 4

All rights reserved. No part of this publication may be reproduced or transmitted in any form or by any means, electronic or mechanical, including photocopy, recording, or any information storage and retrieval system, without permission in writing from the publisher.

Published by
Institute of Public Administration
57–61 Lansdowne Road
Dublin 4
Ireland

First published 1990

Index by Helen Litton
Typeset in 11/12 Bembo by Brunswick Press Limited
Printed in the Republic of Ireland by
Brunswick Press Limited

Contents

Foreword by Dan Murphy		ix
Chapter I	*To the Anglo-Irish Treaty*	1
Chapter II	*1923 - 1935*	29
Chapter III	*1936 - 1950*	74
Chapter IV	*1951 - 1969*	122
Chapter V	*1970 - 1990*	198
Notes		270
Index		274
Plates between		86–87
		198–199

This book is dedicated to all those who served the union loyally during its first hundred years and to those who carry on the work today. It is hoped that, in a modest way, it will serve to record their efforts in the history of the Irish trade union and labour movement.

FOREWORD

History tends to be seen as a record of the doings of kings, presidents and prime ministers. There are wars, battles, revolutions, and great movements from the past — frequently described in heroic terms. The pages of history are littered with the work of famous men — and occasionally of famous women. While there has been a greater emphasis on social and economic history in recent times, history is still seen as something concerned primarily with the mighty in society.

Our story is more mundane, but nonetheless heroic in its own terms. The history of the Public Service Executive Union is not concerned with the famous or the mighty, even though they impinged on the activities of the union from time to time. Rather it is concerned with the lives and affairs of the Little People.

Yet in its own way our history is one that is just as great as the traditional view of history and just as important to the daily lives of our members. Without the union, our members' lives would be significantly poorer in many respects than they now are. Members would have no effective means of countering the decisions of government or management. The union, by providing a collective power to its members, gives them an opportunity to have their rights recognised and respected.

It is appropriate, therefore, at the time of the celebration of the union's centenary, that we are publishing Garry Sweeney's history because it enables the current generation of union members to acknowledge those who, by their willingness to accept sacrifice and — not infrequently — retribution, have created this union. Their sacrifice and their thankless daily grind of organisation and work have provided the current generation with an organisation that assists members collectively on a daily basis.

Without the work of our predecessors, we would not have the organisation we have today. It is against this background that this history is being published. It is a salute to all the unknown, unsung but yet great historical figures who have worked so hard over the past hundred years to build up the union.

Treaslaimis doibh!

Dan Murphy, General Secretary
October 1990

I

To the Anglo-Irish Treaty

The executive or middle management grades of the Irish civil service developed within the imperial civil service. On the transfer of civil servants to the service of the new Irish state, the grades had reached a degree of development that has withstood the passage of time without significant change. The Society of Civil Servants, which represented the executive grades in the United Kingdom civil service, stated in its submission to the Fulton Commission:

... the general executive class, broadly as now constructed, came into being in 1920 as a result of the recommendations of the Reorganisation Committee of the National Whitley Council. Based upon the accumulated experience of all the various enquiries into the Civil Service from 1853 onwards, and being the work of those who on both Official and Staff Sides were intimately acquainted in practice with the work of a wide range of Departments, the Committee's appraisal of the needs of the Service and the proper classification of its function rested upon sound and knowledgeable foundations.[1]

The report of the Fulton Committee states that the UK civil service is fundamentally the product of the nineteenth-century philosophy of the Northcote-Trevelyn report of 1854. Before the implementation of this report, appointments to the civil service had been based on patronage, but there is some evidence that, even within the patronage system, forms of joint action were beginning to develop. As officials became conscious of common grievances, they drew up collective petitions to their superiors.[2]

The civil service as it was in 1922 developed through a series of reports, the most notable of which were:

In Public Service

   Northcote-Trevelyn report of 1854
   Playfair Commission of Inquiry report of 1875
   Ridley Royal Commission report of 1888
   MacDonnell Royal Commission report of 1914
   Report of the Reorganisation Committee of 1920

The need to make representations to these bodies gave an impetus to the establishment of staff organisations — the commissions and committees themselves wished to take evidence from organisations rather than from individuals. It was an organisation set up to prepare an elaborate statement to the Ridley Commission that led to the establishment of the Second Division Clerks Association in 1890. An examination of the reports listed above will show that the executive class underwent a number of changes of title, as follows:

   regulation II clerks
   lower division clerks
   second division clerks
   executive officers.

At various times temporary staff organisations existed for specific purposes, but the first permanent association catering for the class was that set up in 1890.

The privilege of petition had long been established for civil servants. Therefore, although the efforts of the first combinations could be interpreted as an awakening of a trade union movement, the groups' activities actually more closely resembled a simple extension of the traditional petition privilege, revised to meet changes in the framework of the civil service. The limited extent of official obstruction in the early stage of organisation tends to substantiate the latter view. Not until the turn of the century, when associations begin to press for recognition as permanent staff representatives, do we more frequently find the familiar employer objection to employee usurpation of managerial prerogative. The passage of the Trade Union Acts of 1871 and 1876 had little effect on the attitudes of civil servants, except among manipulative workers in the Post Office. As yet, few civil service clerks saw a need for unions that would constantly review working conditions and negotiate regularly with the employer. The first associations

To the Anglo-Irish Treaty

were temporary bodies, created periodically to take over from individuals the task of preparing and presenting memorials.

The 1890s saw the formation of the first permanent staff associations. The Second Division Clerks Association was one of the earliest and, indeed, was the first all-service organisation. The changes in the organisation and functions of the civil service will be described later in this chapter in the context of the various commissions set up to inquire into the service and the staff reaction of these bodies. This led to the establishment of the Association of Executive Officers of the Civil Service and the transfer to the Irish service.

NORTHCOTE-TREVELYN

The centennial of the publication of the Northcote-Trevelyn report was celebrated in the mid-1950s. The civil service unions joined in these celebrations, thus emphasising the importance that present-day civil servants attach to the report.

The principal recommendations of the Northcote-Trevelyn report were:

1. To provide, by a proper system of examination, for the supply of the public service with a thoroughly efficient class of men.
2. To encourage industry and foster merit, by teaching all public servants to look forward to promotion according to their deserts and to expect the highest prizes in the service if they can qualify themselves for them.
3. To mitigate the evils that result from the fragmentary character of the service and to introduce into it some element of unity, by placing the first appointments in other departments than their own and introducing into the lower ranks a body of men (the supplementary clerks) whose services may be made available at any time in any office whatsoever.

In 1870, the chancellor of the exchequer, Robert Lowe, persuaded Gladstone to propose to cabinet that a system of open competition be introduced. The cabinet raised no objection to the proposal, except for one or two departments. At the same time departments were to be organised on the basis of a superior and a lower grade of clerk, with a separate class of copyists or writers. G. A. Campbell mentions that while the

In Public Service

Treasury issued regulations on the staffing of offices, departments had their own views on the class of employee most suitable for their particular work.[3] Some chose to have a staff composed principally of the superior grade, others favoured the lower grade for all duties. Division of work was a novelty in most departments, and a reorganisation of this kind could not be carried through satisfactorily without much more guidance than the Treasury was able to give. No uniform scales of salaries had been introduced and a man on the lower grade in one department might be paid more than his counterpart in another department which had chosen to put its staff on the superior grade. Complaints of the injustice of the arrangements and of the chaos in the departments resounded in Westminster and elsewhere and, in April 1874, the government felt compelled to order a comprehensive review of the whole field by another civil service inquiry commission.

THE PLAYFAIR INQUIRY COMMISSION

The commission of inquiry chaired by Sir Lyon Playfair[4] was set up by letter from the chancellor of the exchequer dated 27 April 1874. The inquiry examined the following matters:

1. The method of selecting civil servants.
2. The principles upon which men should be transferred from office to office, especially in cases where one establishment has been abolished or reduced in numbers, and where there were redundant employees, whose services should, if possible, be made available in other departments.
3. The possibility of grading the civil service as a whole, so as to obviate the inconveniences that result from the differences in pay in different departments.
4. The system under which it was desirable to employ writers or other persons for the discharge of duties of less importance than those usually assigned to established clerks, or purely temporary duties.

The commission found that the work of the offices was carried on by staff officers, by two grades of established clerks appointed under what was known as regulations I and II, and by a fluctuating body of writers. The regulation I clerk was appointed from examination of a higher order from the best class of university merit. The regulation II clerk was selected by open competition in an examination of a more moderate kind.

Staff officers differed very widely in different offices, in numbers, salary and position. They were appointed either from the clerks or from outside the office. In general, examinations were dispensed with.

The commission proposed that the service should be divided into four divisions: staff officers, higher division, lower division and boy clerks. All candidates for the higher division should pass a preliminary test examination open to all persons over the age of seventeen. It was proposed that, in future, entry to any of these levels should be by means of examinations, the degree of difficulty of which would vary from one level to another.

The commission then looked at the possibility of grading the civil service as a whole and remarked on the tendency of grading offices to employ as much inferior labour as possible. The report of the commission stated that beyond the two grades of clerks there should be staff appointments, including such officers as chief clerks and principal clerks; the numbers and pay should be fixed with reference to the work of each department. The selection of men to fill those offices should be left to the heads of each department, with recourse, if necessary, to the outside world.

The commission considered that the pay of the higher division should attract men of a liberal education who otherwise would go into the professions. The concept of 'duty pay' was recommended. This was in accordance with the current practice of the Bank of England and of various private banks and commercial establishments. The duty pay was to be attached to superior duties and work of a special character. It was to be given in annual payments of various amounts, say £50, £100 and £200.

Regarding the transfer of men generally from office to office, and from one branch to another within the same office, the commission considered that transfer could be easily arranged in the lower division of the service where the work and pay would be uniform throughout the different offices, and that every clerk appointed to the lower division should hold himself ready to serve at any time in any office.

Promotion from the lower to the higher division of the service should be a rare occurrence. This would be necessary, if there was to be any educational test for the higher division, and reasonable if only because of the character of the work in the inferior grades, which would be rarely calculated to develop superior capacities. A promotion should not take place without a certificate from the Civil Service Commissioners, granted upon the special recommendation of the head of the department, with the assent of the Treasury, and published in the Gazette. The lower division, however, should be allowed some extension of time beyond that fixed for the outside public, during which it would be eligible to compete for admission to the list of candidates for the higher division. Nevertheless, such a privilege should be extended only to those whose conduct had satisfied the heads of the departments in which they had served.

The report's recommendation of the recruitment of boy clerks had, in at least one respect, significant implications for the development of the service. It was recommended that boy clerks should not be retained after age nineteen, but with approved good service they should be allowed to compete for a limited number of men clerkships of the lower division. There was considerable difficulty in certifying sufficient boy clerks as suitable for such promotion. In an effort to overcome this difficulty, the new grade of assistant clerk was introduced. This grade was later to become the main clerical grade in the civil service.

The grade of lower division clerk was introduced into the permanent civil service by order in council dated 12 February 1876.

THE LOWER DIVISION CLERKS MEMORIALISTS

The lower division clerks rapidly found that their interdepartmental class, with identical conditions of service, emphasised the need for co-operation on grievances. Furthermore, with the grade now centrally controlled by the Treasury, it appeared useless to appeal only to department heads.[5] In June 1880 a

To the Anglo-Irish Treaty

memorial signed by 660 lower division clerks was sent directly to the Treasury. The memorial sought an adjustment of salary increments. The Treasury responded with one small change in the incremental scale. The Treasury minute commented: 'The uniform character of this branch of the Service explains why this memorial, which is also financial in character, has been presented to the Treasury, and why my Lords have consented to receive it, and to deal with it directly.' However, the minute contained the following warning: 'But the Clerks are then warned that they are not encouraged to regard themselves as privileged to act independently of the heads of the offices in which they are for the time being employed. My Lords intend to give no countenance to any such procedure.'

THE RIDLEY COMMISSION 1888

The lower division clerks availed of the opportunity presented by the establishment of the Ridley Commission[6] to organise a general committee with the object of preparing a statement to be set before it. The commissioners listened to representations from lower divison clerks in fifteen departments. The case for the whole grade of almost 3,000 men was then summed up by representations of the general committee.[7] The clerks emphasised the fact that pay and prospects in the lower division compared unfavourably with those of clerks in private business.

The official side point of view was put by the permanent secretary to the Treasury, Sir R.E. Welby. The general service nature of the lower division grade clearly was causing concern to the Treasury. Welby said that 'the Trade Unions you are creating will probably be too strong for the Government and probably too strong for Parliament'. He went on: 'these men act practically like one man, and bring all their political influence to bear. We have seen very formidable meetings from a Government point of view, held in consequence.' The Treasury objected to grading because it might increase the power of combination.

Having reviewed the evidence, the commissioners affirmed that the young men of the grade who had entered the service since the 1876 order in council had been excellent. Yet they were not surprised to find that, partly owing to the keenness of the competition and the expectations aroused by success in it, the prospects of promotion were disappointingly slim. Still, they considered that it would be out of the question to promote clerks when higher service was not required, simply to provide advancement for them. Although individual men in the grade were probably fit for, and were indeed employed in some instances on higher work than had been contemplated in the order in council, the commissioners thought that the grade as a whole was not inadequately remunerated. With regard to promotion from the lower division, the commissioners were emphatic:

> ... we think that routine promotion by seniority is the great evil of the Service, and that it is indispensable to proceed throughout every branch of it strictly on the principle of promotion by merit, that is to say, by selecting always the fittest man, instead of considering claims in order of seniority, and rejecting only the unfit. It is no doubt true that objections on the score of favouritism may arise in the application of such a rule in public departments, and that the intervention of Members of Parliament also presents an obvious difficulty, but we think that such constant vigilance, tact, and resolution, as may fairly be expected on the part of heads of branches and of offices, will meet these objections, and we believe that the certain advantages of promotion by merit to the most deserving man and therefore to the public service, are so great as to be sure, in the long run, to command public support.

The recommendations of the Ridley Commission and the subsequent adoption of some of them by orders in council had profound implications for the civil service and in particular for the grade of lower division clerk. Indeed, in 1890 the title lower division was changed to second division. Other orders in council stabilised hours (seven per day), sick leave and annual leave. The principle of division of labour was reaffirmed, as was that of greater Treasury control.

The following are some of the main recommendations, relating in particular to the lower division:

> Since the lower divison would constitute a still greater measure of the clerical establishment of the various offices, they should be recruited from young men of the same age as the present, and under the existing regulations. The character of the examination

To the Anglo-Irish Treaty

should not be raised since it appeared to afford a sufficient test of a good commercial education. However, a knowledge of shorthand and of a modern foreign language as optimal subjects might be encouraged.

Seven hours a day should be worked in all offices, without exception.

That every possible care should be taken to make the first year a probationary one, since it by no means followed that success in a competitive examination secures a good clerk, and in cases where it was clear that the elements necessary for making an efficient clerk did not exist, there should be no hesitation in at once discharging such a person from further service.

That after a satisfactory probation, the increment of salary should be £5 annually up to £100. Before any periodical increment was granted, a certificate should be furnished, and kept as record, from the officers under whom the clerk was serving, to the effect that the performance of his duty has been satisfactory.

The commission set a new salary scale extending from £80 to £350. An efficiency bar would apply at a salary of £100 when a report on the performance of the officer would be required. Unless this report was satisfactory, there should be no further advance in salary. A further such bar applied at a salary of £190. The maximum of the scale set by Ridley was £350, in place of the previous £250. Duty pay should be abolished. Superior work, or the supervision of the work of others, for which duty was given, would be adequately covered by the salaries proposed by the Commission. However, a limited number of staff appointments, such as accountantship, registrarship, and the like, as well as certain supervisory posts, often assigned to the upper division, could be adequately filled up by, and be reserved for, the best clerks of the lower division.

The effect of the Ridley recommendations on pay was to introduce a new higher section of the second division (formerly lower division). This recommendation divided the work of the division and may have originated the classificiation of work into higher executive and executive.

The commission considered that, with such a system, it would not be necessary to maintain the limit of ten years' service, before which promotion to the higher division was not possible. One obvious objection to the fixing of such a limit was that it not unnaturally led to the expectation that all who reached it had some right to be promoted. The commission considered that no such right should be recognised but that all the prizes of the service should be open to those of exceptional fitness.

With regard to the change of title, the commission accepted that there was a good deal of feeling against the name lower division and it considered that the difficulty might be removed by distinguishing between clerks of the first and clerks of the second division.

FROM RIDLEY TO MACDONNELL

The legalisation of the trade unions by the Act of 1871, on which the first civil service associations were eventually based, did not make a definite change in civil service unionisation. Movements for improved conditions had long been in evidence, and the official attitude was usually discouraging and even obstructive. The real change was that permanent bodies could be set up to look after the staff interests. During the hearings of the Ridley Commission, the lower division clerks had established and maintained an active general committee. With support in some fifteen departments, they were able to represent almost the entire grade. Subsequent to the Ridley Commission's report, the clerks decided to set up a central body continually to review conditions and in 1890 the Association of Second Division Clerks was established.

The previous year had seen the Great London Dock Strike and the strike of the employees of the South Metropolitan Gas Company. During 1889 there were over one thousand strikes in Britain, mainly about wages. In 1890 there were again over one thousand strikes. These strikes presaged the development of the organisation of the unskilled workers and turned people's minds to the question of measures that might be taken to prevent such outbreaks. In 1893 the activities of the Board of Trade were reorganised in a separate department, the Labour Department, which intervened in a number of disputes. The Royal Commission on Labour, which reported in 1894, defined the terms conciliation and arbitration and even discussed the

To the Anglo-Irish Treaty

use of mediation. As early as 1892, the Post Office Fawcett Association[8] proposed the setting up of a Civil Service Federation, but it was many years before this was achieved. It may have seemed an appropriate time to launch the new Association for Second Division Clerks, but it was not in the government's mind to extend recognition to associations of civil servants. W.A. Humphreys writes:

> Blocked within the departments from appealing directly to the Treasury or Parliament, the only bodies which could influence their condition, and chastised by the Treasury when such attempts were made, the Association fought a hopeless battle with the antiquated system of staff appeals and gradually through the 1890s fell into disuse. Within the departments, however, branches of the association continued to act co-operatively, restricting themselves to special issues unconnected with general conditions of employment.

Humphreys mentions that the second division clerks were in a particularly uncomfortable position. Formerly they had been the elite clerical group of the service. By 1895 reforms had reduced their average money rate by twenty-six per cent below the scale in 1875, had increased hours and had reduced considerably their chances of promotion. The morale of the clerks was further lowered by the disastrous results of an agitation among second division clerks in the Post Office Savings Bank in 1891. Following the recommendation of the Ridley Commission, all established lower division clerks in the Savings Bank were assimilated into the new second division in 1890. This meant a considerable setback in pay. Recruitment had been suspended during the Ridley hearings and many clerks were working up to eleven-and-a-half hours a day. The levelling-up from a six- to a seven-hour day meant the loss of one hour's overtime a day, aside from the fact that the second division salary scale was lower than that which had been effective previously. Humphreys writes:

> In the course of an unofficial interview with the Controller, who attempted to persuade them to resign themselves to inclusion in the Second Division . . . the men were informed, that in all probability the number of women clerks would be increased. This information supplied material for an additional, though unsubstantiated,

In Public Service

grievance that men would be pushed out of their jobs by newly engaged women.

The Post Office was the first department to employ women clerks. The reason for this was that when the private telegraph companies were taken over by the Post Office in 1870, their women employees were transferred. A submitted memorial included complaints about the threat of redundancy if too many women were recruited and the possible future reduction of superior appointments. The agitation ceased after the content of the petition had been published in the newspapers before it had been received by the Postmaster General. The petitioners then received a friendly warning from the authorities and the agitation soon died down.

In 1903 a new and more combative clerical association was established — the Assistant Clerks' Association. This was the predecessor of the Civil Service Clerical Association and the Civil and Public Services Association.[9]

The creation of the Assistant Clerks' Association was prompted by a circular from clerks in Dublin, including a memorial they had prepared requesting increased pay. It came into the hands of James Maxwell, an assistant clerk in the Post Office Savings Bank, where work was particularly hard and discipline especially strict. The growth of government activity following the election victory of the Liberal Party in 1908 saw the number of civil service non-industrial staff rise to 280,000 in 1914, as opposed to 116,000 in 1901. In 1906 civil servants began to advocate the establishment of a court of appeal for an independent body to hear their grievances. The initial move came from the Inland Revenue Associations which were agitating for a court of appeal in the form of a standing committee of the House of Commons, composed of members of all parties and representatives of associations. In 1909 the Civil Service Court of Appeal Committee was formed. In the next two years support grew and in 1911 a conference representing the great mass of organised civil servants — more than 100,000 — agreed to set up a federation. With the threat of a post office strike and the teachers joining in the agitation, the government decided that a select committee (the Holt Committee) would be appointed to inquire into the grievances

To the Anglo-Irish Treaty

of the postal staff. In December 1911 the prime minister, Herbert Asquith, agreed to set up a royal commission to inquire into the civil service. The Civil Service Federation came into existence in 1912 and had as its initial purpose the preparation of evidence to place before the royal commission.

The unity of the federation did not last long. The leadership's concentration on political rights did not help the clerical unions, which had envisaged a united bargaining front that would destroy the Treasury's power to play one grade off against another. The second division clerks declined to affiliate. Eventually, in 1916, all the clerical unions withdrew.

THE MACDONNELL COMMISSION

The commission's terms of reference were:

1. To inquire into and report on the methods of making appointments to and promotions in the civil service, including the diplomatic and consular services and the legal departments.
2. To investigate the working and efficiency of the system of competitive examinations for such appointments, and to make recommendations for any alterations or improvements in that system which may appear to be advisable; and
3. To consider whether the existing scheme of organisation meets with the requirements of the public service, and to suggest any modifications which may be needed therein.

The MacDonnell Commission[10] finished its work as World War I broke out. It was evident that the proposals in its four reports could not be fully considered at such a time. When war was declared, the associations were informed that further consideration of pay and conditions would have to be suspended. However, the government did adopt the recommendation that all members of the administrative class should be recruited on common scales of salary, a measure that a number of major departments had obstinately resisted. The commission was the last of the royal commissions to have a direct relevance for civil servants in Ireland and, as such, is of considerable importance. When the war ended in 1918, arbitration was in place in the civil service and discussions were underway on the introduction of the Whitley system of conciliation. Since the

In Public Service

future development of the civil service was greatly influenced by the recommendations of the MacDonnell Commission, they are worthy of examination. The report also draws a profile of the personnel of the service. General principles laid down in the report included the following:

1. Greater facilities should be provided for the progress from the primary to the secondary schools, and thence to the universities, of pupils capable of benefiting from secondary and university training.
2. There should be closer co-ordination between the educational systems and the civil service examinations.
3. The principle of open competition should be adhered to and extended.

A new system of grading was suggested and this would correspond with educational levels.

Although the MacDonnell Commission report was not implemented and was overtaken on industrial relations matters by the Whitley proposals, its views on staff associations probably reflected the change in attitude towards trade unions. Both Playfair and Ridley to an extent had encouraged staff combinations in so far as they received information from groups of civil servants acting on behalf of their colleagues. MacDonnell went somewhat further in stating:

> We do not doubt that generally such associations serve a useful and worthy purpose in promoting co-operation amongst many individuals serving under similar conditions, and we are glad to find that the heads of public departments generally recognise such associations in the sense of receiving from them directly representations affecting their interests.

The commission went on to recommend that a special inquiry should be held to consider the question of trade unions in the service and the desirability of creating suitable machinery for assessing grievances, particularly on pay and conditions.

The commission reviewed developments in the civil service since the Playfair Commission, which had recommended that the service should be divided into four divisions. MacDonnell stressed that, while the order in council of February 1876 purported to deal with the recommendations of the Playfair

To the Anglo-Irish Treaty

Commission, it dealt only with the recommendations touching the lower division. It did not mention the administrative staff or the professional officers and it referred to the higher division only indirectly. In the meantime certain developments had taken place, partly under the power reserved by the orders in council, partly by departmental initiative, and by legislation. These developments were listed under the following five heads:

1. The intermediate class
2. The boy clerks
3. The assistant clerks (abstractors)
4. The women and girl clerks
5. A numerous body of officers employed in the Labour Exchanges, the Unemployment Insurance Offices, and the National Health Insurance Commissioners, the method of whose appointment differed noticeably from the ordinary method of recruitment.

The MacDonnell report commented that attention had already been drawn to what it saw as a serious defect in the arrangements of the examination for entry into the clerical branch of the civil service: their divergence from the actual conditions of education and instruction. The second division examination marked the extreme point of such divergence. The years from seventeen to twenty corresponded to no stage in the organisation of education. Since a complete course of secondary education ended when the pupil was about eighteen years old, it was obvious that the superior age limit was far too high.

One major effect of the MacDonnell Commission report was to confirm as a principle what had previously existed in practice: to strengthen the relations between the establishments division of the Treasury and the establishments officers of the departments in such a way as to make the establishments division the last word in regard to staff problems. The commission stated that a new section should be set up within the Treasury to deal solely with establishment questions. This proposal was carried into effect in 1919 when an establishments division was created within the Treasury. Its functions were to sanction rates of pay, to control salaries, and to issue general regulations relating to the conduct of the service. Each of the

In Public Service

larger departments appointed an establishment officer who was made responsible for dealing with all questions of personnel; moreover, a standing committee of establishment officers, with the controller of establishments as its chairman, was brought into being to advise the Treasury on all general matters concerning the staffing and organisation of the service, and to ensure co-operation between the Treasury and the departments on establishment matters.[11]

This development was an essential precondition for the successful operation of the Whitley system. The first report of the Civil Service Conciliation and Arbitration Board, presented in 1918, remarked on the divergence of view between the Treasury and the departmental representatives. When eventually the official side was restructured to meet the demands of Whitley, it remained for the staff side to restructure too.

THE ROAD TO WHITLEYISM

In examining the number of hours worked in the departments, the MacDonnell Commission had found some diversity in practice and suggested that attendance be fixed at a minimum of 42 hours, possibly with the hours arranged to allow for a half-holiday each week. The Committee on Retrenchment in the Public Expenditure make a similar recommendation in its final report, issued in February 1916: that hours be increased to eight a day, with some increase in salary to existing members of the service in lieu of overtime pay.[12] On 30 March 1916, the Treasury issued a circular that set out its proposal for an order in council providing for an eight-hour day (instead of seven) throughout the service, with a half-holiday on Saturdays.

At the time almost all civil servants were working longer than eight hours a day and receiving overtime payments. They saw the longer official day, without an accompanying increase in salary scales, as an attempt to cut costs at their expense. The effect of the proposal would be to deprive all civil servants of an hour's overtime pay per day while the pressure of work continued and, when the emergency had passed, to lengthen permanently the normal working day without compensation. The Assistant Clerks Association immediately got in touch with

To the Anglo-Irish Treaty

the Second Division Association and, at a meeting on 7 April, they agreed on a full-scale campaign. A petition was sent to King George V begging him to withhold his assent to the proposal until representations had been made and considered; that an all-grade memorial should be signed in each department; that arrangements should be made for a mass protest meeting; that the sympathy of MPs should be sought. The following day the Association of Female Clerks, Female Typists and Intermediate Clerks had agreed to join the other associations. The petition to the King was delivered and memorials were being signed in all departments. On 11 April the announcement of a mass meeting was circulated. On the following day the Treasury withdrew its proposal. Following the success of the eight-hour-day campaign, the two associations called a meeting, also attended by representatives of the women's organisations, at which the Civil Service Alliance was formed.

By April 1917 the alliance had seven affiliates with a membership of 15,000. The alliance was representative of the clerical grades, while the Civil Service Federation mainly represented the Post Office and other minor grades. An Irish Civil Service Alliance was also established to represent the permanent clerical classes in the civil service.

The Irish section of the alliance was not able, of course, to foresee the position that would arise with the establishment of the Irish Free State.

In 1917 the main alliance headquarters in London had to prepare for the introduction of conciliation and arbitration for government employees. The MacDonnell Commission had considered that new machinery should be introduced for dealing with grievances in the civil service. Ramsay MacDonald stated in the House of Commons, when preparing an inquiry into the Post Office, that there was a consensus of opinion in the House that to settle these questions by commissions or committees was not the best method. Postmaster Hobhouse agreed that they would have to create some authority to stand between the House and the servants of state.

The Civil Service Arbitration Board, established as a result of a cabinet resolution, held its first meeting on 12 February 1917. Under the board's auspices, 91 agreements were made; in addition, the board issued 131 awards. The board ceased its

In Public Service

functions in June 1922 following the introduction of the Whitley system.

Following the extension in 1919 of arbitration rights to civil servants on salaries of up to £1,500, three associations were formed in the higher grades: the Association of Staff Clerks and Other Civil Servants, the Society of Civil Servants, and the Association of First Division Civil Servants. Throughout the civil service the number of associations increased from 80 in 1913 to 194 in 1919. In the main, the new additions were women's grade organisations and departmental unions of temporary workers.

On the whole, the service associations were pleased with the personnel of the board, which consisted of three members under the chairmanship of Sir William Collins MP, an experienced arbitrator. With him were Harry Gosling of the Transport Workers' Federation, a well-known figure after his leadership of a big dock strike in 1912 and his efforts to mediate in the Dublin Lockout of 1913, and Sir A. Kaye Butterworth, general manager of the North-Eastern Railway. The board immediately was inundated with claims, nearly all for a 30 per cent increase in the bonus. From 1917 to 1919 it allowed thirteen small increases, but at the end the bonuses were still too small to compensate for the rise in prices. The first award, dated from 1 January 1917, was as follows:

	Men	Women
Wages not exceeding 30 shillings a week	9s	6s
Wages between 30 and 40 shillings	8s	5s
Wages between 40 and 60 shillings	7s	4s 6d
Wages between 60 shillings and £250 per annum	5s	3s 6d

This and similar awards drew the wrath of the Association of Irish Post Office Clerks (AIPOC). Its secretary commented in his report for 1918:

A further unsatisfactory point is the extraordinary differential in the amounts granted to men and women. Your Executive can see no good grounds for this differentiation, and expresses the hope that our lady members will take full advantage of the parliamentary franchise, and make the fullest use of that powerful weapon of democracy, the vote, which, if wielded to proper advantage, must eventually force the recognition of the claim of equal pay for similar work.

To the Anglo-Irish Treaty

In his report for 1920 the secretary of the AIPOC stated:

> An award of 10% increase in War Bonus was made by the Civil Service Arbitration Board. Apparently the Board calculated that the Civil Service generally could be relied upon to accept the dole without any serious murmuring. The calculation was correct. Dissatisfaction was universally expressed in words, but it was laid down by those representing the vast majority of the rank and file that no further action was possible, because, constitutionally, both parties were committed to acceptance. In other words, however absurd and unjust any decision may be, so long as the ethics of constitutionalism are observed, the pressing needs of existence must remain unsatisfied, but quiescent.

WHITLEY

W. J. Brown was appointed as the full-time officer of the Assistant Clerks Association in 1919. He was the first such officer in the service outside of the post office field. In his book *So Far*,[13] he describes the change the war had made to the civil service. Referring to the men who had returned from the war, he comments:

> They came back different men from the men that they were when they went. And they came back to a different Civil Service. They had left a Civil Service so crystallised in tradition, so ridden by routine, that nothing ever appeared to happen to it. It was more than an instrument, that pre-1914 Civil Service. It was an Institution — like the Church. Its wages were from the past. Its vocabulary was stilted and archaic. It had a tremendous veneration for precedent. It moved with stately leisureliness . . . . But the Civil Service to which the men came back was a new and strange Service, a Service which under the stress and shocks of war had been jerked from the nineteenth into the twentieth century. Women thronged the Whitehall offices, and actually sat in the same room as men! A revolution in itself. In pre-1914 days, in the few Departments in which women had been employed at all, they had been rigidly segregated from the men, and it was as much as a man's career was worth for him to invade the quarters reserved for them.

Humphreys also comments on the changes wrought by the Great War, contending that it had two effects on the civil service clerical movement. It sharply speeded up the development of unions by causing greater and more widespread discontent, and it offered better opportunities for obtaining the alleviation of grievances by creating a situation wherein the government was more inclined to act expediently. Long overtime, lack of promotional opportunities and the downgrading of work were sacrifices that might well have been made by clerks without complaint during the war if the cost of living rise had not cut so deeply into an already unfavourable wage structure.

An added cause of grievance was the Treasury's attempt to lengthen the official day without a compensatory rise in pay. The war had a levelling influence: discontent was no longer a grade, class or department problem. The establishment of the Arbitration Board emphasised the need for extensive organisation if full benefits were to be gained. It also created an air of respectability around unionism by allowing associations a function in official procedure. One effect was the rapid formation of associations in the higher grades. Following the setting up of the Arbitration Board, the unions went through an adjustment period in which practical forms of organisation were settled and policies and programmes for the future were renewed and adjusted.

The government was conscious of the serious industrial strains that were likely to arise in the period of post-war reconstruction. In 1917 it appointed a committee under the chairmanship of J. H. Whitley, who afterwards became speaker of the House of Commons. The committee's brief was:

1. To make and consider suggestions for securing a permanent improvement in the relations between employers and workmen.
2. To recommend means for securing that industrial conditions affecting the relations between Employers and Workmen shall be systematically reviewed by those concerned, with a view to improving conditions in the future.

In his book *Industrial Arbitration in Great Britain*,[14] Lord Amulree states that this committee, unlike most of those that had previously inquired into labour matters, heard comparatively few witnesses. Most of the members knew the essential facts and the report of the committee (Cmd 9081) was brief and unpretentious. It was nevertheless epoch-making. The committee began from the assumption that all parties in industry desired

To the Anglo-Irish Treaty

peace, and when this desire was frustrated, it was due mainly to want of knowledge and understanding. What was necessary was that between the employers and those immediately concerned with management, on the one hand, and the workers on the other, there should be a regular interchange of views and a state of mutual confidence. The committee examined various systems of arbitration:

We are opposed to any system of compulsory Arbitration: there is no reason to believe that such a system is generally desired by employers and employed and, in the absence of such acceptance, it is obvious that its imposition would lead to unrest. The experience of compulsory arbitration during the war has shown that it is not a successful method of avoiding strikes, and in normal times it would undoubtedly prove even less successful. Disputes can only be avoided by agreement between employers and workers and by giving to the latter the greater measure of interest in the industry advocated by our former reports (through Conciliation Councils); but agreement may naturally include the decision of both parties to refer any specified matter or matters to arbitration, whether this decision is reached before or after a dispute arises. As arbitration affecting the same trade or section of trades may recur, there are advantages to both employers and workpeople in knowing that the tribunal to which they submit any differences which they may have failed themselves to settle is one to which previous differences have been submitted, and which therefore has become to some extent familiar with the conditions of the trade.

The committee went on to state that it would be obvious that the efficiency of an arbitrator, provided that he possessed the right personal qualifications, increases with practice and the study of the conditions with which he would deal.

The committee's scheme of industrial organisation comprised four stages. In the individual firm, a shop committee, made up of representatives of the various classes of employees, was to be the medium of communication and consultation with the employer. District councils similarly were to provide the means of discussion between groups of employers and workers in districts in which, as a matter of tradition or sentiment, a local organisation was required. For the industry as a whole, there was to be a joint industrial council, an assembly of selected representative employers and workers. The joint industrial council and the district committees were to be formed on the principle of equal representation and it was understood that employers and workers were to be represented through their respective organisations. There were to be no outsiders and the chairman had no casting vote, so that if a deadlock should occur, there was no means of relieving it from the inside. Therefore, the committee recommended the establishment of an appellate tribunal, to which differences unsolvable by the joint industrial councils could be referred.

It has been said that Whitleyism came to the civil service in a fit of absentmindedness. When Whitley issued his report on industrial relations and civil servants, he was asked whether Whitley Councils were meant to apply to the civil service. He confessed that he had never thought of it. The government warmly commended the proposals contained in the report to employers' organisations and to the trade union movement, and meetings were held throughout the country to popularise them. Civil service organisations thought it was anomalous that the government should commend such proposals to employers and employed generally without applying them to themselves and their own employees.

The Civil Service Alliance commenced a campaign for equal treatment with outside industry and, after publication of the committee's second report, was joined by the Post Office groups and the Civil Service Federation. The upshot of this agitation was that Joint Whitley Councils were instituted in the civil service towards the end of 1919. A National Civil Service Whitley Council was set up, consisting of representatives of the unions and of the administration, to deal with issues affecting the civil service and matters common to two or more departments. In each department a Department Whitley Council was established, consisting of representatives of branches of the associations within that department and the departmental administration, to deal with purely departmental matters or with departmental aspects of general matters. Paragraph 26 of the National Council's constitution was to assume great importance in the struggle of the associations in the Irish civil service to restore the Whitley system, which was not carried forward from the imperial civil service:

To the Anglo-Irish Treaty

The decisions of the Council shall be arrived at by agreement between the two sides, shall be signed by the Chairman and Vice-Chairman, shall be reported to the Cabinet and thereupon shall become operative.

When the National Whitley Council was set up, the civil servants in Ireland pressed for a similar council in their country. This request was refused, but an Irish Civil Service Joint Council was established which had no functions of decision, but was empowered to advise the National Whitley Council in London on purely Irish matters, or particular Irish aspects of general service questions.

Over 200 associations were represented on the staff side in 1919 through federations or occupational groupings. A number of new associations were set up in that same year, including the Association of Executive Officers of the Civil Service. The Irish members of this association retained this title on transfer to the Irish civil service.

REORGANISATION

Apart from their resolve to secure Whitley Councils in 1919, the individual associations did not relax their efforts to gain wage increases. Both the Assistant Clerks Association and the Second Division Clerks Association submitted claims which included higher minimum pay, larger increments, revised overtime rates and increased leave. The Treasury's position was that the claims were so bound up with other questions, such as reorganisation of the service, employment of women, and reclassification of work, that the matters should be negotiated within the Whitley machinery. At the first meeting of the National Whitley Council, it was agreed to appoint three joint grade committees to consider the remuneration of assistant clerks, second division clerks and staff clerks. At the same time, the Civil Service Alliance was considering a reorganisation and reclassification of the service. Such a proposal was made to the official side and an agreement was reached at the second meeting of the National Whitley Council on 14 October 1919 as follows:

In Public Service

That a special committee be appointed to consider the scope of the duties at present allotted to the Clerical classes in the Civil Service, to report on the organisation most appropriate to secure the effective performance of these duties; and to make recommendations as to scales of salary and method of recruitment. That it be an instruction to this committee to present a report by 31st January next.

Work on the three previously appointed grade committees ceased and their subjects of inquiry were transferred to the General Reorganisation Committee. The report of the Reorganisation Committee is of considerable importance in so far as it established the basis of the structure that was carried into and maintained within the Irish civil service. The committee looked at the relative pay of men and women and agreed that the minimum of the basic scale in each class should be the same for women as for men, and that the incremental rates should be identical up to a point. It also agreed that women were fully capable of discharging the clerical work of the civil service and should be recruited to the new clerical class through open competition by written examination. However, with regard to recruitment of the administrative and executive classes, the Committee agreed that, subject to review after a period of five years, women should be recruited by a system of selection by impartial and authoritative boards. The staff side insisted on the review procedure. Reporting on the administrative and clerical branches of the civil service, the committee stated:

The Administrative and Clerical work of the Civil Service may be said, broadly, to fall into two main categories. In one category may be placed all such work as either is of a simple mechanical kind or consists in the application of well-defined regulations, decisions and practice to particular cases; in the other category, the work which is concerned with the formation of policy, with the revision of existing practice or current regulations and decisions, and with the organisation and direction of the business of Government.

To handle the work that fell into the two main categories, four different classes were recommended:

(a) A writing assistant class for simple mechanical work.

(b) A clerical class for the better sort of work included in the first main category defined above.

(c) An executive class and } for the work included in the
(d) An administrative class } second main category defined above.

With regard to the executive class, the committee reported:

In this class we would assign the higher work of Supply and Accounting Departments, and of other executive or specialised branches of the Civil Service. This work covers a wide field, and requires in different degrees qualities of judgement, initiative and resource. In the junior ranks it comprises the critical examination of particular cases of lesser importance, and the immediate direction of small blocks of business. In its upper reaches it is concerned with matters of internal organisation and control, with the settlement of broad questions arising and of business in hand or in contemplation and with the responsible conduct of important operations. We are of the opinion that, insofar as it may be desirable to appoint men from outside the Service to the staffs of these Departments and branches, recruitment should be by open competitive, written examination between the ages of 18 and 19. The syllabus of examination should be framed with reference to the standard of development reached at the end of a secondary school course.

On the recruitment of women, the committee members noted that they had already decided that they had not been able to recommend the extension of the mode of recruitment appropriate to men and that they had agreed that women candidates should be recruited during the period of experiment by means of authoritative and impartial selection boards. This experiment was to be reviewed after five years.

The committee considered that entrants of both sexes should be regarded as members of a training grade and that, during the term of their employment in this grade, they should be given the widest possible training in all branches of the work of the department or branch to which they were assigned. The committee also believed that a considerable portion of executive class posts would be filled by promotion from the clerical class. The salary of those serving in the training (executive) grade was recommended to be for men £100 per year (inclusive of overtime), rising by annual increments of £10 to £130 a year, and proceeding therein by annual increments of £15 to a maximum of £400 a year; and for women, £100 a year rising by annual increments of £10 to a maximum of £300 a year. The salary appropriate to the grade to which men and women would normally receive their first promotion (higher executive) was recommended to be (inclusive of overtime): for men, a scale ranging from £400 by annual increments of £15 to a maximum of £500 a year, and for women a scale ranging from £300 by annual increments of £15 to a maximum of £400 a year. The recommended annual leave was (exclusive of the usual public holidays): for the executive class, 36 working days, to be increased to 48 days on promotion to the grade carrying a scale of £400 to £500 (men), and £300 to £400 (women), after 15 years' service in a grade eligible for 36 days.

The recommended hours of attendance were seven hours a day with a half-holiday on Saturday; a luncheon interval of three-quarters of an hour, with discretionary power given to heads of departments to allow up to an hour in special cases.

COST-OF-LIVING SETTLEMENT

During World War I it was not possible for the association to secure a permanent improvement in wages. However, a special war bonus was introduced to compensate for the constantly rising cost of living. Civil servants were obliged to have almost continual recourse to the Arbitration Board to gain increases in the bonus. At the same time as the Reorganisation Committee was set up, the National Whitley Council was appointed to:

Consider the increase in the cost of living and its effect upon the salaries of Civil Servants, whether permanent or temporary, and to report to the Council. The inquiry centred on two issues: (a) the framework of a scheme which would be appropriate and equitable in its general incidence and (b) the provision of machinery for adjustment of the scheme in accordance with future fluctuations in cost of living.

This committee's report, which was implemented and carried forward into the salary structures in the Irish civil service, is of great significance in an understanding of the pay problems in the Irish service leading to the Standstill Order of the Emergency

To the Anglo-Irish Treaty

years and the eventual consolidation of basic pay and bonus in 1946. In its report, the committee agreed that in order to keep step with rising cost of living, it was necessary to adopt a permanent sliding scale bonus geared to the Ministry of Labour's notional cost-of-living index. The figure of 130, as shown in the *Labour Gazette* for 1 March 1920 as the percentage increase in the cost of living over July 1914, was accepted as the starting point for the initial bonus award, to be applied in the following way:

a) 130 per cent of ordinary remuneration where this did not exceed £91.5.0 per annum.

b) Where the ordinary rate exceeded £91.5.0, but did not exceed £200, 130 per cent on the first £91.5.0, and 60 per cent on the excess.

c) Where the ordinary rate exceeded £200, 130 per cent on the first £91.5.0, 60 per cent on the next £108.15.0, and 45 per cent on the excess up to £500.

The bonus was to be subject to revision every four months during the first twelve months, and thereafter every six months. The standard cost-of-living figure was to be arrived at by taking the average of the official figures for the preceding four months, or six months after March 1921. Changes were to be based on increases or decreases of 1/26th for every five full points by which the average cost-of-living changed, and variations of less than five full points in either direction were ignored. Persons earning over £500 were not covered since these grades were outside the scope of Whitleyism, but nonetheless the Treasury agreed informally to include persons on basic salary rates up to £1,000.

TRANSFER

The transfer of administrative services from British to Irish control took place on 1 April 1923. The revenue staff had been transferred as from 6 December 1922. Some 21,000 persons were transferred, of whom more than half were in the Post Office. The annual cost to the new Irish Free State was estimated at £4 million. The terms of the transfer were set out

In Public Service

in Article 10 of the Articles of Agreement for a Treaty between Britain and Ireland:

The Government of the Irish Free State agrees to pay fair compensation on terms not less favourable than those acceded by the Act of 1920 to judges, officials, members of the Police Forces and other Public Servants who are discharged by it or who retire in consequence of the change of Government effected in pursuance hereof.

Provided that this agreement shall not apply to members of the Auxiliary police force or to persons recruited in Great Britain for the Royal Irish Constabulary during the two years next preceding the date hereof the British government will assume responsibility for such compensation or pensions as may be payable to any of these excepted persons.

The Act of 1920 referred to was the Government of Ireland Act. The statutory conditions were set as follows:

a) Retirement must take place within a period of seven years from the appointed day (in this schedule referred to as the transitional period).

b) Notice of the intention to retire must be given in accordance with the Regulations made by the Civil Service Committee.

c) The retirement must not take place until at least six months after notice of retirement has been given, and may be postponed by the Civil Service Committee, if they think fit, to any later date not being more than two years after the date of the notice, within the transition period, and

d) The retiring officer must show to the satisfaction of the Civil Service Committee that he is not incapacitated by mental or bodily infirmity for the performance of his duties, and that he has not attained the age of sixty-five years at the time when the notice is given.

On voluntary retirement, the officer could reckon his years of service and pay as if he had served to the end of the transitional seven years, and had received the benefit of any annual increments due up to date.

The Civil Service Committee (Compensation) held its first meeting on 4 October 1922 under the chairmanship of Mr Justice Wylie. Its activities and the problems faced by transferred officers will be discussed in later chapters.

II

1923-1935

The transferred civil servants were about 21,000 in number, of whom 17,239 were classified as permanent and 3,176 as temporary, the remainder belonging to certain industrial classes. Besides these, there were incorporated into the Saorstát civil service 131 officers who had served under Dáil Éireann in the pre-Treaty period and 88 persons who had formerly been in the British service but who had left it on political or similar grounds.[1] Some 54 per cent of the transferees were in the Post Office. The annual cost of the service was approximately £4 million. About 940 established and 760 unestablished women civil servants were transferred, excluding in each case women engaged on manipulative work in the Post Office and in subordinate employment (e.g. cleaners).

The majority of the established women officers were employed in the Post Office Accounts Branch and the National Health Insurance Commission Office, and the Department of Industry and Commerce accounted for almost all the balance. They were employed principally in the clerical and writing assistant grades. These grades had been introduced only a few years previously, and the typing grades had been almost entirely confined to women for many years beforehand.[2] The transferred civil servants were protected by the provisions of Article 10 of the Treaty.

A dispute between the transferred officers and the Department of Finance led to a hearing by the Judicial Committee of the Privy Council in the famous Wigg-Cochrane case. The Privy Council judgment confirmed that the rights of a transferred officer contained in the Treaty were legal rights and that the duty of determining the amount of compensation to which a transferred officer (retiring in consequence of the change of government) was entitled, fell, if needs be, on the courts. The outcome was that agreement was reached between the two governments and the transferred officers about the basis on which claims for compensation should be effected. The agreements were given statutory effect in Ireland by the Civil Service (Transferred Officers) Compensation Act 1929. Under the provisions of that act, a board, consisting of a judge as chairman and two representatives each of the Minister for Finance and the transferred officers, was established to determine all questions under Article 10. The board's decisions were final and were not subject to appeal or to review by the courts, and the Minister for Finance was bound by law to pay compensation in every case in which the board made an award.

The Brennan report commented that one of the abnormal features of the early days of the Free State civil service was the relatively high proportion of officials who had been recruited either temporarily or without undergoing the usual tests. This was in part a legacy from the previous administration, reflecting a consequence of the Great War, but it arose also from the emergency conditions in which new recruitment had inevitably to be carried on in 1922-23 and from the need to hire staff for a large volume of work that was definitely temporary, in particular for dealing with compensation schemes in respect of both pre-Treaty and post-Treaty damage. From 1 April 1922 to 1 October 1923, apart from the special groups of ex-Dáil and reinstated officers, 2,320 persons were recruited into the civil service, mostly on a temporary basis, of whom 676 were engaged in the Office of Public Works, largely on compensation problems, and 468 in the Office of the Revenue Commissioners, which among other new matters had to provide for the service of a customs land frontier.[3] On the establishment of the Free State, it became necessary to set up a Civil Service Commission. A temporary act was passed for this purpose in 1923. It was replaced by a permanent act the following year and this latter act was in certain respects amended by a further statute in 1926.

The Ministers and Secretaries Act 1924 provided a statutory classification of the functions of government under the several departments of state, thereby establishing the framework to which the organisation of the civil service had to conform. Between 1923 and 1935 there was little variation in the strength of the civil service. The figure of 21,000 in 1923 compares with the following figures supplied to the Brennan Commission by the Department of Finance:

Total personnel employed

1 January 1927	22,708
1 January 1928	23,349
1 January 1929	23,796
1 January 1930	23,430
1 January 1931	23,219

The report supplied the figure for 1 January 1935 at 20,984, of whom 5,449 were female.

The initial examination for administrative officers was scheduled for December 1924. Under the original terms of the advertisement, however, women were prohibited from entering for the examination, and the ensuing protest caused the examination's postponement. The Minister for Finance eventually decided that both men and women should be eligible for the examination, which was held in April 1925.[4]

The cost (including bonus) of the service showed an actual decrease and at the following dates was as follows:

1 April 1922	£4,170,861
1 January 1927	£4,061,666
1 January 1928	£4,040,243
1 January 1929	£4,074,587
1 January 1930	£4,052,049
1 January 1931	£3,962,877
1 January 1932	£3,947,969

In its memorandum to the Brennan Commission, the Department of Finance supplied the following statement, which included both permanent and temporary officers, showing classes and grades and relative strengths at that time:

In Public Service

Class	Number
Administrative and executive above HEO	333
Junior administrative	24
Higher executive	176
Junior executive	429
Staff officers	170
Clericals (including departmental)	2,065
Writing clerks	219
Superintendents of typists	13
Shorthand typists	271
Typists	287
Inspectorial, professional and technical	1,061
Subordinate (messengers, postmen)	7,872
Industrial classes	2,998

In addition, there was a miscellaneous group representing about 6,000 persons in which the principal classes were as follows:

Post office assistants and other departmental post office staff	3,944
Customs and excise officers (of all grades)	756
Employment branch officials	107
District court clerks and summons servers	639

The division of the personnel of some grades as at 1 January 1934 was as follows:

	Male	Female
Junior administrative	26	3
Higher executive	179	2
Junior executive	419	15

Senator Thomas Johnson, in a minority report, stated that, of the 419 male junior executive officers, 155 were unmarried, and of the 1,356 male clerical officers, 682 were married. He asserted that junior executive officers did not marry until their pay reached £350 per year (inclusive of bonus); the figure in the case of clerical officers was £200 per year.

1923-1935
UNION ORGANISATION

With the establishment of the Irish Free State, the staff associations began to reform. The Post Office Workers' Union was formed at a conference held in Dublin's Mansion House in June 1923. Before January 1920, there existed the Postmens' Federation, the Postal Clerks' Association and the Fawsett Association. In 1919 these organisations amalgamated under the title of the Union of Post Office Workers. There was also extant a purely Irish organisation — the Irish Postal Union — which formerly had been the Association of Irish Post Office Clerks. In March 1922 the Union of Post Office Workers convened a conference of their branches in the Irish Free State and proposed either setting up a separate organisation, or alternatively, entering the Irish Postal Union. The conference decided to establish a separate organisation under the title of the Irish Postal Workers' Union. A threatened cut in the cost-of-living bonus led to a strike in the Post Office in 1922, one outcome of which was the amalgamation of the two unions. In the same year the Civil Service Federation was established. The federation comprised the following staff associations:

The Association of Executive Officers of the Civil Service
The Civil Service Clerical Association
The Ordnance Survey Staff Association
The Association of Inspectors of Taxes
The Established Attendants' Association
The Inland Revenue Stamping Department Association
The Irish Waterguard Customs and Excise Federation
The Association of Officers of Taxes
The Civil Service Library Association
The Employment Exchange Managers' Association
The Irish Post Office Controlling Officers' Association
The Head Postmasters Association
The Telephone Contract Officers' Association
Intermediate Education Established Clerks' Association
Association of Junior Officers

Two organisations remained outside the federation: the Institute of Professional Civil Servants and the Post Office Workers' Union. The Civil Service Clerical Association seceded from the federation in 1927. In 1923 the Association of Executive Officers had some 390 members and some 473 members four years later. With the secession of the Civil Service Clerical Association, the Association of Executive Officers became the largest affiliate to the federation and invariably supplied its officers.

The official organ of the federation, the *Civil Service Journal*, first appeared in January 1923. The first editorial, under the heading 'We are Born', commented:

Daily and almost imperceptibly the machinery of Government in the new Free State is altering and expanding. These changes are bound sooner or later to react upon the interests of Civil Servants whose duty it is to see to the smooth running of that complex machinery. Will that reaction be for better or worse? Will the new brooms, in their sweeping, clear away much of the discontent of the past, or will they but add to the accumulation? Quien Sabe? It is too soon yet, perhaps, to endeavour to predict what the future of the Irish Civil Service shall be. But this we can predict:
It shall not be the fault of the Civil Service Federation if the Service is not made a brighter and better sphere than it has been in the past.

Mr M. Smithwick resigned from the honorary secretaryship of the Association of Executive Officers early in 1923 and was replaced by P. J. McElhinney of the Board of Works. It was not long before the new secretary found cause to complain about the members' apathy. In July 1923 he wrote in the *Journal*: 'The failure of certain Departments to forward subscriptions is a trial of patience. We are now in the third quarter when normally arrangements should be in operation to collect the corresponding instalment. In a number of cases, however, the first instalment is still outstanding, and in the great majority the second payment has not been received. The Association has large commitments which obviously it is not able to meet, unless the requisite funds are forthcoming.'

In January 1924 the association again drew attention to the need for the early payment of all outstanding subscriptions. It also underlined the need to recruit to the associations all officers eligible for membership. Those eligible were set out as follows:

a) Officers holding posts in the higher ranks of the executive class — £400 per annum and upwards.
b) Executive officers — £100 to £400 per annum.
c) Second divison clerks not yet assimilated.

1923-1935

The 'Association Notes', published in May 1924, asked corresponding representatives to be aware that executive officers on the upper ranges of salary — £500, £550, £700 — were eligible for membership and that they should be invited to join since it was the only association open to them. At the time of the transfer of staff to the Free State, few, if any, administrative officers were transferred since the function of the Irish offices were mainly executive and clerical. The executive officers on the upper range of salary were mainly departmental and had various titles. The maximum annual pay of a higher executive officer at the time was £500. The grades of general service assistant principal officer and principal officer did not exist. The association's rule book, published in 1928, provided that no temporary or unestablished officers, officers of the clerical class (including the higher grade of the clerical staff) would be admitted to membership. The grade of higher clerical officer was in existence at the time of the transfer to the Free State civil service. The maximum of the scale was slightly below that of an executive officer. The staff officer grade had its origin in circular 44/24. The creation of major staff posts was later to be a cause of great concern to the Executive Officers' Association. The grading of these posts was between that of the executive officer and the higher executive officer.

The 'Civil Service Federation Notes' of November 1924 stated that the number of affiliated associations stood at fifteen, although three had given notice of withdrawal. The total number affiliated were 1,560, a decrease of 130 on the previous year's total. Some other associations, with 500 members in all, had intimated their willingness to affiliate, but affiliation was conditional on a reduced fee. The 'Notes' further commented that the two principal Treasury class associations were much below their potential strengths.

In December 1925 the Executive Officers' Association informed its members that 38 branches were entitled to send representatives to the annual council meeting the following month. In 1927 the association had problems with some of its branches. That August its 'Notes' mentioned that considerable attention had been paid to organisation, especially of the Land Commission and the accountants' branch of the Post Office. The corresponding representative of the accountants' branch resigned and apparently was unable to secure anyone else to take over the duties. A lengthy correspondence ensued between the association and another officer of the accountant's branch, but it was not possible to re-establish a branch of the association in the Post Office. The executive committee was then asked to receive a deputation. It considered the request irregular but, in order not to appear aloof, decided to receive the deputation. Yet, despite the item appearing on the agenda for the two monthly meetings of the executive committee, the deputation failed to appear. A happier outcome ensued in the case of the Land Commission branch. D. A. Kane undertook the duties of corresponding representative, and the reports from the branch improved considerably.

The 1927 annual report of the association stated that, with a membership of 473, it was the largest of the fifteen associations in affiliation with the Civil Service Federation and had representatives on its council and executive, while several members held positions as officers. The report refers to the Civil Service Housing Association, the Civil Service Benevolent Fund, and the Civil Service Guild. Income for the 473 members was £360, of which £105 was expended on honoraria and £125 as an affiliation fee to the Civil Service Federation.

The 1929 annual report showed the membership at 561, the highest in the association's history. The report refers to the opening of the Civil Service Supply Stores. In its initial development, the stores confined itself to the sale of groceries and other ordinary household requirements. Collection boxes for orders were placed in government offices and goods were delivered twice weekly. Arrangements were then made for the supply on favourable terms of ready-made and made-to-measure clothing and electrical apparatus. Despite a strong recommendation from the executive committee and a reduction in the price of groceries, only a fraction of the civil servants in Dublin patronised the stores. Because of financial commitments to do with acquiring new offices for the federation, the executive committee strongly recommended that the subscription for 1930 should remain at £1.

In its submission to the Brennan Commission, the association stated that it existed to safeguard and promote the professional interests of its members. It was a voluntary organisation comprising 514 of the serving executive and higher executive officers. The submission pointed out that membership was open to officers of still higher grades of the executive class, but confessed that the response from the higher ranks had been disappointing. Two main reasons for this were suggested:

a) In the civil service there were normally only two steps intervening between the higher executive officer and the headship (or deputy headship) of a department; the higher executive officer's maximum salary was £500 a year (exclusive of cost-of-living bonus) and the salary scale for heads of departments normally commenced at £1,000 a year. Hence, the intervening grades were so close to ultimate authority that they normally felt constrained to acquiesce in the policy of authority, and

b) Under the system of negotiation between staff organisations and the Minister for Finance, the latter had declined to entertain representations regarding the rate of remuneration of officers in receipt of salaries exceeding £500 a year. This regulation did not favour the adhesion of senior officers to staff organisations.

In January 1930 the Post Office Workers' Union suggested that a Permanent Joint Committee of Civil Service Organisations should be established so that in matters of mutual concern the service could speak with a single voice. The national executive of that union decided to obtain the views on the matter of the Civil Service Federation, the Institution of Professional Civil Servants, the Civil Service Clerical Association and the Government Minor Grades' Association.[5] By February 1930, replies had been received from all but the Institution of Professional Civil Servants, intimating the willingness of these organisations to attend a preliminary conference with the Post Office Workers' Union to consider the question of setting up a permanent joint committee.[6] In July 1930, the general secretary of the Civil Service Federation, T. J. Hughes, issued a circular letter on the matter to members of the council of the federation and to secretaries of organisations outside it. Mr Hughes was later to take up a full-time appointment with the British Institution of Professional Civil Servants. This circular stated, inter alia:

In the opinion of many the Saorstat Service is too small to maintain methods of organisation such as have hitherto obtained following precedents established during the British regime. The total strength of our Service does not exceed the membership of several individual Associations in Great Britain. The multiplicity of small Associations involves considerable duplication of work and the distribution of funds in the maintenance of separate secretaries, journals and premises. It is for consideration whether the establishment of a single union for all Saorstat Civil Servants is or is not practicable at the present time. The advantages of such a Union are obvious. The Executive would have at its disposal large sums of money which are now not spent with great advantage. It would thus be able to maintain an efficient secretariat with a number of full-time officials. Central well equipped and commodious premises could be obtained which would provide for the carrying on of all Service activities. Representations on behalf of constituents could be more effectively made with the service of such a secretariat than at present, and the claims of such bodies could be put forward with the backing of the whole of the staff.

If the Service considers that the formation of a single Union is either not desirable or not practicable at the present time a step forward might be made by the formation of some kind of Confederation in which the various organisations could be associated to deal with matters of mutually agreed common interest. It is not contemplated that the autonomy of bodies affiliated to the Confederation should be restricted. Association would be loose and, in theory, meetings infrequent — say quarterly.[7]

The circular advocated the possibility of a general purposes committee which would be continuously engaged in prosecuting the aims of the Confederation regarding such urgent issues as the safeguarding and improvement of the bonus, conciliation machinery, the retrenchment policies re salaries and grading, superannuation, principles of promotion, civil rights, widows' pensions, differentiated scales, and so on. The circular concluded by suggesting a conference of interested parties. The outcome of the conference and discussions was set out in the Post Office Workers' Union annual report for 1930:

During the year the question of a Joint Committee of Civil Service Organisations has been pursued by the National Executive. A Conference was held on the 29th September last to consider the question, submitted by the Civil Service Federation, of the formation of one Civil Service Union, or, if this was not possible, the formation of a federation of Civil Service Organisations. After giving the matter careful consideration the National Executive decided that it would not be to the advantage of the Union to associate itself with the idea of a single Civil Service Union, nor did it see any value in a costly, rigid scheme of Federation. The Civil Service Clerical Association, and the Civil Service Federation, however, agreed to discuss the question of the amalgamation, but it is understood nothing definite has come from the discussions. The question of proceeding with the setting up of the Joint Committee was re-opened recently, but the Civil Service Federation have indicated that they do not desire to participate in the setting up of such a Committee. The remaining separate Associations outside the Federation, however, are understood to prefer a Joint Committee, and negotiations are proceeding with a view to establishing such a Committee for these bodies.

A joint committee was eventually established, representing the Post Office Workers' Union, the Civil Service Clerical Association, the Association of Officers of Customs and Excise and the Association of Officers of Taxes.

THE STRUGGLE FOR CONCILIATION AND ARBITRATION

The 1930 annual general meeting of the Association of Executive Officers of the Civil Service decided that the title of the association be changed to The Association of Officers of the Executive and Higher Grades of the Civil Service. This decision was taken because some officers, superior in rank to the higher executive grade, were already members of the association, and other officers, who would be willing to join, thought that the existing rules precluded them from membership. The association remained in affiliation to the Civil Service Federation.

The case for the establishment of an acceptable scheme of conciliation and arbitration was represented by the federation and the Civil Service Joint Committee. The Association of Executive Officers made no separate submission on arbitration to the Brennan Commission since the federation had made a submission on behalf of all its affiliates. In its submission to the commission, the Department of Finance, said that when the civil service had been transferred to the Free State there was

In Public Service

no machinery in existence for arbitration on civil service matters. Such machinery had been set up during World War I, the submission stated, but because of the establishment of Whitley Councils, it had been abolished in 1922 (arbitration boards were re-established in Britain in 1925). The submission of the Department of Finance continued:

No demand for the establishment of arbitration machinery was put forward by the Free State Civil Service following the change of Government. The subject was never suggested by staff representatives for discussion at the Representative Council. The first indication of intention by the staff to seek for arbitration was given at a public function held by a staff association early in 1931, and the subject was referred to the Minister for Finance in a debate in the Dáil on 11 June 1931.

It is correct that a firm intention to seek the establishment of an Arbitration Board did not emerge until 1931, although William Norton of the Post Office Workers' Union, in a letter dated 10 March 1927 to the secretary of the Civil Service Federation, stated: '. . . my Executive is prepared to co-operate with your Federation and the Institution of Professional Civil Servants in an endeavour to secure the setting up of an Arbitration Board, but it is not prepared at present to take any steps to amend the Civil Service Representative Council.'

The matter was pursued in an editorial in the same issue of the *Civil Service Journal,* which stated that some kind of arbitration court would have to be established to make conciliation machinery effective. The function to which the Department of Finance's submission referred was the Civil Service Federation annual dinner and dance.[8] All the speakers favoured the principle of independent arbitration. Father Canavan S. J. said that there seemed to be a case for settlement of disputes by arbitration, but that certain clear guarantees had to be given:

1. Their case must in no sense be made a political issue.
2. The civil service must accept the award as final.
3. The authority of Parliament must be supreme. The Board of Arbitrators must not be regarded as having powers superior to Parliament, which might change or reject the award.

1923-1935

A statement made by Ernest Blythe, the Minister for Finance, in the Dáil on 11 June 1931 included the following remarks:

> Suggestions have been made from time to time that any differences of opinion that might arise in relation to the Civil Service bonus or salaries should be submitted to arbitration. In my opinion, in spite of the fact that the arbitration system was established in Great Britain just as the Whitley Council was established there, the system is entirely unsuitable for this particular work and entirely unjustified. The claim for it has no regard to the real facts of the situation. . . . If you were to have an arbitrator to deal with Civil Service salaries only one side of the thing would be looked at. The conditions of affairs relating to the real employer of civil servants would not be looked at at all. It is a fact that the real employer of civil servants is not the Executive Council, the Government or the Oireachtas, but rather the ordinary tax payers of the country. The Government is only a representative, and the only proper arbitrator that you could have for dealing with civil servants' salaries and conditions of employment in the Civil Service is, I venture to assert, the Minister for Finance.

The general election in 1932 brought to power a Fianna Fáil government. This administration set up the Brennan Commission, whose terms of reference included a request to report on: the methods by which arbitration can best be applied for the settlement of questions relating to pay and other conditions of service.

The commission was also expected 'to consider first and submit an interim report on that part of the Terms of Reference relating to the application of the principle of Arbitration already accepted by the Government.'

The demand of the staff associations in 1922 was for a continuation of the Whitley system that had been in place at the time of transfer to the Free State administration. They saw in the Whitley system bodies that had decision-making powers at both national and departmental levels. The constitution of the national council provided that its scope 'shall comprise all matters which affect the conditions of service of the staff. . . . The National Council shall be the only joint body to determine questions of remuneration affecting a class employed in two or more departments . . . decisions shall be arrived at by agreement between the two sides, shall be signed by the Chairman and

Vice-Chairman, shall be reported to the Cabinet, and thereupon become operative.' The council was therefore an executive rather than an advisory body.

In May 1922, staff representatives met General Michael Collins of the provisional government to seek the continued operation of the Whitley Council. Collins made it clear that he could not commit the as yet unborn Free State government to accept any machinery such as Whitleyism. However, he admitted that some body should function during the transitional period in place of the defunct Whitley Council. As a result of this meeting, a joint consultative body was established. The Civil Service Federation never took kindly to that temporary arrangement and the experience of the staff representatives during the period of its existence proved the inadequacy of the body for dealing effectively with staff representations.

On 10 December 1923, a deputation from the federation met Ernest Blythe and pressed him to introduce an acceptable scheme of conciliation. The immediate outcome of the interview was that the minister extended an invitation to the federation to formulate proposals for a scheme that would receive his personal attention. The proposals were duly submitted. The federation was unable to depart from the principle of Whitleyism and the minister, unwilling to accept this principle, undertook to submit a conciliation scheme.

In July 1924 the vote for the estimate of the Ministry of Finance was moved in the Dáil and Deputy Thomas Johnson said:

When this matter was under discussion last week the question was raised as to the position of Civil Servants, as to means of access to the Ministry in matters affecting the service, and as to whether the Ministry was prepared to re-institute the Whitley council system or something equivalent.

Deputy Johnson proposed a proper negotiating system. The President of the Dáil, William T. Cosgrave, who replied on behalf of the Minister, stated that he did not consider it was desirable or necessary to have in the Free State civil service bodies such as the Whitley institutions. He indicated that the minister was most anxious that there would be created for the civil service, some body, similar to the Police Representative Council, that could bring before the Minister for Finance, and in that way before the Executive Council, any representations the staff desired to make affecting their conditions of service. The Minister for Finance promised to prepare a draft of the arrangement. On 6 September he notified the federation that 'the draft of the scheme for the future is complete. Before communicating the draft to the staff . . . it is my intention to bring it before the Executive Council at their next meeting, and as soon as their decision is obtained the proposals will be communicated to your Association and other representatives of the staff.' The proposals were not communicated to the association and on 4 December the Ministry of Finance issued circular 48/24. The Civil Service Federation gave close attention to the scheme and, in view of what were considered to be its defects and shortcomings, it was considered necessary to issue to affiliated associations a warning not to take any steps that might be construed as an acceptance of the scheme. One beneficial result of the issuance of the scheme was that the different branches of the civil service were brought into closer relationship and a provisional staff side was formed, consisting of representatives of the federation, the Institution of Professional Civil Servants and the Post Office Workers' Union. The new staff side considered the combined views of the three main bodies and a letter, signed jointly by the three secretaries, was addressed to the secretary of the Department of Finance on 2 February 1925.

The minister's reply was first considered independently by the three main constituents of the provisional staff side, and then by the full staff side, who decided that, before the final decision on the circular was taken, the minister be asked to receive a deputation from the provisional staff side. A joint communication to this effect was forwarded to the department on 26 February 1925. The reply of 11 March stated:

. . . I am directed by the Minister for Finance to inform you that the decisions arrived at in this matter were taken in full view of the arrangements previously in operation for representation in the Civil Service, and the statement conveyed to you in the letter of the 14th ultimo was made after careful consideration of the views already expressed in your communication of the 2nd February.

If you desire to add anything to the statement last mentioned, the Minister will be glad to receive it, but he does not consider it necessary to ask you to send a deputation to discuss the subject and thinks the interests of the staffs will best be served if action is taken on the lines of the Circular letter from this Ministry of 4th December last (E.100/4).

The Civil Service Federation subsequently convened a special meeting of its council to determine the federation's line of action in regard to the proposed conciliation scheme. The resultant decision by a large majority vote was that, as far as the federation was concerned, the scheme was to be given a trial.[9] The Association of Executive Officers commented:

The Scheme, undoubtedly, has its shortcomings but the Minister for Finance has stated in the Dáil that he is prepared to remedy any defects discovered in the working. In the interests of efficiency, economy and contentment in the Service, may we express the hope that the trial gallop will justify the optimism of the Federation in supporting 'A scheme devised expressly to meet Irish needs'. The effective operation of the scheme depends on the goodwill of Official and Staff Sides. Capital and Labour circles will be keenly interested in results.

The provisional staff sides met on a number of occasions and, after the federation had decided to accept the scheme, the following responses were received from the Post Office Workers' Union and the Institution of Professional Civil Servants:

Institution of Professional Civil Servants
25th June 1925

Secretary
Civil Service Federation

Dear Sir,

I am instructed by my Council to inform you that at its meeting last Tuesday evening, it was unanimously decided not to accept the Government's Scheme for Conciliation Machinery.

They regret to learn from their representative that the Federation, as was announced at the joint meeting last week, have decided to act on their own initiative in accepting and attempting to work the

Scheme, and hope that it may not yet be too late for united, instead of individual, action upon the part of the three bodies concerned.

Yours faithfully,

(sgd) W. J. Adams
Secretary

Post Office Workers' Union
8th July 1925

Mr P. J. McElhinney
Civil Service Federation
19 Upper Merrion St., Dublin

Dear Mr McElhinney,

As arranged at the last Joint Meeting, I acquainted my Executive of the decision of the Civil Service Federation to give the Government's Representative Council Scheme a trial, explaining the reasons stated by you for your decision, and I asked my Executive to indicate its attitude towards the Scheme in the light of your decision.

The feeling of my Executive was that the Scheme in its present form was utterly worthless and its deficiencies make it altogether unacceptable to use. We have, therefore, decided not to take any action whatever to work the Scheme and we regret very much that your Federation has not seen its way to stand firm on this matter and thus indicate to the Government generally, and the Minister for Finance in particular, that a united Civil Service would not accept such a miserable and reactionary Scheme.

Yours fraternally,
W. Norton,
General Secretary

The federation then applied to the Department of Finance for official recognition for the purpose of representation on the representative council. The first meeting of the council was held on 15 March 1926. The *Civil Service Journal* of April 1926 stated that it was the unanimous opinion of the 'recognised' associations that the constitution of the council was unsatisfactory to the staff in several respects. The minister on several occasions had signified his willingness to consider carefully any amendments to the constitution of the council which the staff might suggest. The *Journal* also included a statement that proposals for amendment had been agreed upon by the staff side and were being sent forward to the minister, with a request that he receive a deputation to discuss them.

The secretary of the federation in fact had written to the Post Office Workers' Union and to the Institution of Professional Civil Servants on February 1927 and a conference of the groups had been held on 3 March. The points discussed at the conference and forwarded to the different executives included:

1. Provision should be made for the setting up of departmental councils or committees to deal with departmental matters.
2. The chairman of both local and central councils should not have the right to decide which matters should be placed on the agenda for discussion.
3. That the councils should have power to come to decisions.
4. Provision should be made for the attendance at council meetings of the full-time officers of associations.
5. That an appeal body should be set up to which matters on which disagreement had been reached might be referred.[10]

Within a week William Norton of the Post Office Workers' Union replied as follows:

Your Memorandum of the 4th instant was considered at a Meeting of my Executive which was held last Tuesday, and I have been instructed to inform you that my Executive is prepared to co-operate with your Federation and the Institution of Professional Civil Servants in an endeavour to secure the setting up of an Arbitration Board, but it is not prepared at present to take any steps to amend the Civil Service Representative Council machinery. . . .

The memorandum was sent to the Minister on 26 May 1927, but a reply was not received until 30 September. The Department of Finance attributed the delay to pressure of other matters (there were two general elections in 1927). Meanwhile the staff side decided that, until the suggested amendments had been dealt with, no matters would be put down for discussion at the council meeting. Merely formal meetings were held to comply with the constitution. A meeting with the minister did eventually take place on 12 December 1927, but the sole outcome was a marginal improvement in the arrangements to enable departmental classes to represent their views.[11]

In the meantime, the Civil Service Clerical Association had seceded from the federation in September 1927 because its affiliation hampered its activities and its internal organisation. This association withdrew from the council because of its dissatisfaction with the minister's refusal to amend the council's constitution. From that time, the council ceased to represent the majority of civil servants.

In July 1928 the Civil Service Clerical Association decided to write to the Post Office Workers' Union suggesting a joint approach with the Institute of Professional Civil Servants to the Department of Finance on the subject of conciliation machinery. This approach drew the following response from the general secretary of the Post Office Workers' Union:

> Your letter of the 18th instant on the subject of the setting up of conciliation machinery was considered by my Executive at its meeting on the 22nd and 23rd instant, and I have been instructed to inform you that my Executive considers that what is really required is an Arbitration Board. My Executive fears, however, that progress in the direction of getting such an Arbitration Board will be impeded by the 'Civil Service Representative Council', the existence of which, in the view of my Executive, will be used by the Department as an argument to show that conciliation machinery in some form exists. My Executive is prepared to consider co-operation in the direction of establishing an Arbitration Board, but the first step in this direction must be the withdrawal of existing staff organisations from the Civil Service Representative Council. My Executive is prepared to co-operate with your organisation and the Institution of Professional Civil Servants in approaching the Civil Service Federation and the other organisations who have representation on the Representative Council, with a view to requesting them to withdraw from that body, and to ask for the setting up of an Arbitration Board which is really what the Service requires.

The Civil Service Clerical Association and the Civil Service Federation then made a joint approach to the Minister for Finance. A deputation met him on 6 June 1929. The Civil Service Clerical Association was represented by Archie Heron,

In Public Service

its new general secretary, and some clerical officers. The deputation raised the following matters with the minister:

1. The admission of full-time officers to the council.
2. The inclusion of members of the Dáil on the council.
3. The minister's decision was to be based on agreed reports.
4. Official views to be discussed at the council.
5. Delays in obtaining agreed minutes.
6. Departmental machinery.

The *Civil Service Journal* commented as follows:

Having waited for close on two years, the Minister has at last given his decision on the suggested improvements in the Representative Council. His reply will be regarded everywhere as utterly unsatisfactory. We do not qualify that remark, for we cannot but believe that even his own advisers must recognise that the situation as it stands is rather forced and cannot be maintained.

The result of the general election of 16 February 1932 was: Fianna Fáil 72 seats, Cumann na nGaedheal 57, Independent 11, Labour 7, Farmers 4 and Independent Labour 2. William Norton was chosen to replace T. J. O'Connell, who had lost his seat, as leader of the Labour Party in the Dáil. The party decided to support Fianna Fáil in forming a government. Before the election, both parties pledged to support the civil service demand for arbitration and, on 22 June the Department of Finance announced the appointment of a commission to inquire and report on the organisation of the civil service. Its terms of reference were as follows:

To inquire into and report on the Organisation of the Civil Service, with special reference to the arrangements for ensuring efficiency in working; the general standard of remuneration of Civil Servants; the age of retirement from the Service, and the methods by which arbitration can best be applied for the settlement of questions relating to pay and other conditions of service.

The commission advertised in the press on 9 July, inviting persons or associations who desired to submit evidence to communicate with the secretary. Memoranda bearing on the subject of arbitration were submitted to the commission by the following: Department of Finance; Civil Service Joint

Committee; Civil Service Federation; The Institute of Professional Civil Servants; clerical officers (formerly members of the Districts Board Staff); the chairman of the Revenue Commissioners; the secretary, Department of Posts and Telegraphs; Association of Chambers of Commerce of the Irish Free State; a committee representing all grades of women civil servants; and the Association of Officers of Taxes.

The committee was asked to consider first and to submit an interim report on that part of the terms of reference relating to the application of the principle of arbitration already accepted by the government.[12]

The Civil Service Federation, on behalf of the Association of the Executive and Higher Grades and its other affiliates, submitted that, in view of this request, it was unnecessary to repeat the arguments used by the federation in the campaign it had carried on for the establishment of a Civil Service Arbitration Board. Those arguments were directed to demonstrating the justice and expediency of giving effect to the principle, now recognised, of arbitration when disputes arose between the government and civil service staff organisations regarding conditions of service of civil servants. The submission therefore was confined to a brief exposition of the views of the federation as to how a system of arbitration could be devised for the civil service which would operate to the best advantage of all interests. (In the Fianna Fáil 1932 election manifesto, issued over the signature of Eamon de Valera, it was stated that a Fianna Fáil government would establish an arbitration board to deal with the grievances of the civil service.) The staff organisations were substantially in agreement on the proposals put forward to the commission on the constitution of the arbitration board:

1. The chairman to be appointed by agreement between the government and the staff organisations.
2. Each party to be free to select its representatives on the board and its advocates before the board.
3. Each party to have the right to bring before the board any claim, within a previously agreed category, without veto by the other party, the board alone having power to decide whether a particular claim fell within the agreed category.

In Public Service

4. The government to give effect to the awards of the board, subject to the authority of Parliament.
5. In the event of a dispute about the meaning of an award, the board would determine its own findings.

In its submission, the Civil Service Federation pointed to the need to provide additional machinery for negotiations regarding the conditions of service of civil servants. Such negotiations, it was pointed out, if they did not result in agreement, would at least serve a useful purpose in revealing to the board the exact ground covered by a dispute and thus save time in the hearing of the cases.

It became evident at an early stage in the proceedings of the commission that there was a fundamental disagreement between the Department of Finance and the staff associations about the extent of the government's commitment. The commission's interim report, signed on 5 February 1934 by a majority of its members, said inter alia:

The intimation conveyed to us that the principle of arbitration was already accepted by the Government obviously constitutes an advance towards the staff viewpoint on the shortcomings of the existing system. We find ourselves, however, in a position of having little or no assistance from the evidence in defining any agreed extent to which it can be said that the policy of arbitration for the Civil Service has been advanced by this intimation. On the one hand, it was stated in evidence by the Assistant Secretary of the Department of Finance that the intimation was given without prior investigation in that Department of the practical possibility of devising a scheme of arbitration that would be suitable in the case of the Civil Service, and it seemed to be the view of that witness that that intimation did not in itself contribute or purport to contribute anything towards elucidating the actual framework of any method of arbitration for the Civil Service. Staff witnesses, on the other hand, claimed to interpret the intimation as involving a much deeper commitment of the Government, and at times when answering questions on aspects of their proposals they argued that practical points raised by the questions should be assumed to have been settled by implication in the prior acceptance of the principle of arbitration.

The commission took the view that the reference to it was of an open character and that there was no good reason for supposing it was debarred from giving full weight to any considerations that would have a practical bearing on the framing of a scheme of arbitration. In the event, the commission's majority report proved to be totally unacceptable to the staff associations.

The view expressed in this report was that staff proposals would vest in the arbitration tribunal an authority that would be excessive, and that no arrangement should be made whereby the award of an independent arbitration tribunal should be recognised either legally or de facto as binding upon the executive council or upon the Minister for Finance. It was considered inevitable that the discretion of ministers who were responsible for the budget had to prevail in the last resort over any subordinate authority, however constituted. The executive council therefore should be free to adopt, or not, the findings of an arbitration board.

It was also considered that arbitration should take place only on specific issues to be agreed on each occasion between the Minister for Finance and the body of civil servants concerned and to be set forth in a formal reference to the tribunal. In that way the minister would be afforded an opportunity to see that any issue submitted to arbitration was of a character that seemed to him to be suitable for settlement in that manner. The *Civil Service Journal*, the official organ, commented: 'The Service has been deeply shocked by the Report of the Brennan Commission on Arbitration.'

The Minister for Finance proposed that the interim report should be discussed at the Civil Service Representative Council. The federation rejected this proposal because it considered that it could not be drawn into a discussion about whether or not the principle of arbitration should be applied to the settlement of disputes regarding the conditions of employment of civil servants. It was considered that reopening a controversy ended by the mandate expressly sought and obtained from the electorate for the establishment of an arbitration board would lend some credence to the interim report. This decision was conveyed to the minister in a letter from the federation on 4 July 1934. The letter also indicated that the federation would not take part in any further proceedings of the representative

In Public Service

council as then constituted. It was suggested that a special conference of government and service representatives be held to discuss the scheme of arbitration that the federation had placed before the commission. In a reply, dated 4 September, the minister made no reference to the suggested conference but noted, with concern, the decision to take no further part in the council. The letter concluded by stating that if the staff side declined to attend meetings of the council, the minister might be obliged to postpone action on the report indefinitely or, alternatively, to proceed to a decision without its assistance. The Civil Service Representative Council thereupon effectively ceased to function. The Department of Finance subsequently did produce a draft scheme of arbitration which the staff organisation rejected as unsatisfactory and unacceptable.

COST-OF-LIVING BONUS

Soon after the 1932 election, the Fianna Fáil government set up a number of bodies to examine aspects of the public service. One such committee caused great alarm among civil servants. The 'Cuts Committee' was set up in September 1932 to make recommendations to the Minister for Finance about the reductions that could be made in the present year in the pay of the civil service, army, Garda Síochána and primary school teachers, having regard to the general financial and economic position of the state and to the circumstances and conditions of service in each of the services and the relations of the services to each other. The majority report, presented in October 1932, recommended substantial cuts in the pay of the army and teachers, but recognised the special position of the civil service as being radically different because the variation in the cost of living had been reflected in the salaries; by that means, a substantial contribution to the national economy had already been made, and would be made to a further degree in that financial year.

The Brennan Commission was later to make a similar point. Paragraph 160 of the report states: 'There is an obvious lack of consistency in the application of the bonus system by the State. It has no application to numerous classes of persons whose remuneration is defrayed from the Exchequer. School teachers, the Civic Guard and the Army all receive an inclusive rate of pay which has no element of bonus.'

The government set up two other bodies in 1932. The Committee on the Cost of Living Index Figure, which reported in May 1933, and the Commission of Inquiry into the Civil Service (Brennan Commission), which made its final report in November/December 1935. The Civil Service Federation, on behalf of its affiliates, including the Association of Officers of the Executive and Higher Grades, made submissions to both bodies. In its submission to the Brennan Commission, the Department of Finance set out the official view of the bonus system as follows:

The pay of the Civil Servant is made up of two different elements, viz. a scale of fixed salary not liable to fluctuation, and an addition thereto by way of supplement related to the current cost of living which varies up and down in accordance with the ascertained index figure. The bonus is based on a cost of living index figure ascertained quarterly on the basis of current prices. Until 1922 the bonus paid to Irish Civil Servants was calculated on the same cost of living index figure as in Great Britain. In 1922 a cost of living index figure based on Free State conditions was ascertained and applied. The basic salary, generally speaking, represents what would be paid to the official had there been no increase in the cost of living since 1914. The bonus is intended, in the case of officials receiving a higher basic salary than £91 per annum, to make up in part the increase in the cost of living ruling from time to time as compared with 1914.

The submission continued:

The use of the word bonus to describe this element of Civil Service remuneration was unfortunate. It has always tended to give the impression that the payment it represents was something over and above what the official really earns by way of salary or wages — something to which he is not entitled in the sense in which he is entitled to his basic salary. Further, the impression has prevailed that the bonus makes up to all officials the full difference in cost of living as compared with conditions prior to the European War. This is not and never has been the case.

The Department of Finance directed the attention of the Brennan Commission to what was known as the super-cut. In

In Public Service

August 1921, the British government had reduced the bonus on basic salaries exceeding £500 a year and had laid down that a bonus should not be payable at a rate that would raise an officer's total remuneration above £2,000 a year. This cut was retained by the Free State government. While the arrangements regarding salaries up to £500 had been the subject of agreement between the associations and the government in Britain, the super-cut was imposed without consultation with the associations.

In June 1931, the Dáil discussed the following motion proposed by Deputy Richard Anthony:

> That in view of the discontent prevalent amongst the lower grades in the Civil Service, the Dáil is of the opinion that the Executive Council should set up a Commission of Inquiry to investigate and report on the present method of computation of the cost of living bonus and its application to Civil Servants' salaries and wages.

The motion was supported by Fianna Fáil and Labour deputies, but on a snap division it was defeated by 57 votes to 42. During the 1932 election campaign, Fianna Fáil promised that, if it was voted into office, the party would review the salaries and pensions of civil servants in general, and the higher paid civil servants in particular. The government invited Senator Thomas Johnson to preside over a Committee on the Cost of Living Index figure. This committee's terms of reference were:

> To enquire into and report on any complaints addressed to the Committee by organisations representative of persons employed in Government Service whose remuneration is regulated, in whole or in part, by the cost of living index figure as to the principles and methods according to which that figure is computed.

The Post Office Workers' Union, which had sponsored the Dáil motion in 1931, expressed disappointment and said that the limited terms of reference would make its work of little value to civil service organisations. The committee was precluded from inquiring into the method of applying the cost-of-living bonus to basic wages and salaries.[13] In the event, the only memoranda submitted came from the Civil Service Federation and the Irish Government Workers' Union (Minor Grades).

The kernel of the case made by the Civil Service Federation was that the average civil servant's household budget included items that did not appear at all, or only to a negligible extent, in that of a working-class household. These items included travelling expenses, life insurance, restaurant meals, medical expenses, books and maidservants. It was argued that the circumstances of a civil servant's household differed greatly from that of a working-class household. At least one maidservant was normally employed in the former and the period of dependency of the children was more extended than in a working-class family.

In its recommendations, the committee went some of the way to meet these complaints. It was recommended that a budget inquiry should be undertaken with a view to revising, if necessary, the weighting used in the computation of the wage-earning class index figure, and that middle-class budgets should also be obtained for the purpose of computing a middle-class figure. The committee thought it well to examine the effect of the inclusion of alcoholic drink in the index figure. It was not included in the existing computation, but it was estimated that the national drink bill represented about $9\frac{1}{2}$% of the total national income. It was recommended that an inquiry on drink expenditure should be specifically included in the form of inquiry. If an allowance equivalent to ten per cent of household expenditure was made for alcoholic liquor, it would have increased the official figure by eight points. It was not accepted that insurance premiums or income tax should be budget items.

The federation made the following submission to the Brennan Commission:

(a) sacrifice of full compensation under the 1920 agreement for the decreased purchasing power of money, however it might have been considered desirable in the circumstances of 1920, needed amelioration . . . having regard to the subsequent unanticipated decline of the cost-of-living index figure on which the bonus was payable.

(b) The bonus super-cut imposed in 1921 on the already substantially scaled-down compensation on basic (pre-1914) remuneration above £500 per annum could not be defended in the circumstances and should be withdrawn.

(c) The automatic relation of civil service remuneration to the cost-of-living index figure had, in the light of experience, been shown to have inflicted on civil servants big reductions of pay not sustained by other state employees nor by non-state employees, which could not be defended on the principle of a fair relativity between civil service and outside remuneration.

(d) Having regard to outside practice, no further reduction in civil service remuneration below that payable on the current cost-of-living index figure of 55 was justifiable.

(e) Having regard to the finding of the Johnson Committee on the cost-of-living index figure as to the inclusion of alcoholic liquor in the national cost-of-living index figure, the payment of civil service bonus on an index figure eight points higher than the current figure was justifiable and should be immediately effected.

(f) The preparation of the index figures recommended by the Johnson Committee should be commenced as soon as practicable.

(g) That no revision of the bonus system would be equitable which did not take into account the exceptional sacrifices suffered in the past by civil servants.

The majority report of the Brennan Commission came to the radical conclusion that steps should be taken to terminate the bonus system at an early date and that discussions towards this end should be undertaken with the staff organisations through the Civil Service Representative Council.[14] The commission had noted the evidence that, in a number of occupations outside the civil service, rates of remuneration that had moved upwards in times of rising prices had since been maintained without serious reduction, notwithstanding subsequent downward movements of the cost of living. The report pointed out that the operation of the bonus system during the previous fifteen years effectively ensured that the remuneration of the civil service would not be open to criticism for exhibiting so questionable a rigidity. However, while the bonus system could be said to have justified itself in the past in times of more or less violent fluctuation in the cost-of-living, it seemed pertinent then to inquire whether, in view of the more settled price-level of recent years, it could be considered to have outlived its usefulness. Members of the commission had asked a number of witnesses who appeared on behalf of staff organisations about their attitude towards the possible discontinuance of the bonus system. As might be expected, these witnesses considered that the answer would depend very much upon which terms of discontinuance would be proposed.

The terms on which the commission proposed to effect the consolidation of pay and bonus clearly would not have been acceptable to staff organisations.

Senator Thomas Johnson, who had chaired the Committee on the Cost of Living Index Figure, was also a member of the Brennan Commission. He did not accept the recommendations of the majority that the bonus system should be abolished. In a minority report he recommended that:

1. The bonus system should be continued.
2. The method of fixing the index number should be modified in accordance with the recommendations of the Committee on the Cost of Living Index figure.
3. The full amount of the increase in retail prices as indicated by the cost-of-living index figure should be added to the first £160 of ordinary remuneration (or basic pay) instead of on the first £91.5.0.
4. The pay of the lower grades should be adjusted so as to provide a minimum rate for whole-time staff (male) at the age of 25 years of:

	£ s d
For officers on weekly wages of :	40. 0
which with bonus (calculated on an index figure of 55) :	60. 7
For officers on annual salaries of :	100. 0. 0
which with bonus (calculated on an index figure of 55) :	152. 9. 0

In the event, the government did not implement the recommendations of either report. The reduction in bonus due on 1 July 1933 was suspended for six weeks to enable the associations to make recommendations on the report of the Johnson Committee. The reduction was enforced as from 13 August 1933. When the cost of living increased as a result

In Public Service

of the wartime conditions, the government stabilised the bonus by an Emergency Power Order in 1940.

ALTERATIONS IN BASIC PAY-DIFFERENTIATED SCALES

In its submission to the Brennan Commission, the Association of Officers of the Executive and Higher Grades agreed that the progressive salary scale was the proper system of remuneration, but it expressed emphatic condemnation of the empirical methods adopted in framing the salary scales for the Saorstát civil service, especially with regard to the executive grades. The association pointed out that there were no less than four separate scales in operation for executive officers and no less than five for higher executive officers, namely:

Executive Officers
(a) £100 - £10 - £130 - £15 - £400 (undifferentiated). Applied to officers transferred in their grades from the British service. This was the London rate.
(b) £95 - £9$^{1/2}$ - £123$^{1/2}$ - £14$^{1/2}$ - £380 (undifferentiated). Applied to officers transferred as (a) above but on a special provincial scale applied to Dublin and provincial British towns in 1920.
(c) £90 - £7$^{1/2}$ - £105 - £10 - £175 - £15 - £310 - £10 - £350 (undifferentiated). Applied to officers promoted or recruited to the grades since the Treaty of 6 December 1921.
(d) 1. £90 - £7$^{1/2}$ - £210 - £10 - £250
    2. £90 - £7$^{1/2}$ - £105 - £10 - £175 - £15 - £310 - £10 - £350 plus children's allowances.

1. Applied to women promoted or recruited to the grade since the Treaty and for single men recruited after 1925.
2. Applied to married men recruited after 1925.

Higher Executive Officers
(e) £400 - £15 - £500 as (a) above ⎫
(f) £380 - £14$^{1/2}$ - £475 as (b) above ⎬ Undifferentiated
(g) £350 - £15 - £500 as (c) above ⎭
(h) £285 - £14$^{1/2}$ - £380 — applied to women only — transferred post-Treaty.

1923-1935

(i) £250 - £10 - £350 - applied to women only — promoted or recruited post-Treaty.

On 21 November 1924, the Department of Finance issued a circular (No.44/24) that stated that the Minister for Finance did not consider that 'the conditions in the Saorstát' warranted the payment for future appointments to the typing, clerical and executive classes of scales of salary as high as those then obtaining. The reduced scales were set out in the circular. The new scales were imposed without prior negotiation with the staff associations, and no reason beyond the statement in the circular was assigned for the change. From the setting up of the Free State to the issuance of the circular, many vacancies had to be filled. Promotions to these were made on an 'acting' basis only. Subsequent to the appearance of the circular, these promotions were confirmed permanently in their appointments, but on the reduced salary scales.

The circular also provided for a considerable reduction in the amounts of allowable annual leave. The following examples show the extent of the reduction.

	No. of Days before the change of government	No. of Days fixed in 1924
Administration class	36-48	30-36
Higher executive grade	36-48	30
Executive grade	36	21-24
Clerical grade	24	15-21
Writing assistant class	18-21	12-18
Shorthand-typist class	21-24	15-18
Typist class	18-21	12-15

The Civil Service Federation took the line that the minister should hear the staff's views on all conditions of circular 44/24. The federation was particularly concerned about the effect of the circular on the rights of the transferred officers who, according to the minister, on acceptance of a higher office than that enjoyed under the British government, would forfeit the right to claim to retire in consequence of the change of government. The Department of Finance contended that provision had already been made through the Civil Service Representative Council to enable the views of organisations representative of the civil service to be communicated to the Minister for Finance. It was not until the council first met on 15 March 1926 that the staff side had an opportunity formally to discuss the terms of the circular.

At this meeting the staff side objected to the reduced scales of pay and allowances of leave laid down in circular 44/24. They pointed out that at the time of the change of government, the Whitley Reorganisation report had not been applied to all Irish departments, the result being that, though certain new posts had been recognised, they were not actually filled. At the same time the officers, who might reasonably have looked forward to promotion to the newly created posts, were actually discharging the duties of those posts. A number of these officers were later promoted, but at scales of pay lower than those they would have received had the original reorganisation schemes proceeded. The staff side held the view that the existence of several types of officers belonging to the one grade doing the same class of work, but remunerated according to different scales, was not conducive to efficiency. The design of the circular was to effect economies in the cost of the public service, but the staff side submitted that no immediate economies could be secured by the new scales.

Officers who had been promoted on an acting basis to the clerical and junior executive grades suffered hardship because of the fixing of the reduced salary scales and leave allowances. They had interpreted the acting nature of their appointments solely as precluding them from claiming enhanced compensation under Article 10 of the Treaty of 6 December 1921, and not carrying with it any liability to reduction of scales or leave on conversion to substantive rank.

The official side maintained that the Whitley Reorganisation report was framed mainly with regard to conditions in Britain and that it did not bind the Minister for Finance. It could not, for example, conceivably be held to govern the cases of 700 recently recruited clerical officers. The new scales had been fixed in line with rates generally paid in the Saorstát. The government felt that it could recruit suitable material for the grades dealt with in the circular at the pay specified, and in the circumstances it could not justifiably offer more. The salaries laid down in the circular were not in all cases lower than those provided for in the Whitley reorganisation scheme — e.g. the maximum of the higher executive grade was fixed at £500, as against £475 in the Whitley report. Generally, of course, the scales were reduced, but this was in conformity with the general practice governing the remuneration of public servants in the Saorstát. The official side could not admit that promotion to an 'acting' appointment carried any guarantee that, on being given substantive status, officers would still retain unchanged the scales and pay attaching to the acting posts. The liability to modification was implicit in the 'acting' condition. The official side stated that the nature of the duties of the general service grades, generally speaking, would be as defined in the Whitley report. Higher executive officers, however, would be expected to do more responsible work than higher executive officers in the British service.[15]

The system of differential scales, whereby a discrimination in rates of pay was established between married men and single men and women was introduced in 1925. It was at first applied to the clerical, junior executive and junior administrative grades, but was afterwards extended to a number of other grades. In its submission to the Brennan Commission, the Executive Officers' Association expressed its uncompromising hostility to the principle of differentiation, which, it contended, was introduced on the plea of marriage endowment but in fact had been used solely for the cheapening of labour and so tended to aggravate the social evil it purported to combat. The association asserted its conviction that equal scales for equal work was the only honest basis of remuneration. Its submission went on:

> If discriminatory measures must be taken against celibates of both sexes in order to remedy the social evil of the late marrying age, the social problem should be attacked logically on natural lines by means of differentiated taxation. There may, for example, be every moral and social justification for a per capita supplementary direct tax of a punitive amount levied on the whole celibate population, but the arbitrary imposition of such a penalty on one small section of the community alone by means of differential scales is clearly indefensible.

In Public Service

In its final report, the commission set out its general considerations affecting civil service pay. The pay of the civil service, taken in conjunction with other benefits of state employment like superannuation, should be sufficient to provide a reasonable expectation that it would attract recruits in the number and of the kind required by the government. The commission also stated that, in the case of all posts in the civil service, the pay should be related to the nature of the actual duties of the officer concerned. How then to justify the existence of different rates of pay for the performance of similar duties? The report asserted:

> The relation of pay to duties arises also in connection with the claim advanced by several witnesses to equal pay for equal work. Prima facie, it appears to be reasonable that persons performing the same task should receive the same reward and we think that this principle should always receive due recognition. It would, however, be wrong in our opinion to attribute to it any absolute or over-riding authority which would exclude regard to other considerations that may also merit attention. In any given case there may be a number of competing factors which ought to be recognised in due proportion for the purpose of determining actual rates of remuneration . . . .
>
> We may note that one intelligible if not complete explanation of it is that the wage of the average man tends to be influenced by the fact that, unlike the average woman, he is usually the head of a dependent household.

With regard to other factors that could influence civil service pay, the commission held that the pay of civil servants could not be readily and objectively measured by reference to comparable posts in the outside world. Yet, although no simple rule of that kind was available for ascertaining the appropriate pay for any given civil service post, it was, according to the commission, right and feasible that the fixing of civil service pay should have regard to the need for giving civil servants a standard of living that bears reasonable comparison with the standard of the community in which they lived. Regard, however, must be had to the fact that the civil service was a sheltered occupation that was not subject to the curb of competition as far as costs were concerned, but was maintained at the expense of the community by the exercise of the taxing power of the state.

Almost all classes of civil servants who were represented in evidence before the commission made claims for increases of salary. The commission in some cases noted that these claims were expressed in direct and unambiguous fashion, but in other cases they were of an indirect character, such as proposals for regrading which would have resulted in improved scales of pay for those concerned. The commission concluded that these claims were not sustainable and it felt bound to say that demands for increased pay were entirely out of place, given the prolonged period of economic difficulty and strain that the great mass of the community was suffering. The commission report goes on to state: 'we have indicated strong reasons of a fundamental and national character which render it inopportune that the cost of the Civil Service should be increased at the present time and we think that in such circumstances Civil Servants would be ill advised to seek concessions upon any wide front or to urge any individual claim which could not be supported by exceptionally strong reasons.' The commission maintained that the real problem with the general standard of remuneration of the civil service was not whether it could be raised in accordance with the demands put before it, but whether it could be maintained, as the commissioners thought it should be, at the level that then prevailed.

In its report on differential scales, the Brennan Commission noted that it had been informed that the introduction of what was called 'this novelty in the methods of remuneration of Civil Servants was effected without any previous discussion with representative bodies of the Civil Service and that no reasoned explanation was given at the initiation of the system of the considerations which were thought to be in its favour.' The new system was at first applied to the clerical, junior executive and junior administrative grades, but was afterwards extended to a number of other cases. In 1934 it was extended to clerical officers appointed from the open competition examination held in December 1925 and subsequently when promoted to staff officer posts.[16] The commission reported:

... while not oblivious of the fact that some arguments may be urged in support of the view that the responsibilities of a married man afford a ground for giving him higher remuneration than his unmarried colleague on the same work, we are of the opinion that for practical purposes this ideal is one which the State is not justified in attempting to enforce at least in present circumstances. It finds no recognition in the community generally and to impose it on Civil Servants tends to create a feeling of discontent through the impression that they are expected to allow themselves to become the object of an experiment of which the ultimate results must be doubtful. It also disregards to an unwarranted extent the principle of equal pay for equal work.

In the commission's view, the system ought to be abandoned and a reversion made to the old method whereby officers were paid without reference to their domestic circumstances and without special provision for children's allowances.

Many decades would elapse before differentiated scales ceased to apply.

PROMOTION

The Association of Officers of the Executive and Higher Grades gave considerable thought to the principles that they thought should govern promotion. In a submission to the Brennan Commission, the association stated that there had been a too apparent tendency on the part of candidates to concentrate on (a) methods of creating more numerous opportunities of advancement, and (b) complaints as to bias in the minds of selectors. On the other hand, the selectors were too prone to resent reflections on their discretion and to discount criticism as an expression of purely personal disappointment. However, the association asserted, considerable research had established the fact that much of the dissatisfaction with the machinery of promotion could be traced to the defective methods of the selectors. The association emphasised the difficulty of promotion for two reasons. In conjunction with other bodies affiliated to the Civil Service Federation, it had attempted to reach reasonably definite conclusions on a promotion policy but, unfortunately, the considerations affecting promotions in the lower, middle and higher grades appeared to differ so widely that even prolonged discussions had failed to produce tangible results. Secondly, the association was anxious that the commission should appreciate that the difficulties were not local or personal, but would be found in civil and municipal services and in the larger commercial establishments of every civilised country, and that, if some measure of experiment must be ventured, the proposals submitted by the association represented an earnest attempt to provide for the difficulties of the state and not merely the ambitions of the civil servant. Indeed, it was pointed out, the acceleration of promotion for executive officers would be achieved, if at all, by securing adequate ratios between the numbers in the higher and lower grades and not by the use of a finer sieve for selection.

Two postulates were stated:

1. In the selection of an officer for promotion, merit shall be the sole consideration. (Seniority, as such, should influence promotion only in the rare event of a choice between candidates of equal merit.)

2. Merit should be assessed according to strictly utilitarian standards. (The mere possession of university degree or an analogous qualification should not be a passport to advancement. Academic attainments should be viewed mainly in relation to the requirements of the post to be filled, and the candidate who most perfectly satisfies those requirements should secure the appointment.) The association was concerned at the absence in the civil service of instructions pertaining to the methods of assessing merit.

In its submission to the commission, the association stated: 'In a discussion ad hoc as to the qualifications of a candidate for promotion, two or three officers may form opinions based on entirely different factors.'

The association considered that three principal requirements should be satisfied: (1) the full range and degree of the qualifications of candidates should be stated; (2) a uniform standard of appraisal should be applied; and (3) the bona fides of the selectors should be above question. It strongly urged the experimental adoption of what was known as the Probst Efficiency Rating Report. This type of efficiency reporting was named after a former civil service commissioner in St Paul, Minnesota, who conducted his researches under the auspices of the Spelman Foundation of New York. This system contemplated the use of one form by three officers on a particular candidate. Three reports on a single candidate, it was thought, would produce a fair average rating. The reporting officer was not invited to grade a candidate and the report would be confined to known facts as far as possible. Apparently, the system was undergoing official trial at the time in the British Inland Revenue Service. The association urged that the forms relating to each candidate should be collated for three or four years preceding the occurrence of a vacancy. This material should then be reviewed by a promotion board which should be set up in each department. The board should comprise four officers of principal and assistant principal, and a fifth member elected by the staff. Finally, the association strongly urged the necessity to provide for an appeal system against decisions of the board.

The Brennan Commission examined in some detail the various methods of promotion without offering a radical alternative to the already existing methods. It maintained that it would be a useful measure of progress towards a better arrangement if the system of promotion boards then applied informally and somewhat haphazardly in certain departments were placed on a formal footing and prescribed for general use in all cases where neither examination nor any other formal procedure for promotion was available. The Brennan Commission considered that the promotion board should be formed ad hoc on each occasion when a particular promotion was to be made, and that it should usually be presided over by the establishment officer or his deputy, and that the other members should include an officer or officers of a rank immediately superior to that in which the vacancy existed, but that normally no member should rank lower than higher executive officer. The commission looked at the possibility of making a more effective use of the Civil Service Commission in promotion procedures. Under the Civil Service Regulation Acts, it was the primary duty of that body to issue to every permanent civil servant a certificate of his qualifications for the situation to which he was appointed and that certificate must indicate, amongst other things, that the candidate possessed the requisite knowledge and ability to do the work.

1923-1935

The commission stated that a certificate of the Civil Service Commission was sometimes of a very wide scope so that, for example, a person recruited to a junior post and being certified for that situation may afterwards be promoted through several grades up to a higher administrative post without the need for any further certificate. This is what happened in the case of a customary promotion. The commission considered that this arrangement was unsatisfactory and that a much narrower interpretation should be placed on the phrase 'customary course of promotion' so that there should be a requirement of a fresh certificate of the Civil Service Commission in most cases, where a person already certified for a particular situation was being advanced to any other situation which demanded higher qualifications than were necessary in the lower situation. Many of the witnesses who appeared before the commission referred to the use of examinations as a method of regulating promotion. The commission stated that the method of examination was liable to certain defects in so far as, while affording a fair test of intelligence, it might fail to measure other qualities that were of decisive importance in the matter of promotion. It might also confer an undue advantage upon candidates who had most recently left school and thereby prejudice the chances of officers of longer service and wider experience. These defects, however, could be eliminated to a great extent by a proper choice of syllabus for the examination.

The commission considered that the equitable distribution of the available volume of promotion throughout the civil service was a matter of much importance and urged that the Department of Finance should insist on a sufficient measure of interdepartmental promotion.

THE ADMINISTRATIVE CLASS AND THE ROLE OF THE EXECUTIVE OFFICER

The Association of Officers of the Executive and Higher Grades in the period covered by this chapter were wedded to the principles of the 1920 reorganisation, which distinguished qualitatively between the classes that comprised the civil service. The association claimed to represent the executive and administrative classes, but it accepted that the functions of each class were widely different. The introduction of the junior administrative grade in 1925 was accepted on the basis that both the executive and administrative officers were separate trainee grades. The association made a submission to the Brennan Commission and the junior administrative officers made their own submission. The higher administrative grades were later to be defined as assistant principal and principal officer grades. In their submission, the junior administrative officers stated that the total number of such officers was 27, of whom 18 were in the Department of Finance, four in the Department of Local Government and Public Health and one each in the Departments of Justice, Industry and Commerce, Education, the President and in the Office of the Revenue Commissioners.

The Executive Officers' Association considered that the executive officer's function was primarily to carry out a defined policy. Organisation, direction and the production of results were within the officer's discretion, but the formulation and crystallisation of policy were the concern of the administrative class. Nevertheless, it was thought appropriate to point out that, in the consideration of policy, an important contribution was always required from the executive officer. In the evolution of every policy a stage arrived when the executive officer had to be consulted on the practicability of the conception, cost, machinery and co-ordination of the policy. The officer's normal reaction would be departmental and he would pronounce on the resources required for specific results. (Both submissions referred to officers in male terms. The first female administrative officer was appointed during the sitting of the Brennan Commission.) However, in the course of such consultation, the executive officer would be invited and would tend to reach out to embrace extra-departmental considerations in order to respond more completely to the proposed idea. Some officers would be more supple and responsive. Some would display a particular aptitude for the full perspective, the more governmental and less departmental view, and these officers were of prime value as administrators. A remarkable proportion of higher administrative officers had graduated with distinction from the executive class. Clearly, therefore, the executive class is one source from which administrative officers should be recruited. The administrative officer on promotion should be engaged exclusively on higher administrative work. With regard to the separateness of administrative and executive functions, the Executive Officers' Association in its submission to the Brennan Commission stated:

> Consideration has been given at some length to the recruitment and disposal of Junior Administrative Officers because it is desired to show that an adequate and useful career is available to them in purely Administrative work. In practice it is found that the allocation of these officers is somewhat haphazard. They are permitted to encroach on purely Executive posts for which they have not been fitted but for which Executive Officers have been expressly recruited and expensively trained. It is necessary to enter a strong protest against this encroachment on the purely Executive domain. Not only does this militate against the advancement of Executive Officers for whom promotion is, at best, relatively slow and modest, but it is definitely wasteful of both administrative and Executive capacity.

In their submission to the Brennan Commission, the junior administrative officers stated that their members were recruited and were in training for higher administrative duties: those to do with the formation of policy, the co-ordination and improvement of government machinery, and the general administration and control of the departments of the public service. With regard to recruitment, the submission stated: 'Since the setting up of the Civil Service Commission in 1923, recruitment to the Junior Administrative grade has been by means of open competition and by the promotion of Junior Executive Officers through the medium of inter-departmental selection boards.'

The submission had made clear earlier that the principle involved in the existence of a separate administrative class had been endorsed by a recent Royal Commission in Britain (the Tomlin Commission) and that in the United States civil service the employment of staff of the highest qualifications for administrative work was becoming a factor of increasing importance. The number of university graduates employed in business was a further indication of the general trend of the time. Nevertheless, the recruitment to the grade by way of confined competition was accepted.

The submission of the junior administrative officers went on: 'It is important, however, that there should be opportunities for advancement to the grade for persons already in the Service who show early proof of real ability and promise of being able to discharge higher administrative functions. In our view it would be in the interests of the Service that such opportunities should continue to be afforded from time to time.' The officers accepted the broad distinction between higher work of the administrative type and the executive type. They asserted:

We think that consideration will indicate the desirability of organisation based on a separation of the administrative and executive arms to as great a degree as possible. Under the present system, administrative officers of the Assistant Principal or analogous grades and upwards, who should normally be discharging mainly administrative duties, have also to deal with a considerable volume of executive problems. This position is essentially wrong as it is a negation of the principle underlying the creation of a separate administrative class.

The junior administrative officers further considered that the distinction between the types of work should be established in an organisation corresponding generally with that then obtaining in the Department of Finance. Below the secretary and assistant secretaries in that department, there were two grades of principal and assistant principal above the junior administrative grade. The junior administrative officers proposed that the two grades whose function would correspond generally with those of the two mentioned should intervene between the permanent head of a department or his deputy and the lowest line of the administrative class. They wished to designate as principals the members of the lower of these grades. Under the proposed organisation, they would be discharging comparable duties in the various departments and so should be remunerated on a common scale. A similar argument was applied to members of the other grade, whom, they thought, should be designated senior principals. This grade should have a higher remuneration. Some departments might be organised solely on an executive basis, while others could be organised on administrative-cum-executive basis. The point up to which executive work should be arranged on a self-contained basis would depend on the general circumstances of the department, in particular on the ratio of the administrative and executive work. The main considerations would be that the work finally transferred from the executive arm

(a) should not be of such volume as would interfere with the efficient working of the administrative arm; and

(b) should roughly correspond in complexity with the administrative problems dealt with at that stage.

The junior administrative officers went on to argue that, as members of a general service grade, they should be freely transferable on promotion from department to department and that, in view of their comparatively small numbers, there should be little difficulty in considering all officers on merit.

THE CLERICAL STRUCTURE

In its submission to the Brennan Commission, the Executive Officers' Association also referred to what it called the clerical sub-structure. The Civil Service Clerical Association had argued that there were too many grades in the service. They identified the general service grades as follows: writing assistants, writing clerks, clerical officers, minor staff officers, junior executive officers, major staff officers, higher executive officers, junior administrative officers, assistant principal clerks, principal clerks, assistant secretary and secretary (exclusive of the typing grades and certain unestablished officers). The Clerical Association stated that three grades would be sufficient, with avenues of promotion from class to class. It recommended that the service be reorganised to provide for three grades — grades 3, 2 and 1.

The duties of grade 3 would be performed exclusively by women. Large numbers of women entered the service and subsequently retired to get married; the association argued that it was undesirable that those who remained in the service should spend a lifetime on work of a purely routine or mechanical nature. The conditions of the grade would be so designed as to ensure that normally the women should pass into the grade above after having reached a reasonable standard of efficiency and experience.

Grade 2 would cover the broad range of duties then assigned to clerical officers, departmental clerical officers, staff officers, superintendents of typists and junior executive officers. Officers in this grade would be recruited by open competitive examination between the ages of 17 and 19 on a leaving certificate standard and by promotion from Grade 3.

Grade 1 would comprise a small class of higher officers. The duties of the grade would broadly correspond to those laid down for higher executive officers. Officers would be recruited exclusively by promotion from grade 2. Above grade 1 there would be certain higher administrative and supervisory posts, such as principal clerks, accountants and secretaries, which would be filled as they then were. The Executive Officers Association had a different view. In its submission to Brennan, it stated that the base of the office organisation was a force of workers engaged on routine clerical work of a simple and frequently mechanical nature — copying, checking, recording, compiling and digesting data, disposing of routine returns in a prescribed manner; the application of well-defined regulations to straightforward cases was the scope of the clerical grade.

The point the association wished to emphasise was the magnitude of the work, which involved the engagement of bodies of subordinate employees on masses of work on which they would tend, under economical disposal, to become highly but narrowly specialised; in other words, mass production of clerical work. This type of employee could be given a wide range of duties of the same quality. The work was simple and the training relatively brief. The direct supervision of such work would be a natural extension of clerical work and would provide a promotion outlet for the clerical employee. The number of supervisory posts ordinarily would be in a stable ratio to the number of lower posts, but manifestly a proportion of efficient lower-grade workers would not achieve advancement. Therefore, in order to get an adequate return for a salary scale that must be sufficient to provide a decent standard of living for the economic unit, it would be necessary to make use of the individual to the fullest extent by devolving to him or her a range of duties up to the point at which the work would be executive in character. Recruitment to the clerical force should not be stimulated by any undue emphasis on prospects. The standard of the entrance examination should continue to be that of a 'clerk' standard, i.e. the intermediate certificate. The Executive Officers' Association conceded that the clerical class would always include some brilliant officers for whom an opportunity of advancement should be provided in their early years while they were receptive and adaptable and before their higher capabilities had atrophied.

III

1936-1950

The period from 1936 to 1950 was of great importance to the development of staff associations. It included the beginning of the Civil Service Alliance and also the commencement of its decline, the demise of the Civil Service Federation, and the birth of such organisations as the Civil Service Staff Officers' Association, the Association of Higher Civil Servants and the organisation of the staff of the Houses of the Oireachtas. The period concluded with the establishment of the Civil Service General Council Staff Panel.

On the outbreak of war on 3 September 1939, the government introduced the Emergency Powers Act (1939). Section 2(1) of the act provided that:

The government may, whenever and so often as they think fit, make by order (in this Act referred to as an emergency order) such provisions as are, in the opinion of the government, necessary or expedient for securing the public safety or the preservation of the state, or for the maintenance of public order, or for the provision and control of supplies and services essential to the life of the Community.

Within the provisions of the Act, the government issued Emergency Powers Order (1940) which suspended the operation of the Civil Service (Transferred Officers) Compensation Act 1929; under Section 14 of the Act, this had invested in transferred officers a statutory right in respect of the cost-of-living bonus. Furthermore, with effect from 1 July 1940, the government introduced Civil Service (Stabilisation of Bonus) Regulations which made stable the bonus on the basis of an index figure of 85, even though the bonus to be applied to wages should have been based on an index figure of 105. The

1936-1950

legality of the government's decisions subsequently was contested in the courts (see p. 116). The pay of employees generally was not stabilised until the introduction of Emergency Power Order No. 83, which came into effect on 7 May 1941. In the period between July 1940 and May 1941 the cost of living rose by 35 points. The post-war years were to see the consolidation of basic pay and bonus.

In 1939 the Civil Service Alliance offered to co-operate with the government in organising the civil service to cope with the many difficulties that had arisen because of the state of emergency. The Civil Service Alliance also proposed the setting-up of a joint council for the discussion of staff matters, pending the resumption of negotiations regarding an arbitration and conciliation scheme. The Minister for Finance, Seán MacEntee, while expressing appreciation of this token of goodwill, regretted that it was necessary to defer the establishment of such machinery for the duration of the Emergency, and declined to entertain the proposal of a joint council. Later, however, he consented to an informal body being constituted, but from which any claim involving increased remuneration was excluded.[1]

With effect from 26 May the hours of attendance were increased for general service classes (the details were set out in Department of Finance circular No. 9/41). The purpose of this increase was to provide trained staff for emergency services. The representatives of the association expressed their willingness to co-operate with the government in the Emergency and agreed that, in the case of all classes that were conditioned to a working week of 42 hours, the hours of attendance be increased by half-an-hour on weekdays. The circular concluded:

... it will be apparant that the addition of two and a half hours to the present working week of 41 hours is approximately equivalent to a staff increase of 1/16th of the numbers employed in the grades affected. It is anticipated that a proportionate number of staff will now be available for assignment to vacancies in essential services and the Minister would accordingly be glad to be furnished, not later than the 9th proximo, with particulars of the number of staff in the grades affected serving in your Department and the number which can now be released, as a result of the increase in hours of attendance for assignment to vacancies which may arise in future. In making transfers from one Dept. to another the Minister would be

In Public Service

glad if regard were had to the domestic circumstances of the officers concerned. In particular married men, who in their present Departments can conveniently visit their homes for the mid-day meal, should not be disturbed unless this is unavoidable, and so far as practicable, regard should be had in all cases to the distance of the new Department from the Officer's normal place of residence.

The widespread incidence of tuberculosis engaged the attention of staff associations during the 1940s. They called for the immediate provision of sanatoria, for the early diagnosis of the disease by mass X-Ray, for financial allowance for tuberculosis patients and for special sick pay. Special sick pay regulations applicable to officers suffering from pulmonary tuberculosis were set out in Department of Finance circular 9/45. The main features were:

1. Established Officers
   Six months on full pay, followed by six months on three-quarter pay, and by six months on half-pay.
   Unestablished Officers
   Those eligible under approved conditions of service for ordinary sick pay and who had completed not less than three years paid service: Three months on full pay followed by six months on three-quarter pay less, in each case, deductions, where applicable, in respect of National Health Insurance Benefit.
2. The qualifying period of three years' paid service for unestablished officers ordinarily should be continuous. In certain circumstances, however, breaks in service of not less than twelve months would not be regarded as disturbing the continuity.
3. The granting of special sick pay was to be subject to the usual conditions.
4. The special sick pay was to be allowed only once to any officer and would not be affected by, or reckoned for purposes of calculation of, ordinary sick pay.

The special sick pay arrangements were applied to all forms of tuberculosis from 1 April 1948.

The question of the inclusion of civil servants in the social welfare system came to the fore in October 1949 following the publication by the inter-party government of a White Paper containing proposals for a social security scheme. Civil servants speculated about how the scheme would apply to them. Their position was referred to in paragraph 55 of the White Paper:

1936-1950

The position of Civil Servants, teachers, gardai, members of the Defence Force and, perhaps, certain employees of local authorities is receiving further consideration. The problem is being examined to see whether, having regard to the existing schemes of Welfare which apply to these classes they should be included in the scheme or whether it might be advisable to exclude them.

The *Civil Service Review* of October 1950 reported that the Civil Service Staff Panel had discussed the question of whether civil servants should participate in the scheme. After much debate, a resolution was adopted, the substance of which was conveyed to the Department of Finance in a letter dated 26 September:

The Staff Side consider that Civil Servants should be included in the proposed scheme on the same basis as other classes of employed persons, i.e. with full participation in all benefits in return for full contributions. . . .

The Taoiseach, John A. Costello, received a deputation from the Irish Conference of Professional and Service Associations. (The Civil Service Alliance was affiliated to this body.) It consisted of A. P. Dempsey, president, P. Linehan, INTO, P. Crowley, Assurance Representatives Organisation, J. B. O'Quigley, Civil Service Alliance, W.A.K.H. Peard, Irish Bank Officials Association, and D. F. Murphy, Railway Clerks' Association. The deputation said that, without certain information, it was difficult to come to a definite conclusion about the scheme. J.B. O'Quigley said that his members were perturbed lest regulations that had been applied in Britain, on foot of the introduction of the National Health Service, would be applied to the civil service in Ireland. He pointed out that the conditions of service of British civil servants had been worsened by the reduction of the National Health contribution for sick leave. The Taoiseach said that the government had not made any decision on the inclusion of those groups specifically exempted in paragraph 55 of the White Paper. The government was anxious that the social security scheme, when implemented, would be acceptable to those covered by it, and wished to avoid any just grievances. The government, he said, was intent upon putting through a social security scheme, but a final decision had not been reached on the inclusion or exclusion of

In Public Service

certain groups. (The Social Welfare Act eventually became effective in 1953 under the aegis of a new government. The act was not as comprehensive as the bill introduced in 1951.) William Norton, Minister for Social Welfare in the inter-party government, stated at the annual conference of the Post Office Workers' Union in 1952 that the scheme would now provide only for unemployment benefit, sickness benefit and widows' and orphans' pensions. Since established civil servants were not likely to qualify for unemployment benefit under the act and because they received sick pay, they were not likely to receive sickness benefit as well. They were already insured for widows' and orphans' pensions. The staff side asked that civil servants be excluded from the scheme and the government agreed.

'The growth of the civil service' was the title of an article by Thomas P. Linehan, published in *Administration* (Volume 2, Number 2, Summer 1954). It showed the number of civil servants serving on 1 January in the following years:

$$
\begin{array}{rl}
1934 & 21,522 \\
1940 & 25,387 \\
1947 & 28,832 \\
1953 & 33,828
\end{array}
$$

The numbers serving in various categories were shown as follows:

Administrative and Executive

	Established			Unestablished			Total		
	Men	Women	Total	Men	Women	Total	Men	Women	Total
1934	1,684	43	1,727	13	–	13	1,697	43	1,740
1940	2,110	89	2,199	17	1	18	2,127	90	2,217
1947	2,194	94	2,288	15	–	15	2,209	94	2,303
1953	2,554	141	2,695	29	2	31	2,583	143	2,726

Clerical, Writing Assistants Etc.

	Established			Unestablished			Total		
	Men	Women	Total	Men	Women	Total	Men	Women	Total
1934	2,216	1,249	3,465	424	86	510	2,640	1,335	3,975
1940	2,911	2,269	5,180	420	106	526	3,331	2,375	5,706
1947	2,683	2,262	4,945	824	832	1,656	3,507	3,094	6,601
1953	2,641	3,394	6,035	518	388	906	3,159	3,782	6,941

The total number of civil servants serving on 1 January 1953

1936-1950

included 16,510, or almost 50 per cent, who were unestablished. The numbers for all years included those who were serving in the Post Office.

UNION ORGANISATION

The preliminary notice for the 1936 annual general meeting of the Association of Officers of the Executive and Higher Grades stated that the executive committee had decided to make no nominations for the officerships. It would move that a special general meeting be convened at an early date for the specific purpose of amending the rules. A sub-committee had been appointed to examine revision of the rules, but would not be able to lay comprehensive proposals before the annual general meeting. The executive committee considered that the defects were so numerous that the introduction of a completely new set of rules was inevitable. The new rules were again to change the name of the association to the Civil Service Executive and Higher Officers' Association. This title was to be retained for almost forty years. The 1936 annual general meeting was well attended and proceeded with little controversy. The last business of the meeting concerned the filling of a vacancy for an assistant principal officer in the Department of Justice and the decision of the meeting was reflected in a letter addressed to the Secretary, Department of Finance, dated 25 February 1936:

I am directed to inform you that Finance Circular, 4/36, relative to the filling of the vacancy for an Assistant Principal Officer in the Department of Justice was under consideration at the Annual General Meeting held on 21st instant, when it unanimously decided that an emphatic protest should be entered against
(a)   the proposed restriction of candidature to male officers;
(b)   the proposed admission of Junior Administrative Officers to competition for an Executive Class position.

The subscription for 1936 was fixed at the then existing rate:

Officers in receipt of salaries not exceeding £200 per annum inclusive of bonus   15 shillings

All other officers   £1

In Public Service

John Kelly (Local Government) was elected chairman and P.F. Patten (Local Government) was elected honorary secretary. In September 1936 the executive committee wrote to the Department of Finance pointing out how necessary and desirable it was that facilities should be afforded to the honorary secretary to enable him to do some part of his association duties in official time. Reference was made to the statement in the Brennan Commission report that civil servants were afforded adequate facilities for devoting time even during official hours to the business of staff associations with which they were connected. The minister was requested to identify the facilities he was prepared to afford the honorary secretary.[3] The *Civil Service Journal* of December 1936 reported that a very unsatisfactory reply had been received to this letter; despite having been asked twice to state specifically the facilities that he was prepared to afford the honorary secretary, the minister had evaded the question. The association continued to pursue this matter, but the failure to secure adequate facilities was later to lead the association to consider appointing a full-time general secretary.

A special general meeting was held on 7 December 1936 to revise the rules. The *Civil Service Journal* of January 1937 reported a poor attendance. The Department of Agriculture branch was congratulated on the thorough manner in which it had criticised the executive committee's draft rules and for its many useful amendments.

The 1937 annual general meeting was held under the new rules. The annual report dealt with such matters as arbitration, service unity, the final reports of the Brennan Commission, acting appointments, salary scales on promotion, and sick leave regulations. The membership was reported to be 535, an increase of 68 on the previous year's figure and the highest recorded since 1929.

The report was unanimously adopted and the following officers were elected for 1937: chairman: J. Kelly (Local Government and Public Health); vice-chairman: Miss H.F. Spence (Industry and Commerce); secretary: M. P. Russell (Industry and Commerce); treasurer: J. O'Keeffe (Agriculture).

The executive committee of six was elected at the council meeting on 19 March 1937. The election was the first conducted under the principle of proportional representation. The report of the council meeting published in the *Civil Service Journal* admits that, while the election was certainly interesting, judging by expressions heard at the meeting, it was hardly as popular as the previous system.

In the June 1937 issue of the *Civil Service Journal* there is mention of the imminent general election:

> With the General Election at hand the Civil Service Alliance will no doubt inaugurate a big publicity campaign to focus attention on our chief grievance — the denial of a just measure of Arbitration and Conciliation machinery. Advantage will naturally be taken of the opportunity offered to derive the maximum benefit at a time when we assume the unusual role of being courted for a few days, instead of being spurned, as we usually are, for a period of five years. The alliance may be relied on to carry out a canvas of the candidates in order to ascertain those in favour of conceding our legitimate demands as regards Arbitration and Conciliation. Thus we will know where we stand when it comes to the polls.

The same issue records that a special general meeting had been fixed for 28 June 1937 to consider a recommendation from the executive committee that the resolution passed at the annual general meeting, providing for the appointment of a clerical assistant to carry out the organisation and office work, be rescinded because of various commitments and the state of the association's finances.

In September 1937, the 'Association Notes' returned to the matter of the appointment of junior administrative officers, saying that it was intended to appoint such officers to the Department of Industry and Commerce:

> It is a grave issue for our members when it becomes the declared policy of a Department to favour the appointment of such officers to posts hitherto reserved for the Executive Grade. It is our contention that the Administrative and Executive Grades are intended to perform different classes of work with their own salary scales and their own avenues of promotion. It was never contemplated that the former class should deviate from their prescribed course and infringe on Executive Grade Posts.

The same 'Notes' contained a paragraph relating to representations made to the Department of Finance for the extension of the 1909 Superannuation Act to women civil servants. The 'Association Notes' in the August issue of the *Journal* extended congratulations to Deputies William Norton and Archie Heron on their success in the general election.[4] In the election Fianna Fáil secured 62 seats, Fine Gael 48, Labour 14 and Independents 13. The association commented:

Not since the establishment of the Free State have the prospects of our being conceded an equitable measure of Arbitration and Conciliation machinery been brighter. In the meantime there has been an accumulation of grievances which would keep any Board that may be set up to deal with these matters busy for a long time. A real note of warning must, however, be struck at this stage. It is quite conceivable that our claims may not be regarded as of first-class importance and that others may take precedence over them. Such a situation may arise and, in that event, we can remain wandering in the desert.

The October 1937 issue of the *Journal* contains a report of an interview given by J. Leydon, the secretary of the Department of Industry and Commerce, to a deputation from the departmental branch of the Executive Officers' Association. The department was represented by the secretary and T. R. Price, establishment officer. The deputation consisted of T. J. Hughes, chairman, M. P. Russell, B. Molloy and D. Meade (branch secretary). The subject of the interview was the consequences of the appointment of a junior administrative officer to the department. The deputation stated that the executive officers in the department were gravely concerned at the reported intention to revert to the junior executive grade one of the acting higher executive officers, in order to assign a junior administrative officer to the work in question. J. Leydon replied that, following representations by him, the Department of Finance had agreed that there was work of an administrative character in his department and consequently consented to assign there a number of junior administrative officers. This decision immediately necessitated the revision to his substantive rank of one of the acting higher executive officers.

The deputation contended that merely to send junior administrative officers into the department was not a recognition of administrative work. Industry and Commerce was still organised on a clerical-executive basis, unlike the Department of Finance which adopted a clerical-administrative structure. The secretary said that, as the head of an expanding department, his concern was to obtain the best qualified people available for the work to be done and he did not consider it advisable that he should be restricted in his selection by having to consider old methods of organisation or of what was customary in regard to promotion. There was work in the department on which he considered junior administrative officers would be useful. As regards promotion, these officers must be eligible with other officers for whatever higher posts there were in the department.

The question of the appointment of a non-civil servant as an official of a staff association had been a subject of controversy with the Department of Finance since the foundation of the state. There were two such officials — William Norton, general secretary of the Post Office Workers' Union, appointed in 1923, and Archie Heron, general secretary of the Civil Service Clerical Association, appointed in 1928. The Department of Finance refused to recognise either official. In an effort to resolve the problem, in 1932 the Department of Finance proposed to appoint both to permanent posts in the civil service on the understanding that they would be seconded for association work on a whole-time or part-time basis according to the requirements of the association. Both officials rejected the proposal. Heron resigned his post as from 1 January 1939. The December 1940 issue of the *Journal* of the Civil Service Clerical Association described his departure in the following terms:[5]

Heron is leaving us and with his departure there is closed an eventful chapter in the history of the C.S.C.A. To the month it is just 12 years since he was appointed General Secretary. Heron goes from us to the Irish Local Government Officials' Union. He is a realist and he saw that so long as the Minister for Finance refused an independent General Secretary recognition, so long would we be impeded in our work.

The Civil Service Clerical Association also took a realistic view and decided that the new general secretary would be a seconded serving civil servant. By arrangement with the Department of Finance, the appointed member would be seconded to the association and would have access to all departments in order to make staff representations. The association would be required to refund to the state an amount equal to 'the mean of the scale' of the officer appointed, plus 15 per cent in respect of superannuation. The association decided to add £100 to the appointee's service pay. This was increased to £150 in 1942. The appointment of D. O'Conaill was ratified by a special conference. The question of recognition had been referred to the Brennan Commission, which commented:

> There has been raised before us the question of the recognition of a non-Civil Servant as a member of the executive committee or as an official of a Civil Service Staff Association. The existing position is that a non-Civil Servant Secretary acting in this capacity will not be officially received by any Minister or in any Government department for the discussion of any matter in which the association may be interested. Civil Servants are afforded adequate facilities for devoting time even during official hours to the business of staff associations with which they are connected. There is accordingly no need in this connection for any association to have resort to outside personnel. We are not, in fact, aware of any argument of considerable weight which would seem to favour the recognition of a non-Civil Servant. On the other hand, it is our view that there is argument of outstanding weight against recognition, namely, the strong probability that any association which admits a non-Civil Servant in the capacity mentioned will inevitably find itself involved in infringement of the rule against political activity. It is, we think, a sufficient confirmation of this to point out that in the case of the Civil Service Clerical Association which appears to have a considerable membership of Civil Servants the secretary, a non-Civil Servant, was some time ago a candidate for election as a member of Dáil Éireann. We understand also that the General Secretary of the Irish Post-Office Workers' Union is at present a member of Dáil Éireann. We are strongly of the opinion that it should be a condition of the recognition of staff associations for official purposes that their members, executive officers, and other officials who might be required to represent the association on any official occasion, should be drawn exclusively from the Civil Service.[6]

The Executive Officers' Association immediately wrote to the Department of Finance referring to the commission's statement and enquiring if the minister would be good enough to state the exact nature of the facilities that he was prepared to afford to the association's honorary secretary. In the course of lengthy correspondence, the department maintained that, subject to conditions in the department in which the officers were serving, the Minister for Finance had always been favourable to granting serving civil servants such facilities as were necessary for staff representation. However, despite repeated requests, the department had refused to state the exact nature of the facilities that would be made available. The executive committee concluded:

> It is obvious from the correspondence with the Department of Finance regarding the provision of facilities for the Secretary and Treasurer of the Association that no effective recognition is intended to be extended to the Association. In other words, that Department desires that the organisation should die of senile decay. Such an attitude is all the more difficult to appreciate when it is borne in mind that the Report of the Brennan Commission specifically pointed out that Civil Servants were afforded 'adequate facilities for devoting time even during official hours to the business of Staff Associations with which they are connected' and further reference to the fact that 'there is, accordingly, no need in this connection for an Association to resort to outside persons'. But as in fact no such facilities are afforded, the Association is fully justified on the lines of reasoning of the Brennan Commission, in appointing a General Secretary who is not a Civil Servant.[7]

The executive committee argued that a general secretary of the kind it had in mind would go a long way to remedy the unenviable state of affairs in the life of the association. Unfettered by the shackles of service discipline, he would be able to resort to propaganda to a degree that could not have been attempted previously. His energies could be devoted to securing a real measure of arbitration and conciliation machinery. He would be involved also in the organisation of the association, particularly since the younger entrants to the executive class had not had the benefit of the tradition of service agitation and association activity and, therefore, it would be a heavy task to get them to realise what an association meant to them. The executive committee also faced practical questions relating to the appointment. The article in the *Civil Service Journal* stated:

> To secure the right man to fill the post, the Association must be prepared to pay an adequate salary. Cheese-paring in this instance would be a mistaken policy, and so much is at stake that it would

be extremely foolish to contemplate such a course. The fact of the appointee having a pension should not be taken into consideration for after all the training in, and experience of, service matters which he acquired while in the Service should prove invaluable to the association.

It was the intention to restrict selection to ex-civil servants since a stranger to the peculiar nature of the conditions under which civil servants worked would require considerable training before he could acquire the necessary familiarity and understanding. The executive committee pointed out that to pay a reasonable salary and to cover incidental expenses such as clerical assistance and typing, it was necessary to raise the annual subscription to 30 shillings a year. This was regarded as the minimum subscription on which the appointment could be safely made. The committee noted that clerical officers paid their association a subscription of two shillings per month and that surely nobody could plead that an extra sixpence was too much for an executive officer to pay to his professional association. An editorial in the same issue of the *Civil Service Journal* identified the obstacles that would have to be overcome before an effective appointment could be made. The editorial concluded:

We can see interesting possibilities and rather intriguing prospects in the engagement of an 'outsider' as the spokesman of the Executive Officers' Association. For the moment, judging by the unanimous approval given by the Council of that Association, the proposal has had the great merit of arousing a large amount of badly-needed enthusiasm. It is a proposal at least to do something in circumstances which urgently call for action but in which none the less the methods of useful action are very limited. And the fact that something will no doubt meet with the grave disapproval of the Minister for Finance will, we suspect, not diminish its attractiveness for the general body of Executive Officers.

Indeed, the minister's reaction may be gleaned from an editorial in the May 1943 issue of the *Civil Service Review* in which it was stated that the association had been threatened with immediate ostracism if it had dared employ an outsider in the management of its affairs. The association's annual report for 1939 stated that two special general meetings had been held during the year to consider the circumstances surrounding the

A stark message from the October 1925 issue of The Civil Service Journal.

IRIS SEIRBISE AN STÁIT
(THE CIVIL SERVICE JOURNAL)
IRISLEADAR OIFIGIUIL COM-CUMAINN SEIRBISEAC SCÁIC
(*Official Organ of the Civil Service Federation*)

IMLEADAR 3. UIMH 10.   DEIREAD FOGHMAIR (OCTOBER), 1925.   DÁ PINGIN

ORGANISE

We have as the existing law of the Saorstat the judgment given in the Supreme Court in favour of the Attorney General in the Wigg and Cochrane case. The effect of this judgment is, that despite the Act of 1920, the Treaty, and the Constitution, a Civil Servant cannot appeal to any court against any salary or pension decision of the Minister for Finance. A Civil Servant is earning say £200 per annum ; the Minister may order his reduction to £50 ; may then refuse to allow him to retire under Article 10 of the Treaty, and if he insists on retiring, may refuse to allow him any pension. That Civil Servant has no appeal.

These are powers which the Transferred Officers cannot, in justice to themselves, allow any Minister to hold over them.

The T.O.P.A. has been formed to support financially a petition to the Privy Council for a Declaration of the rights of Transferred Civil Servants under Article 10 of the Treaty. It needs and deserves the the support of all concerned—that is putting it at the very lowest.

* * * *

The statement recently issued by the Irish Labour Party on the Shannon Wage crisis makes it plain to all that our Government stands for a policy of wage reduction. Either the " Fair Wage " clause was not inserted in the Contract made with the German contractors, or if inserted, its observance is not being insisted on.

We had already seen that the allocation of the Road Board Grants to County and Borough Councils was made contingent in each case on the definite lowering of the local standard or trade union rate of wages.

These are texts. There is no need for a sermon. Sensible people in the Service can draw the moral for themselves.

A typical page of advertisements from The Civil Service Journal in 1929.

EXTERMINATE EXAMS !

Who wouldn't if they could. It would be splendid to pass without pressure—to advance without being pushed—suppose we only had to answer familiar questions. Such as :—

What Makes an Uncivil Civil Servant Civil ?

WOULDN'T WE ALL ANSWER

They see McHugh Himself about a Bike and pass without being pushed !

EXPERIMENTS

You wouldn't look for a gas leak with a lighted candle ? Your knowledge prevents that—or else—!

Why should you experiment in your Cycle needs ? Our 25 years of Satisfying Service assures your satisfaction. You pass all experiments by "Seeing McHugh."

Supplier of all makes of Cycles.

1929 MODELS
with a full and personal guarantee for 10 years from

£3 - 18 - 6
to £12

——— ON THE "SERVICE" GUILD ———

McHUGH'S SERVICE STORE, 39 Talbot-st., DUBLIN
— McHUGH HIMSELF.—

Cumann Gaolach na Stat Seirbhise	Electric Lighting to Electricity Supply Board Specifications
Clar na mBuidhean, 1929-30. Árd Rang I. Dia Máirt ... 8 —9.30 p.m. do. II. Dia h-Aoine ... 8 —9.30 p.m. Meán Rang I. Dia Céadaoin 8 —9.30 p. n. do. II. Dia Máirt 5.30—6.30 p.m. Bun Rang. Dia Luain is Dia Céadaoin 5.30—6.30 p.m. AG 6 SRAID FHEARCHAIR Tosnú Dia Mairt Iadh Deireadh Foghmhair	Quotations Free * 12 Months Guarantee P. F. McINTYRE 8 TRINITY STREET, DUBLIN Phone 4523.

OUR TEAS are the pick of the market; are unvarying in quality, and give universal satisfaction.

PRICES—1/6, 1/8, 1/10, 2/-, 2/2, 2/4, 2/6, 2/8, 2/10, 3/-, 3/2 (Highest).
CHINA TEAS—2/8 and 3/2.

BECKER BROS., Ltd. 8 Sth. Gt. George's St., C.1 and 17 North Earl St., C.8

Signing of the Arbitration Agreement, 26 March 1955 (seated l-r) L.M. Fitzgerald, Chief Establishment Officer, G. Sweetman, Minister for Finance, J.C. Horgan, principal staff representative; (standing) M. Dooney, F. Robinson, W.J. Farrell, D.N. Ó Cléirigh, H. Sullivan, W. Bell, C. O'Sullivan, C.J. Tunney, P. Breathnach.

At the 1962 annual general meeting: P.J. O'Grady, treasurer, Dympna Headen, general secretary, and Seán Ó Mathgamhna, chairman. To date, Dympna Headen is the only woman to have held the office of general secretary.

Seán Strattan, chairman, and Kevin Nolan, treasurer, at the 1964 annual general meeting.

A gaggle of general secretaries gathers outside Government Buildings on the occasion of the one-day public service stoppage on 15 October 1985. Included are: Jim Dorney (Teachers Union of Ireland), Gerry Quigley (Irish National Teachers Organisation), John O'Dowd (later of the Civil and Public Services Union) and Dan Murphy. Beside Dan is Kieran Mulvey (Association of Secondary Teachers). Fourth right is Michael Foster, former union A.G.S., and facing him with back to camera is John Dowling (Association of Higher Civil Servants).

General secretary Dan Murphy holds a union placard outside Government Buildings while sharing a joke with Greg Maxwell of the UPTCS on the occasion of the one day public service strike.

Two assistant general secretaries Tom Geraghty (left) and Billy Hannigan at the 1986 conference.

May O'Doherty (second right) accepts a gift from the union to which she had given stalwart service. Also pictured left to right, in 1969 are: Carmel Dunlea (treasurer), Tom Maher (chairman), Dan Murphy (general secretary), J.C. Tucker, and Des Hickey (vice-chairman).

In 1979 trade unionists took to the streets to seek reform of the tax system. Here Seán Ó Conail and Nabla McGinley step it out on behalf of the CSEU.

The late Michael Magner (left), general secretary 1964-1968, seen here with Tom Leahy, member of the executive committee. Michael Magner died at a tragically young age in 1979.

Incoming president of the ICTU, Dan Murphy, the union's general secretary, addresses the 1980 ICTU conference. On the left is the late Ruairí Roberts, general secretary of the ICTU.

appointment of a secretary. At the second meeting the executive committee was instructed to ascertain from the Department of Finance what facilities would be offered by them to a serving civil servant who might be appointed secretary, and a deputation from the committee went to the Department of Finance for that purpose. Subsequently the committee appointed a secretary who would act up to the date of the annual general meeting, and the question of facilities was left over for further examination.

In October 1939, D. O'Colman (Department of Agriculture) was appointed honorary secretary. He resigned the following year to take up the position of secretary to the Civil Service Alliance and was succeeded by D. O'Conchubhair, Office of Public Works. Seán Ó hEidirsceoil, Widows and Orphans, Department of Local Government and Public Health, was appointed to the position in 1941. He became the association's first full-time official at a secondment cost of £250 per annum.[8] On his appointment as public relations officer of the Department of Social Welfare in 1948, Mr Ó hEidirsceoil resigned as president of the Civil Service Alliance, as wholetime general secretary of the Executive and Higher Officers' Association, and as editor of the *Civil Service Review*.[9]

Full representation was granted to the Post Office Workers' Union in 1946 in the course of a discussion on the consolidation of pay for civil servants.[10] This opened the way for the appointment of non-civil servants as association officers. The Executive and Higher Officers' Association appointed J.B. O'Quigley as general secretary in 1949. Subsequently he became a member of Seanad Éireann. It will be recalled what when the association had previously considered the employment of a non-civil servant, the move brought a bitter response from the Department of Finance. The department also had sought to write into a draft scheme of arbitration provisions that would have precluded members of the Oireachtas from becoming association secretaries.

The report of proceedings of the 1940 annual general meeting was brief and dealt almost exclusively with a resolution deploring the continued enforcement of salary scales differentiated on a marriage basis. The meeting noted that, since the report of the Brennan Commission, professional civil servants had

In Public Service

been relieved of the infliction, but that the general civil service was still suffering.

Other matters discussed at the meeting included: medical benefit schemes and group insurances; reductions in pay and leave of officers by circular 44/24; and the continued failure of the government to establish conciliation and arbitration machinery for the settlement of staff claims.

The redeployment of staff during the early period of the Emergency brought new problems. The 'Association Notes' for February 1941 referred to the secondment of officers of Customs and Excise to junior executive posts, notably in the Department of Defence. Branch officers were warned to keep a special eye open to ensure that the interests of executive officers were not thereby adversely affected, and on the first indication that such a danger threatened, it was of the utmost importance that immediate action be taken. A case in the Office of Public Works was held up as an example. A higher executive officer post in that Office was given to a customs officer over the heads of a large number of eligible officers of the junior executive grade. The executive committee promptly submitted a sharp protest. This matter was referred to again in the annual report when all branches were warned to seek assurances that these secondments were to be purely temporary and would not affect the executive grade adversely.

The annual report also referred to the Emergency Powers (No. 30) Order 1940 which ordered the suspension of the Civil Service (Transferred Officers) Compensation Act 1929 and provided that, during such suspension, no action or other legal proceedings should be instituted in any court of law for or on account of any matter which, if the act were in operation, could have been the subject of an inquiry, determination or decision of the Civil Service (Compensation) Board. The annual report stated that the Order was to be tested in the High Court. The stabilisation of the cost-of-living bonus was also referred to and an indication was given that the validity of the government's action was to be tested in the courts. The High Court hearings are referred to in another section of this chapter. The problem arising from Emergency promotions caused a special general meeting to be called for 4 April 1941 in Jury's Hotel, Dublin.

1936-1950

The immediate difficulty was the stated intention of the Department of Finance to set up an interview board to select officers to fill three principal officer posts, three supervising officer posts, and six higher executive posts in the Department of Supplies. Particular exception was taken to the fact (1) that departmental grades and staff officers were eligible for executive positions; (2) that the method of appointment — nomination by the head of the department for interview by the selection board — meant the effective exclusion of some departments and the over-representation of others; (3) that such an unrepresentative panel of nominations should be considered as a basis for possible further Emergency appointments. Letters to the Department of Finance and discussions with its representatives failed to resolve the problem, so the following letter, dated 7 April 1941, was addressed to the department:

> Further to our recent discussions on the question of Emergency Promotion, I am directed by my Executive committee to enclose a copy of a resolution, unanimously adopted by a Special General Meeting of the members of my Association on the 4th inst. As an indication of the resentment and uneasiness caused throughout the whole service by the method of promotion adopted and its possible extension to further posts, I might point out that the Special General Meeting, with only one day's clear notice, filled beyond standing capacity the largest room in Jury's Hotel — a room which normally seats more than 120 persons.
> Mise le Meas
> S. Ó hEidirsceoil

The following is the text of the resolution forwarded to the Department of Finance:

> That this Special General Meeting protests against the method adopted for the recruitment of three Principal Officers, three Supervising Officers and six Higher Executive Officers for the Department of Supplies, and against the inclusion of Departmental Officers amongst those eligible for promotion to these posts, and, in view of the inequitable nature of the existing panel, demands that its use be restricted to the filling of the twelve posts specified.

The 'Association Notes' for June 1941 records the success of the protest in the following terms:

In Public Service

The vigorous protests of the Association against the method of promotion adopted to fill 12 posts in the Department of Supplies, have not been without result. The unrepresentative panel then set up has been abolished in favour of a more equitable one drawn from all eligible officers in the Executive grade. Also the use of the first panel was restricted to the appointment of the 12 posts specified and did not extend, as was feared at the time, to the filling of further emergency vacancies.

The new arrangements for the filling of temporary posts were set out in Department of Finance circular 7/41. The superintending officer mentioned in the circular was of assistant principal grade. The persons eligible to apply for inclusion in the panels were:

1. For the principal officer panel: substantive or acting assistant principals, superintending officers and equivalent general service grades.
2. For the assistant principal and superintending officer panel: junior administrative officers, substantive or acting higher executive officers.
3. For the higher executive panel: junior executive officers and staff or senior staff officers.

However, the circular did make clear that the arrangements would apply only where no officer of appropriate grade could be loaned from elsewhere, and where the vacancies could not be filled by normal promotion, either of officers on the normal establishment or of loaned officers (including officers of departmental grades) serving within the departments concerned at the time the vacancy arose. The association did not accept the possible promotion of departmental officers envisaged in the circular.

The 'Association Notes' for November 1941 indicate that the offices of the association would be made available on certain evenings for the teaching of languages. The 'Notes' also indicate that the medical benefit scheme was proceeding, but that it had been decided not to proceed with a dental scheme because of the poor response.

The association's annual report for 1943 contained the news that the Civil Service Federation had decided to wind up its affairs and to cease publication of the *Civil Service Journal* after the March 1943 issue. *The Civil Service Review*, the successor to the *Civil Service Journal*, first appeared in April 1943. The annual report stated that the advantages to the association of owning and controlling the *Review* could hardly be overstated. For some years various affiliates to the Civil Service Alliance published notes in the *Review*. The same annual report referred to the comparative failure of the association representatives on the Civil Service Alliance council, through the inherent limitations of the informal talks machinery, to effect any fundamental settlement of major service problems.

The 1943 general election gave the alliance an opportunity to canvas the political parties on the subject of arbitration. It received the following responses:

Fianna Fáil: Arbitration was being considered by the Minister for Finance, and his views and those of the government would be communicated to the Civil Service Alliance as soon as possible.

Fine Gael: The party had given evidence of its views on arbitration by moving a resolution in the Dáil for its introduction.

Labour: Agreement with the Civil Service Alliance's claim that, subject to the overriding authority of the Oireachtas, matters in dispute should be determined by the Arbitration Tribunal.

The treasurer's report for 1943 showed a membership of 718 and a subscription income of £487.17.10. The *Civil Service Review* of March 1944 contains a paragraph about the decision of the Civil Service Alliance council to apply for affiliation to the Trades Union Congress. This followed closely on a decision taken at the annual general meeting of the executive committee to affiliate to the TUC if and when it thought fit. (There is no evidence that an application for affiliation was lodged. In 1944 a schism occurred in the trade union movement. This led to the establishment of the Congress of Irish Unions. In a situation whereby two trade union centres existed, it would have provoked controversy to seek affiliation to either congress.)

The 1944 annual report referred to the growth of the association in the following terms:

In Public Service

In the last ten years, a period which may be divided by the Emergency to cover extremes of normal and abnormal conditions, the membership and subscriptions income of the Association have been almost trebled. That this is so, proves not only that there is a growing consciousness of the value of the Association, but also that each new accretion of strength enables your elected representatives to perform with ever-increasing effectiveness the duties allotted to them. As a further general observation it is to be pointed out that this is the first year since the appointment of a full time Secretary that the Association has been able to meet its increased expenditure out of income. This, in the opinion of your Executive Committee, means that if organisation is maintained at a high level, the most difficult part of our struggle for organisational self-sufficiency is over.

The treasurer's report for 1944 showed a membership of 734 and a subscription income of £602.8.10. The main items of expenditure were:

Secretary's secondment	£250
Honoraria to officers	£110
Wages	£93.13.4

There was an excess of income of £1.3.11.

The cost of the *Civil Service Review* was shown as £605.8.10, with an income from sales and advertisements of £611.10.4. The items mentioned in the annual report included:

- Cost-of-living bonus
- Arbitration
- Civil Service Alliance fighting fund
- Sick leave
- Children's allowances
- Stamp duty
- Promotion of departmental grades in the service
- Fortnightly pay
- Local Defence Force and volunteer force special leave
- Superannuation
- Junior administrative officers
- Hours of attendance
- Acting appointments
- Reversion of officers after Emergency
- Irish in the service

The 1946 annual general meeting heralded the end of the Emergency, but some unpleasant matters had to be mentioned. First, the annual report stated that arbitration still peeped shyly from behind the accumulated promises of thirteen years. Secondly, the government had still made no move to recompense the service for the huge loss inflicted by the stabilisation in 1940. Thirdly, junior administrative officers, staff officers and officers of departmental grades continued to move blithely along the highways and byways of executive promotions. But on the other hand there was an association victory in having the ceiling for bonus awards removed, thus reintegrating the whole service as a satisfactory response to the fighting fund appeal launched by the Civil Service Alliance. The substantial improvement effected in the conditions applicable to officers unfortunate enough to contact tuberculosis was also noted.

As from 1 July 1946, the voluntary increase in the working hours, as set out in the Department of Finance circular 9/41, was reduced by one-half to a quarter-of-an-hour a day on weekdays; the remaining quarter-hour was removed on 1 July 1947, on which date the pre-war hours of attendance were restored. The introduction of children's allowances financed entirely by the state out of general taxation under the Children's Allowance Act of 1944 caused some members of the association to seek a review of the civil service arrangements. Under the state scheme, allowances became payable only to a head of a household in which there were three or more children. However, there was no upward limit. The civil service arrangements limited allowances to a maximum of five children. The *Civil Service Review* of May 1946 commented:

> Since all our efforts to date have failed to secure the abolition of the differentiated scales, some of our members are pressing to have certain minor adjustments made within the framework of the present scheme, without prejudice to our claim for its ultimate abolition. Of these adjustments, the most important is the removal of the limitation on the number of children in respect of whom allowances are granted at present. There is no such limitation in the National Scheme and we hope to have a discussion on the question with the Official Side at the earliest opportunity.

In Public Service

The limitation on the number of eligible children was later removed.

In October 1946 the association announced that Trinity College, Dublin had instituted a Diploma in Public Administration, to provide a specific university qualification for employment and promotion in the central and local government services, statutory undertakings and corporations. In order to facilitate the work of those already employed in the service, provision would be made for the lectures to be delivered after office hours and for exemption to be granted from lectures delivered during office hours. Special privileges and exemptions would be granted to holders of the Diploma who wished to proceed to the degrees of B.A. and B.Comm. The fee for the Diploma course would be six payments of £4.4.0 over a two-year period.

The numbers employed in the various grades on 1 January 1946 were as follows:

Over £500 per annum — general service	383
Junior administrative officers	28
Higher executive officers	323
Junior executive officers	649
Staff officers	512
Clerical officers	2,194
Writing clerks	58
Writing assistants	1,045
Temporary clerical assistants (male)	644
Temporary clerical assistants (female)	926
Superintendents of typists	19
Shorthand typists	367
Typists	400
Messengers etc.	499

The association's annual report for 1946 contained a paragraph that later was to create controversy. It read:

> During the course of the year it became clear that there were large numbers of Officers (Departmental, Technical etc.) with salaries and responsibilities approximating to those of the Executive Class but without any organisations catering adequately for them. The Executive Council therefore decided to open membership of the Association to such officers either individually or in groups subject to being satisfied that no conflict of interest would exist between the

1936-1950

newcomers and the present membership. It is not our intention or desire to attract officers away from any existing organisation but rather to induce officers who feel the present imperative need for organisation into one which will cater adequately for them. This does not, of course, preclude the possibility of future amalgamation with other established groups pursuing the same broad objects as ourselves. In the odd arithmetic of trade unionism, two associations are in no positive sense superior to one, rather the contrary.

There was clearly some heated discussion at the 1947 annual general meeting on this matter because the May 1947 issue of the *Civil Service Review* reported as follows:

The section in the Annual Report which suggested that the Executive was considering the possibility of organising within the Association certain unorganised Departmental classes, led to a serious debate on policy, pressed to a vote to have the offending paragraph excluded from the Report. The fact that the motion to exclude this section was lost does not mean a slackening of the opposition to admitting departmental classes to Executive posts. The Executive view as to the interpretation of the section prevailed only following a most explicit assurance from them on this point.

The association's annual report for 1949 showed a membership of 875, an increase of 10 per cent on the previous year. In arbitration cases, the association was recognised to act on behalf of the general service grades of the executive and higher executive officer and the departmental grades of assistant auditor and auditor in the Office of the Comptroller and Auditor General and assistant examiner and examiner in the estate duty branch of the Office of the Revenue Commissioners. Recognition was accorded on the understanding that the association retained its representative character and did not affiliate to any political organisation. The following salary scales applied from 1 November 1948:

Higher executive officer	Scale A	£550 — 17 — £765
	Scale B	£720 — 25 — £965
Executive officer	Scale A	£265 — 10 — £285 — 15 — £550
	Scale B	£265 — 15 — £295 — 20 — £455 — 25 — £655 — 20 — £720

The 1948 salary agreement provided for the abolition of what was known as the '255 scales', which were introduced after the salary agreement of 1946. Entrants to the service after November in that year were to be paid salaries based on a cost-of-living index number of 255, instead of the figure of 270.

This arrangement was vigorously opposed by the staff representatives. Finance circular 9/49 enabled holders of these scales to be placed at the salary points that they would have reached had they entered on a scale based on a 270 cost-of-living index number up to 31 October 1948 and on a 290 cost-of-living index number from the following day.

The annual report for 1950 showed a membership of 873; a new branch had been formed in the Department of External Affairs. The 1949 annual general meeting had directed the executive committee to initiate a drive to recruit officers of the assistant principal rank. The annual report stated:

> Officers of this rank have of late become acutely aware in certain Departments of the need for being members of a general service organisation and reports from Branches to date indicate that the response to the latest drive is encouraging. The Executive has suggested to these officers that if a sufficient number of them became members, a board to advise on the problems peculiar to their rank will be established.

This attempted recruitment drew a sharp response from the Association of Higher Civil Servants. Its annual report for 1950-51 said:

> As regards Assistant principals, the Council [of the AHCS] regrets that the Association of Executive Officers saw fit to issue a circular to these officers some months ago. The circular was issued without consultation with the Council despite the fact that it contained a specific reference to this Association.

In the same report the executive committee of the Executive and Higher Officers' Association announced that during the year a request had been received from members of the staff of the Houses of the Oireachtas to be admitted to membership of the association, and a branch was duly formed from among officers of the grades of junior and senior clerk, translator, reporter and librarian. It consequently transpired, after an application had been made for recognition of the association to represent these grades in the scheme of conciliation and

1936-1950

arbitration, that part of the rules of the association governing eligibility for membership did not cover some of the grades in respect of whom recognition was sought. The Ceann Comhairle of the Dáil indicated that if the executive gave an understanding to have the rules amended to cover these grades, recognition would be provisionally granted. The members of the Oireachtas staff regarded this arrangement as not satisfactory and decided to form an organisation exclusively for the staff in the Houses of the Oireachtas.[11]

At the 1949 annual general meeting a number of resolutions were passed calling on the executive committee to take action to secure the discontinuance of recruitment to the administrative officer grade. A claim on the matter was tabled for discussion at the general council. Individual branches made separate representations to heads of departments.

The Civil Service Alliance was formed in 1937. The 1949 annual report of the Executive and Higher Officers' Association indicated that sixteen organisations were affiliated to the alliance:

Executive and Higher Officers' Association
Association of Attendants -- Dundrum Asylum
Association of Officers of Employment Branch
Association of Officers of Outdoor Branch (Social Welfare)
Ordnance Survey Staff Association
Postmasters' Association
Postal Inspectors' Association
Post Office Controlling Officers' Association
Civil Service Temporary Clerks' Association
Cumann Lucht Meteoriochta na hEireann
Irish Civil Aviation Radio Officers Union
Civil Service Library Association
Social Welfare Supervisors' Association
Prison Officers' Association
Civil Service Staff Officers' Association
Air Traffic Control Officers' Association

At the alliance's 1949 annual council meeting, the revenue group announced that it would be leaving the alliance at the end of the meeting. The chairman of the group said that because of the impending implementation of the scheme of conciliation and arbitration, the need for the alliance had ceased, and it should be dissolved. This view was not shared by the other constituents. At the September 1949 council meeting of the Executive and Higher Officers' Association, relations with the alliance were discussed at length and it was decided, for the time being, to continue in affiliation and be represented on the staff panel through the general secretary of the association, as a permanent representative of the alliance, and the chairman of the association at two out of every three panel meetings.

In May 1949, the alliance's headquarters was transferred to the office of the Executive and Higher Officers' Association at 19 Upper Merrion Street, Dublin. The association's annual report for 1950 maintained that the alliance continued to be the medium through which the affairs of the association were conducted on the general staff side and that the arrangement had proved satisfactory. It also reported that, at the time, nineteen organisations were affiliated to the alliance and that the post of secretary of the alliance was held by the secretary of the association; the association's vice-chairman was vice-president of the alliance, and a member of the association's executive was elected to the alliance executive committee. The September 1950 issue of the *Civil Service Review* reported that the alliance had affiliated to the Irish Conference of Professional and Service Associations. This body was described in the *Review* as follows:

> The Conference is a body which may be said to cater particularly for the interests of the salaried middle classes who are at present without any organisation to express collective views on matters which vitally affect them. The Conference has received Ministerial recognition and has had discussions with Ministers of State on matters such as housing, income tax, etc.

In 1942 the Executive and Higher Officers' Association received a request for affiliation from a newly formed organisation of staff officers. The association replied that the request could not be acceded to because the rules did not permit it. It was also felt that an attempt should be made to heal the rupture between this section of the staff officers and the Civil Service Clerical Association in order to preserve unity within the service. The association's 1950 annual report was glad to record that the long-drawn-out dispute in regard to which the association should be recognised as speaking on behalf of the staff grades in the civil service had been brought to an end during the year and that the Staff Officers' Association was the recognised association for all representations that might be made on behalf of these grades.

A dispute between a section of the staff officers and their recognised association — the Civil Service Clerical Association — surfaced in 1942. The CSCA issued a statement in March 1942 which set out its view of the disagreement:

> Recently some Staff Officers have adopted the unusual course of calling meetings for the purpose of forming a separate organisation solely for Staff Officers. It is within the knowledge of the Executive Committee that among those who attended these meetings were some who were not members of any Service staff organisation and consequently the Executive committee were precluded from dealing with the matter from an Association point of view. The efforts of the Civil Service Clerical Association to improve conditions of the Staff Officer grade are too well known to merit repetition, but it may not be out of place to clear up any misunderstanding which may have arisen over this point. Over a number of years Staff Officers in general have been dissatisfied with their grading and prospects of promotion to the Executive grade. The grade, it will be remembered, came into being as, more or less, an expedient to offset the ban on promotion to the Executive grade, but when the ban was removed no steps were taken to adjust the position in favour of existing Staff Officers. The examination system of promotion continued for a number of years, until, again through the efforts of the Civil Service Clerical Association, the present Interview Board system was introduced. This alleviated somewhat the position of Staff Officers, and it is of interest to note that of those who qualified at the 1940 and 1941 Boards over 50% in each case were Staff Officers. In addition, Staff Officers are normally eligible for promotion to the HEO grade and this right has been zealously guarded by the Association and remains up to the present.[12]

However, the staff officers went on to establish their organisation. In June 1942 they applied for recognition to the Department of Finance. This was granted the following month, but the recognition was illusory since the Department of Finance would receive representations only through the Civil Service Alliance. In a letter dated 29 August 1942 the secretary of the alliance, D. O'Conaill, replied to the application of the staff officers for affiliation to the alliance, stating that because of objections by the Civil Service Clerical Association, the application could not be accepted. The president of the Staff Officers' Association referred to this matter in his address to the fifth annual general meeting as follows:

The Association failed to secure the 2/3 majority required for election to that body [Civil Service Alliance] because of the opposition of two other Associations out of a total of 18 Service Associations. We had the extraordinary position that an Association formally recognised by the Minister could not be granted a hearing by him primarily because two other Staff Associations took a certain line of action.[13]

The Staff Officers' Association made a further application for affiliation to the alliance and in May 1948 it was admitted. In the meantime, the Civil Service Clerical Association had left the alliance and was in the same position as the Staff Officers' Association had been in so far as the minister would not receive representation independently of the alliance. The staff officers took the opportunity to strike at their erstwhile opponents. In an article in the January 1949 issue of the *Civil Service Staff Officer*, under the heading 'Home to Roost', the following appeared:

For over seven years the Civil Service Clerical Association opposed the admission of the Staff Officers' Association to the Civil Service Alliance, as far as lay in their power preventing the proper functioning of our Association. They also endeavoured — for a long time with success — to keep the temporary Clerks Association out of the Alliance. Here again, the object was to imperil the very existence of an organisation of fellow workers — a strange activity for a body affiliated to the Trade Union Congress, since we believe it to be a just principle of trade unionism that all workers should be organised. Now the Civil Service Clerical Association is wrathful because the Minister for Finance will not receive its representations independently of the Alliance. It does not appear to appreciate the arrogance of its attitude.

However, both associations were received by the Minister for Finance in the course of discussions on the establishment of the conciliation and arbitration scheme and both were accorded recognition.

1936-1950

The Association of Higher Civil Servants was established in 1943. Its objectives, set out in its constitution which was adopted at the 1947 annual general meeting, were: 'To safeguard the interests and to promote the welfare of the members.' Membership of the association was stated to be: 'Open to all grades in the General Service above the Higher Executive Grade and to corresponding Departmental Grades as determined by the Council.'

The annual report for 1950-51 stated that, in practice, any established civil servant on a salary scale proceeding to a maximum in excess of the maximum of the higher executive officer (married) was eligible for membership. This annual report went on to state that many members of the association were also members of organisations catering for their own particular needs, e.g. Association of Inspectors of Taxes, Association of Local Government Auditors, and the Institute of Professional Civil Servants. The interests of these members were catered for by the Association of Higher Civil Servants in so far as those interests coincided with the interests of the general body of members, and in that respect many items of vital importance to all higher civil servants, such as widows' and orphans' pensions, the allocation of pensions to dependants, the abolition of supercut imposed on the cost-of-living bonus and the securing of better salary scales, were engaging the association's full attention. The impetus for setting up the association came from the need of the higher civil servant to remedy the injustice caused by the imposition of Supercut in 1921. The Supercut affected any civil servants above the higher executive officer grade and the higher officers took the view that the Civil Service Alliance representing civil servants up to higher executive officer was not an appropriate body to seek the Supercut's removal.

The first meeting of the Civil Service General Council staff side took place on 1 December 1949 at 27 Adelaide Road, Dublin. Present were: W. Bell, M. J. McPartlin, M. G. Keyes, T. K. Igoe, P. Horan and P. McCann (Post Office Workers' Union); J. S. Evers and W. Delaney (Government Employees Federation); K. O'Higgins and J. McAdam (Irish Post Office Engineering Union); John J. O'Kelly and T. O'Sullivan (Irish Professional Civil Servants' Association); J. Martin, J.B.

In Public Service

O'Quigley, M. Lonergan and C.S. Ó Dubhthaigh (Civil Service Alliance); M. F. Swallowe, W. J. Farrell, B. Ahern, D.A. Morrissey (Civil Service Clerical Association); P.S. O'Braonain and L. Ó Muirgheasa (Revenue Group of Departmental Associations).

The draft constitution was unanimously adopted. It provided for representation on the following basis: Civil Service Alliance (4); Civil Service Clerical Association (4); Irish Professional Civil Servants' Association (2); Irish Post Office Engineering Union (2); Post Office Workers' Union (6); Revenue Group (2). L. Ó Muirgheasa was elected chairman and W. J. Farrell was voted in as secretary on a pro tem basis. The chairman told the meeting that he had sent a letter to the Department of Finance, seeking the full-time free secondment of a civil servant for the purpose of carrying out the duties of secretary to the staff panel. The chairman announced that the department had been requested to receive a deputation on the matter. At the panel meeting held on 12 January 1950, the chairman said that the latest reply from the Department of Finance indicated that the minister was not prepared to agree to the full-time secondment of an officer to perform the duties of staff side secretary. However, the minister was willing to release an official for this purpose for three half-days per week, or, alternatively, he would agree to full-time secondment on a repayment basis. The chairman suggested to the panel that perhaps the best policy to adopt would be to use the minister's offer as a basis for further bargaining. They could seek to have the offer increased to three full days with a view to having it extended still further when the general council was formally established. It was agreed that the chairman would raise the matter again with the official side and report back. At the panel meeting on 5 April, the chairman reported on the discussion with the Department of Finance. He said that the impression was gained that the department would be prepared to improve on its offer of three half-days per week if the panel put forward definite proposals. Following further discussions, during which the acting secretary said that he was finding little difficulty in carrying on without secondment, it was agreed to leave the matter to the chairman, who undertook to discuss it again informally with the department at the first suitable opportunity.

1936-1950

The chairman reported to the panel on 15 May, and stated that the matter again had been raised and that, following lengthy talks, the department had made the following offer which could be taken as final:

That, for a period of three months, an officer would be granted special leave with pay on six half-days per week to allow him to devote himself to the duties of Secretary to the Staff Side, on the clear understanding that no extension of this concession would be sought by the Staff Side on the expiration of the three-month period.

The alternative to this offer, the chairman said, was three half-days per week for a trial period of one year or full-time secondment on a repayment basis. After discussion, the following resolution was adopted: 'That the Staff Panel accept the offer made by the Department of Finance and proceed to appoint a Secretary under the terms of that offer.' The resolution was passed by seven votes to six. At a meeting on 22 May 1950, W. J. Farrell was elected secretary with an allowance of £120 per annum over and above his ordinary remuneration. The Civil Service Clerical Association provided office accommodation at a rent of ten shillings per week and allocated £1 per week for a typist who would work for the panel in her own time. Finance was provided by way of a temporary charge of £20 per seat, pending a review of the panel's likely financial commitments. Both L. Ó Muirgheasa and W. J. Farrell were re-elected at the panel's first annual meeting held on 14 December 1950. At this meeting a presentation not exceeding twenty guineas was voted to the chairman.

The appointment of the first chairman of the proposed Arbitration Board took up much time at panel meetings during 1950. At the 12 January 1950 meeting the chairman reported that the Department of Finance had announced that Mr Justice Davitt was unable to accept the post of chairman of the board. The chairman then suggested that delegates should express the views of their respective organisations on six names that had been mentioned by the official side; J. Collins, J.C.M. Eason, J. Ingram, John Maher, J. J. O'Leary and J. J. Robinson.

The Post Office Workers' Union favoured O'Leary. The Civil Service Alliance favoured either Collins or Ingram, but would not support a businessman. The Civil Service Clerical Association would not accept an ex-civil servant or a businessman. The Irish Post Office Engineering Union objected to Ingram.

The chairman intervened to say that since there was no apparent support for Messrs Eason, Maher or Robinson — all businessmen — their names would be eliminated. He enquired if any delegates desired to put forward additional names for consideration. The following persons were suggested: Professor J. A. Coutts, Trinity College; Basil Chubb, Trinity College; Mr Justice Wylie; J. J. O'Donovan, Assistant Secretary, ESB; Mr Micks, SC, chairman of Bank Officials Arbitration Board; Mr Casey, SC, chairman of ESB Manual Workers' Arbitration Board; Michael Binchy, SC; Mr Justice Kingsmill Moore; D. O'Sullivan, former conciliation officer, Department of Industry and Commerce; Rev. Father Coyne; Dr McKevitt, Professor, Maynooth College; R. J. P. Mortishead, chairman of the Labour Court; Judge Roe.

Following a lengthy discussion on the suitability of these names, it was decided that the following should be placed on the tentative panel for further consideration: Professor Coutts, Judge Roe, Mr Justice Wylie, J. Ingram, M. Binchy, J. J. O'Leary and Mr Justice Kingsmill Moore.

A further meeting was held on 27 January 1950 when the chairman reported that the Department of Finance wanted to short-circuit the matter and to see if the panel would accept Mr Ingram. If he was not acceptable, other names would have to be considered. At a meeting on 24 February, Mr Ingram's nomination was rejected. The panel adopted the following resolution:

That the Department of Finance be asked in writing to receive a deputation from the Staff Panel with the object of discussing the list of names submitted by the Panel and with a view to eliciting from the Department a list of several names acceptable to them. In the event of a refusal by the Department to receive the deputation, the Minister for Finance to be communicated with requesting him to instruct his officials to receive such a deputation. Should the Minister fail so to instruct his officials, An Taoiseach to be written to in the matter.

1936-1950

At the panel meeting of 5 April 1950, the chairman reported that, following discussions with the Department of Finance two further names had been put forward for consideration by the staff side: A. W. Baynes and Frederick C. King. Since Mr Baynes was not acceptable to any organisation, the panel voted on a proposal to agree to Mr King's nomination. In the ballot, 12 voted for, and 10 voted against, Mr King.[14] *The Postal Worker* of May 1950 described Frederick King as follows:

Mr King, who received his earlier education at Clongowes Wood College, is a graduate of Trinity College, Dublin. He became a member of the Indian Civil Service in 1911, and held various posts, including the chairmanship of the Assam Labour Board and the Commissionership of the Central Excises and Salt, Northern India. He edited 'Public Admistration in Ireland' and is also the author of various works on Indian Administration. Mr. King is a member of the Creameries Joint Labour Committee, the Cancer Association of Ireland, the Civics Institute of Ireland, the Committee of the Dublin University School of Social Science, the Dun Laoghaire Vocational Education Committee, the Central Catholic Library and the National Children's Hospital.

CONCILIATION AND ARBITRATION

Writing in *The Bell*[15] in 1946, Mark Osborne discussed what he termed the most astonishing feature of the entire organisation of the civil service, namely the one which was often put in the form that 'a Civil Servant has no rights'.

To appreciate the position, it is necessary to take a very brief glance at the historic development. Originally the persons who transacted the affairs of State were personal servants of the King, not different in the legal theory from those who prepared his meals in the royal kitchen. The King was not answerable for his conduct in the Courts of Justice and in any event the Courts took the view that the relationship between the King and the servants in his employ was clearly not one that should be inquired into by them. If a servant therefore was ill-treated by his master he had no remedies, and the Royal master was not above taking frequent advantage of this rule of immunity . . . .

It should be noted also that there is at present no formal system for negotiation between the Staff and the Department of Finance, the controlling body representing the Government. This is in contrast with the British system where the Whitley Councils still

In Public Service

function effectively. These Councils, which were also functioning in Ireland, were abolished in 1924 by the Minister for Finance on the grounds that they were 'unsuitable to Irish conditions'. It is also the official view that under the Offences against the State Act 1939 it would be illegal to organise a strike of Civil Servants. This combination of the absence of arbitration machinery, the prohibition of strike action as illegal, and the fact that a Civil Servant in his dealing with the Executive is not protected by the law leaves matters in a peculiar, almost dangerous, position. The Government however argues that an association with the powers of an ordinary trade union might have the effect of coercing the Government into laying proposals for expenditure before the Dáil of which it did not approve.

Following the failure of the Brennan Commission to recommend an acceptable system of arbitration and the government's failure to offer such a system, the staff organisations resumed their agitation. The staff case was largely built on the statement made by the president of the Executive Council, Eamon de Valera, before the 1932 general election. Speaking at Rathmines Town Hall, Dublin on 28 January, the President had declared: 'I believe it is only right that there should be an Arbitration Board for the Civil Service to deal with matters between the Service and the Executive. We would be prepared to agree that an Arbitration Board be set up.' The *Civil Service Journal* repeated from the staff organisation's letter to the President, dated 27 August 1936, the essential features of any genuine system of civil service arbitration:

1. The chairman of the board to be appointed by agreement between the government and the staff organisations.
2. Each party to be free to select its representatives on the board and its advocates before the board.
3. Each party to have the right to bring before the board any claim within a previously agreed category without veto by the other party, the board alone having power to decide whether a particular claim falls within the agreed category.
4. The government to give effect to the awards of the Board, subject to the authority of parliament.
5. In the event of a dispute about the meaning of an award, the board to determine its own findings.

1936-1950

The matter was discussed on a number of occasions before the 1937 general election, notably on the debate on the Appropriation Bill in July 1936 and on a debate on a motion put forward by William Norton in April 1937. The new Dáil assembled in October 1937. That month's *Civil Service Journal* remarked that the new Dáil would need to tackle a very heavy agenda mainly made up of measures connected with the new Constitution, which was due to come into effect on 29 December, but that civil servants nevertheless would await with some impatience an opportunity to test the feeling of the recently elected legislators on the long-pressed demand for the establishment of effective negotiation and arbitration machinery for dealing with service grievances. The *Journal* referred to a motion put down by Deputy J. A. Costello in the following terms:

That the Dáil is of opinion that the Executive Council should immediately establish machinery whereby conditions of employment in the Civil Service, and other matters which may from time to time be in dispute between the Government and the Civil Service, would be settled by agreement between representatives of the Government and of the Civil Service Associations, and, in default of such agreement, would be submitted for decision to an independent Arbitration Board, the awards of which, subject to the over-riding authority of the Oireachtas, the Government would undertake to implement.

A vote on this motion was not taken until 25 May 1938 when it was carried by 52 votes to 51 votes. On 27 May the commission constituted under Article 57 to exercise the powers and functions of the President, on the advice of the Taoiseach, declared a general election. Polling was fixed to take place on 17 June. The outcome of the election was that Fianna Fáil secured a majority of five over all other parties combined. A stalemate existed until late in 1938 when the Civil Service Alliance decided to approach the Department of Finance to put the service case for proper arbitration and conciliation machinery.

The first meeting took place on 11 January 1939, when the staff side reiterated its claim for the establishment of machinery providing for facilities for negotiation and, in the absence of agreement, recourse to an Arbitration Board. The official representatives said that they would put the staff views before the Minister for Finance. At further meetings, held on 25 May and 8 June 1939, the official representatives outlined the minister's reply to the staff side's case, which did not represent any very considerable advance upon the original position. When the Civil Service Alliance received the report from the deputation, it decided to seek a further meeting with the minister's representatives with a view to pressing for further concessions and procuring a complete scheme in writing for submission to the staff associations. Owing to the absence on leave of some of the official representatives, there was a delay in fixing a date for a further meeting; meanwhile, the commencement of hostilities in Europe and the consequent state of emergency led the Department of Finance to postpone the discussions. On 26 September 1939, the alliance addressed a letter to the Department of Finance offering co-operation during the Emergency and pointing out that such co-operation would be possible only if the staff associations had a means of access to the department and suggesting the establishment of a temporary joint council.

The department's reply stated that the minister did not consider discussion at a joint council to be practicable, but it did intimate the minister's willingness to resume the negotiations that had been held up because of the Emergency and undertaking to arrange a further meeting with the staff representatives. A meeting was held on 31 October when the staff side was informed that, in the circumstances, the minister could not undertake to proceed with the establishment of formal machinery and that no claim for increased remuneration could be entertained. It was hinted to the staff side, however, that the minister would be willing, without prejudice to the ultimate outcome of the negotiations, to arrange for informal discussions between the staff and official sides, and it was agreed that a small deputation should meet representatives of the department to work out a scheme. The official memo contains an outline of the facilities offered by the Department of Finance for the duration of the Emergency:

The staff side stated that they wished it to be placed on record that they could not agree that the establishment of formal conciliation

1936-1950

and arbitration machinery should be deferred until the end of the present emergency, and that they intended to press for the establishment of such machinery. Discussion took place as to the best method of enabling staff organisations to make oral representations to the Department of Finance during the continuance of the present emergency, and it was agreed that informal consultation with Official Representatives should take place in accordance with the following arrangements:

1. No claims for increases in remuneration may be discussed. Subjects which may be discussed will include such questions as the absorption, without examination, of Writing Clerks and certain Writing Assistants and Shorthand Typists into the Clerical Officer Grade; the extension of the list of candidates successful at a limited competition; the channel of promotion from the Clerical Officer to the Junior Executive Grade; and the discharge of temporary staff owing to emergency conditions. Departmental matters with general service aspects may be discussed, but not otherwise.

2. It is desirable to have a clearing house for proposals which the Staff wish to discuss, and it is agreed that the Civil Service Alliance would prove a suitable medium for this purpose.

3. Meetings will be held as and when necessary.

4. At least one week's notice will be given by the Staff Representatives of a desire to have a meeting with the Official Representatives. The nature of the subjects which the Staff Representatives wish to discuss will be indicated by them in advance of each meeting.

5. The number of Staff Representatives will normally be three, and it was agreed that it would be convenient, in order to preserve continuity, if one of the Staff Representatives attended all the meetings with the Official Representatives. The Staff Representatives will be serving Civil Servants.

The matter of the Arbitration Board was discussed at length during the debate in the Dáil on the 1945 Finance Estimates. Subsequently, the Minister for Finance proposed a further scheme, but once more the staff side found it unacceptable. The matter had not been resolved when a general election took place in February 1948. Fianna Fáil failed to secure a clear majority and was unable to form a government. The outcome of the election was as follows:

In Public Service

Fianna Fáil	61
Fine Gael	29
Labour	13
Clann na Poblachta	10
Clann na Talman	8
National Labour	4
Independent	12

An alternative inter-party government was formed, representative of five parties and some independent deputies.

John A. Costello was elected Taoiseach and William Norton, general secretary of the Post Office Workers' Union, was appointed Tánaiste and Minister for Social Welfare. Only two members of the new government had previously held ministerial office, General Richard Mulcahy and Patrick McGilligan. The *Postal Worker* of February 1948 stated that William Norton wished to continue to serve the union of which he had been general secretary for 25 years. However, the Labour Party thought that it was imperative that he be a member of the government. Within a matter of two months, Norton announced that the government had accepted the principles on which an arbitration scheme would be based.

A number of meetings took place between representatives of the staff side and representatives of the Minister for Finance, and an agreement was signed on 30 July 1949. The following signed the agreement: Patrick McGilligan, Minister for Finance; W. Bell on behalf of the Post Office Workers' Union; D.A. Morrissey on behalf of the Civil Service Clerical Association; Tomas O'Suilleabhan on behalf of the Institute of Professional Civil Servants; S. O'Donnchadra on behalf of the Government Employees' Federation; S. Mac AnBhaird on behalf of the Irish Post Office Engineering Union; Michael A. Lonergan, John B. O'Quigley, and Michael Meade on behalf of the Civil Service Alliance.

The *Postal Worker* of September 1949 set out the following as some of the more important changes from previously proposed schemes:

1. The prior veto of the Minister for Finance on claims to be referred to arbitration was removed.

1936-1950

2. The prohibition on associations with outside labour bodies such as the Irish Trade Union Congress was removed.
3. The prohibition on the political affiliation of staff associations was removed, provided the organisation was affiliated to the political body before 1 April 1949.
4. The prohibition on the representation of staff by persons other than serving civil servants was removed.
5. The Arbitration Board would consist of two official representatives and two staff representatives, presided over by an agreed independent chairman.
6. The scheme would be reviewed at the end of twelve months.
7. Subject to maintaining the overriding authority of the Oireachtas, the government would accept the principle of arbitration for the settlement of disputes between the government and the civil service organisations, with suitable machinery for conciliation and negotiation.

The first meeting of the general council took place on 1 June 1950. The Civil Service Arbitration Board first met in December 1950 to adjudicate on a claim for steeper increments presented by the Post Office Workers' Union.

PAY AND COST-OF-LIVING BONUS

The Cost-of-Living Bonus Agreement of 1920 provided that the bonus should be based on an index figure of 130 over the 1914 figure. The agreement provided for an increase or decrease of one twenty-sixth or five one-hundred-and-thirtieths in the bonus for every movement of not less than five points in the index figure above or below 130 on (normally) six-monthly review. The index figure peaked at 165 on 1 March 1921 and then gradually decreased to 60 at 1 January 1936. The index immediately before the stabilisation of the bonus on 1 July 1940 was:

January 1937	65
July 1937	70
January 1938	75
July 1938	75
January 1939	75
January 1940	85

In Public Service

When the pay of employees generally was stabilised under the terms of Emergency Powers (No.83) Order as from 7 May 1941, the index figure had reached 120, an increase of 35 points. The first indication that the government had under consideration the question of stabilisation of the bonus was given by the Minister for Finance in his concluding speech on the Second Stage of the Finance Bill in Dáil Éireann on 29 November 1939, when he stated: 'The Government is determined to set its face against the efforts of any class to obtain compensation for the rise in prices at the expense of the community. Action to the same end is in contemplation with regard to all classes of Public Servants, and if the war continues for a long time, the Government may be forced to adopt more drastic measures.'

The minister's statement was the matter of correspondence between him and the Post Office Workers' Union. In the course of a reply dated 11 December 1939, he stated:

If the need arises for discussion of the bonus question, the arrangements recently agreed to for ascertaining during the emergency the views of the Civil Service on matters of General Service interest will be utilised. Under these arrangements the Civil Service Alliance, with which it is understood the Post Office Workers' Union is associated, acts as a clearing-house in connection with matters to be discussed. It would appear, therefore, that, should the occasion for discussion of the bonus question arise, your Union will have ample opportunity of having its particular interests and views represented at the discussion.[16]

The Department of Finance invited representatives of the various associations affiliated to the Civil Service Alliance to a meeting in the Department of Agriculture on 11 April, in order to clarify the statement made by the minister in the Dáil on 29 November 1939. The Association of Officers of the Executive and Higher Officers was represented by J. Kelly and M. P. Russell. J. J. McElligott made the following statement:

On behalf of the Minister for Finance, I desire to welcome you and to thank you for accepting his invitation to this meeting. The matter for discussion is a very important one, and we are glad to have such a representative attendance. You will recall that the Minister, when introducing the Supplementary Budget in Dáil Éireann on 8 November last, adverted to the danger to our economic position which would arise if the initial increase in prices caused by war conditions were allowed to be reflected in wages, salaries and profits.

'The effect', he said, 'would be to increase prices still more, and to give occasion for new demands. In that way an artificial price structure would be built up, which would inevitably collapse at the end of the war, if not before, leaving behind widespread unemployment and depression.'

Mr McElligott indicated that, in an endeavour to avert such a development, the government would 'set its face against the efforts of any class to obtain compensation for the rise in prices at the expense of the community.' He stated that action to the same end was contemplated with regard to all classes of public servants. In a later speech, on the second stage of the Finance (No.2) Bill, the minister had said:

. . . when further consideration has clarified the general position, in so far as the Civil Service may be affected, consultation with the Service will take place before proceeding. The present meeting has been called in fulfilment of the Minister's promise. The statement in the Minister's Budget needs little elaboration. Those of you who remember the last war and its economic aftermath are already familiar with the dangers of inflation. For this country, these dangers today are even greater than they were twenty-five years ago.

During the last war, no effective steps were taken to control the prices of our exports for the first three years almost, and even after the termination of the war, they continued to rise, while imports of most commodities, though dear, were difficult to procure. The consequence was that, in spite of higher costs of production there was a great increase in our national savings — which incidentally, has enabled us to come through some very difficult periods since. Now the position is completely different. The prices of our exports have been rigorously controlled since the beginning of the war, and on a lower level on the whole than that of the goods we import. We have succeded in maintaining a more plentiful supply of imports than might have been expected — an advantage in some ways, but one for which we have to pay dearly by a depletion of our national savings. Furthermore, the costs of production, already abnormally high here, have risen seriously because of higher prices of raw materials and fuel, and higher wages. Although the war has been in progress for little more than seven months, the result of these factors may be plainly seen in the latest trade returns, which reveal a

In Public Service

disturbing increase in the adverse balance of trade. Inflation had certain compensations for us during and after the last war; this time, it would have none, and unless we can avert it, we shall find ourselves far less able to meet the inevitable difficulties than we were in 1919 and after.

Mr. McElligott continued:

Do what we will, the conditions created by the war will involve us in sacrifices — we may congratulate ourselves that they are likely to be much less severe than those which every other neutral nation in Europe has had to endure. Our problem is to minimise the sacrifices and to ensure that they are spread as fairly as possible. To minimise them, we must keep costs of production at a level which will enable us to maintain and increase our export trade and conserve our resources. To ensure that they are fairly distributed we must avoid the development of a position in which some sections of the community are obliged to bear the share of others as well as their own. Broadly speaking, that means, in the economic sphere, that the State, while doing its utmost to prevent avoidable increases in prices, has also the duty of opposing the claims of sections of the community to obtain at the expense of the rest of the community compensation for such increases in prices as cannot be avoided. It will be obvious that the State could not fulfil this duty if its own employees were to continue to be compensated automatically for rises in the cost of living. As you know, the cost of living bonus has already been allowed to rise ten points above the level at which it stood when the war began. It is not proposed to withdraw that increase, but the Government has come to the conclusion that further increases cannot be allowed during the emergency, and it is proposed to take at once the measures necessary to stabilise the bonus at the figure of 85.

The president of the Civil Service Alliance, C. O'Sullivan, replied on behalf of the staff organisations.

At our meeting [held the previous night] there was absolute unanimity on the subject under discussion — a remarkable condition of affairs at a meeting of all grades of the Service. In the first place, I may say that our people were amazed that the Minister should have chosen the present of all times to take the initiative in raising the question of stabilisation. The present period is described in the Department's letter as a period of emergency, and the Minister must surely know something of the history of the bonus as applied to Civil Service remuneration. He must surely be aware that the sliding-scale principle was first introduced during a similar emergency, in order that Civil Servants should receive partial compensation for rapidly increasing prices. I use the word 'partial' advisedly, because the full bonus is only paid on the first thirty-five shillings per week of a Civil Servant's pay. After that it is scaled down to give less compensation as the index figure rises. Our people had indeed contemplated making a demand to have this defect removed, and to have adopted some of the recommendations of the Johnson Commission so as to make the bonus more equitable and fair to the staffs. In refraining from taking this course during the emergency, we consider we have already made a very large contribution to the national economy. In this connection, I should like to remind the Minister's representatives of the statement made by Mr. McElligott in 1931, when he said that 'the various reductions in the bonus since 1922 had resulted in cumulative saving of nearly £2,000,000 to the Exchequer' and that 'no other section of the community has so substantially contributed to the national economy.' It would be safe to say that a further £1,000,000 has been saved since that year. Apart from this, the Minister must be aware that practically all grades of the Civil Service have suffered reductions in basic pay since 1924, and those who suffered additional losses in basic pay under the Temporary Economies Act, at a time when the bonus was falling, never had their losses restored to them. At the present time the bulk of the lower and middle grades of the Service are suffering under a definite sense of injustice in the matter of scales of pay.

The staff side decided not to resume discussions. Following the meeting with Mr McElligott, the staff associations corresponded with the Department of Finance on the matter of stabilisation. In a letter dated 7 May 1940, addressed to the general secretary of the Post Office Workers' Union, Seán Ó Muinneacain of the department wrote:

Civil Servants, more than any other class of the community, have a special interest in the financial stability and general welfare of the State, and bearing in mind that every increase of five points in the Cost of Living bonus costs the Exchequer at least £100,000 per annum, it is not too much to expect that they would be disposed to take their share in the sacrifices which the present emergency requires of the general body of the people. The Minister regrets that he is unable to find any of the arguments advanced against the proposed stabilisation any grounds which, in present circumstances, would justify him in recommending a modification of the proposal of the Government.

In the light of the government's refusal to alter its decision to stabilise the bonus on the basis of an index figure of 85, even though the bonus to be applied to wages as and from 1 July 1940 should have been based on an index figure of 105, the staff organisations decided to contest the legality of the government's decision. The report of the proceedings and the judgment in the case were published by the Civil Service Alliance in May 1941 and were reprinted in service journals. Mr Justice Gavan Duffy expressed the opinion that the Minister of Finance, in making the Regulations of 1940 that had stabilisd bonuses, had acted strictly within his statutory rights, and that the plaintiffs were suing for relief to which they had no legal title.

The question of appeal[17] to the Supreme Court against Mr Justice Gavan Duffy's judgment was carefully considered by the staff associations in conjunction with counsel. They were advised not to bring an appeal to the Supreme Court.

Following the court decision, the Civil Service Alliance sought a meeting with representatives of the Department of Finance. The Post Office Workers' Union made separate representations.

Representatives of the alliance met with representatives of the Department of Finance on 4 July 1941. At this meeting the secretary of the department, J. J. McElligott, stated that since the time when the bonus question previously had been discussed, the country's general financial position had certainly not improved and the position of the exchequer had rather deteriorated. When the discussions were resumed on 19 September 1941, Mr McElligott said:

> The report of the discussion on 4 July has been read by the Minister and the position has since been discussed with him on several occasions. The possibility of having something done for married Civil Servants on the lowest scales of pay has been fully explored. The Minister was sincerely anxious to give a favourable response to the pleas made on behalf of these men at the July meeting. He has, however, felt compelled to decide that nothing can be done in present circumstances.

The staff organisation, together with the Irish Local Government Officials' Union, then decided to organise a public meeting to protest against the government's decision. The following advertisement appeared in the *Civil Service Journal*:

STABILISATION OF CIVIL SERVICE COST-OF-LIVING BONUS

MASS MEETING OF PROTEST
Round Room, Mansion House, Dublin
Thursday, 8th January, 1942, at 7.30 p.m.

Under the combined auspices of
The Civil Service Alliance, The Post Office Workers' Union
and the Irish Local Government Officials' Union

UNITY IS STRENGTH

Eventually the Department of Finance decided that the following increases should apply as from 1 June 1942.

(a) Married and widowed wholetime officers on basic salaries not exceeding £1 per week — an increase of 3/26ths.
(b) Married wholetime officers on basic salaries exceeding £1 and not exceeding £2 per week — an increase of 2/26ths.
(c) Married wholetime officers on basic salaries exceeding £2 and not exceeding £5 per week — an increase of 2/26ths on the first £91.5s.0d.
(d) Married part-time officers on basic salaries not exceeding £3 per week — an increase of 1/26th on first £91.5s.0d.
(e) Single wholetime officers on basic salaries not exceeding £3 per week — an increase of 1/26th on first £91.5s.0d.

For the purpose of (b), (c) and (d), 'married' included widows with one or more dependent children. A married person included a widower. The number of officers affected was 16,368 and the estimated annual cost was £90,665. The decision did not apply to overtime payments.

It was taken that a one-twenty-sixth increase represented one shilling in the £ on basic wages.

The Postal Worker of July-August 1942 described the decision as being typical of the niggardliness and unreasonableness that

In Public Service

had characterised the government's attitude on the question. The periodical declared that the fight for the normal operation of the bonus agreement would continue with undiminished vigour.

The government made a further announcement on 19 December 1942, detailing increases as from 1 January 1943. The official decision was:

The Government, in view of the increase in the cost of living, has reviewed the remuneration of certain persons in the Public Service and of National Teachers, and has decided on certain emergency increases. These increases which in the case of Civil Servants include any amounts granted last June under the Civil Service (Stabilisation of Bonus) (Amendment) Regulations, 1942, will be given to wholetime employees whose total remuneration does not exceed £5 (five pounds) a week plus bonus or equivalent inclusive pay, and to part-time employees with total remuneration not exceeding £261 per year. In no case will the increases now granted be such as to bring the total pay over these figures. The increases are:

Civil Servants

Wholetime employees — married — 7s. a week, unmarried — 5s. a week
Part-time employees — married — 5s. a week, unmarried — 3s. a week
Juveniles — 2s.6d. a week.

The Postal Worker commented:

Even if the above increases were now granted in full they would make an infinitesimal contribution to what the staff have lost by the Government's repudiation of the Bonus Agreement, but bear in mind that the increases include those granted in June last and thus the amounts to be paid under the decision will again be but a fraction of what is due to the staff under the Bonus Agreement to which the Government was partner.

The Stabilisation Order was again modified with effect from 1 January 1945. This modification was significant in so far as it recognised the claim of the associations that it was unfair to discriminate against the staff by imposing the bonus stabilisation regulations from July 1940, when the government had not applied the Wages Standstill Order to workers in private

1936-1950

industry until 7 May 1941. The government's official announcement on the subject was as follows:

As from January 1, 1945, Civil Service sliding scale bonus will be calculated on the basis of a bonus figure of 110, to be paid at the rate which would in the normal course have applied on May 7, 1941, when the pay of outside workers was first stabilised by Government Order. Since January 1, 1940, Civil Service sliding scale bonus (which was designed to compensate for the increase in the cost-of-living since 1914) has been paid on the basis of a bonus figure of 85. It has also been decided to increase the rates of Emergency Bonus for Civil Servants by 1/= a week. The present maximum rates of Emergency Bonus are 10/= a week (married) and 8/= a week (unmarried) for wholetime officers and 8/= a week (married) and 6/= a week (unmarried) for part-time officers. The grant of a further 1/= a week has been decided by reference to the maximum bonus of 11/= a week payable to workers in outside employment under the provisions of Emergency Powers (No.260) (Fourth Amendment) Order, 1943. The ceiling of £500 inclusive (whole-timers) and £365 inclusive (part-timers) will still continue so far as emergency bonus is concerned, but in applying the ceilings the addition now made to sliding scale bonus will not be reckoned.

The ceiling for the receipt of emergency bonus had been increased to £500, which was the maximum (basic) of the higher executive officer scale. Subsequently the government permitted the payment of an emergency bonus of 15 shillings per week, instead of the former maximum bonus of 11 shillings per week. Following representations from the associations, the government agreed to increase the emergency bonus payable to civil servants by 4 shillings a week with effect from 1 January 1946. Unfortunately, the government retained the discrimination against unmarried officers, who again were penalised to the extent of 2 shillings per week less than married officers. When, at the end of the war, the government introduced the Supplies and Services (Temporary Provisions) Bill, to replace the Emergency Powers Act, and indicated its intention to abolish the General Standstill Order, the associations sought to restore the sliding-system of salary payment. During the discussions that followed, the minister asked the staffs to consider the principle of pay consolidation. Following negotiations, the following proposals emerged and were recommended by the Civil Service Alliance:

All officers previously conditioned to a sliding-scale system of payment will be placed on consolidated scales calculated on a cost of living index figure of 270 coupled with withdrawal of Emergency Bonus, with the following provisions:

(a) No whole-time adult Civil Servant in the classes represented by the organisations at present paid on the basic and bonus system will receive an increase of less than 7s.6d. a week on his present total remuneration, or less than 25 per cent on the remuneration appropriate to his grade in 1939. The minimum increase in respect of juveniles will be 3s. per week in the case of an officer under 18 years of age and 5s. per week between 18 and 21 years of age.

(b) In the case of officers already on inclusive scales of pay, an agreed adjustment will be made later.

(c) The increase in pay will have effect from the 1st November 1946.

(d) The matter will be reviewed at the end of two years from the 1st November 1946, or at any time thereafter, if the cost of living index number is then as high as 30 points above the figure for consolidation or as low as 230. If in the meantime the figure increases substantially the matter will be open to review.

(e) In order to ensure the application of these terms to Transferred Officers it is necessary to have a majority vote of Transferred Officers authorising the signing on their behalf of an agreement accepting the terms. Such an agreement would contain a provision consenting to the introduction of special legislation which would exclude the stabilisation of bonus during the Emergency and the consolidation of basic pay and bonus from the grounds for retirement under the Transferred Officers (Compensation) Act, 1929. With these two exceptions, the Act of 1929 would be restored so that, in effect, Transferred Officers would then have their new position under the proposed agreement fully protected. In connection with sub-section (a) above it should be noted that the distinction between adult and juvenile was strongly resisted by the Alliance representatives, but unfortunately despite a special meeting with the Minister on Thursday the 12th December they were unable to induce the Minister to waive it.

1936-1950

The ballot conducted on the proposals resulted as follows:[18]

	For	Against
Civil Service Alliance	5,164	844
Transferred Officers Protection Association	4,059	743
Post Office Workers' Union	3,360	1,259
Association of Higher Civil Servants	353	99

The effect of the settlement on the administrative and executive grades relative to the 1939 salaries was as follows:

Salaries exclusive of bonus	1939	1946	Increase over 1939
	£	£	£
Higher executive officer (single)	532. 1.0	726. 8.0	194. 7.0
Higher executive officer (married)	683.19.0	917. 0.0	233. 1.0
Junior executive officer (single)	369. 1.0	519.18.0	150.17.0
Junior executive officer (married)	495. 0.0	678.14.0	183.14.0
Assistant principal (single)	683.19.0	917. 0.0	233. 1.0
Assistant principal (married)	788.19.0	1,028. 5.0	239. 6.0

The consolidated agreement was reviewed in 1948 and the following agreement emerged:

1. From 29 May 1948 to 31 October 1948 subject to a ceiling of £350 per annum (inclusive) —
   (a) 11/= per week to all married men and to unmarried men on undifferentiated salary scales
   (b) 5/6d per week to all other unmarried men and to women and juveniles

2. From 1 November 1948 to 31 October 1950 without a salary ceiling, consolidation of basic salary with bonus 290 (i.e. 20 points above the figure operative since 1 November 1946) subject to minimum increases as at (1) above.

3. Interim review of (2) above if the cost-of-living rises to 330 or falls to 50.

This offer was accepted by the council of the Civil Service Alliance by a large majority. The Civil Service Clerical Association opposed the agreement and seceded from the alliance.

IV

1951-1969

The Devlin report set out the numbers employed in the Irish civil service on 1 January 1934 and on 1 January 1969:

1934		1969	
Civil servants	19,600	Civil servants	34,400*
Fee paid, industrial etc.	3,000	Fee paid, industrial etc.	12,000
Total	22,600	Total	46,400

*16,000 in Post Office

On 1 January 1969 the numbers in the general service grades were:

Secretary	19
Deputy secretary	11
Assistant secretary	58
Principal officer	169
Assistant principal officer	345
Administrative officer	69
Higher executive officer	683
Higher executive officer (restricted)	59
Executive officer	1,060
Staff officer	628
Clerical officer	1,582
Clerk typist	4,043

The association's annual report for 1951 stated that, for the first five months of the year, the association had been working under the scheme of conciliation and arbitration — mainly on a cost-of-living pay claim. For the remainder of the year, in common with other staff organisations, it was endeavouring to have the scheme restored. The scheme had been suspended arbitrarily at the end of May and, the annual report avers, no justification, theoretical or practical, was put forward for its suspension. In his address to the 1952 annual general meeting, the chairman, P. Costelloe, said that considerable interest had been aroused by the reply to a parliamentary question on the strength of the civil service, when a figure of 41,000 had been cited. The press complained that this was too high. The chairman commented that civil servants viewed the expansion of the civil service with anything but a favourable eye. They knew from experience that the higher the cost of the civil service, the smaller would be the proportion of compensation for increases in living costs which a Minister for Finance would offer them. While the civil service undoubtedly had expanded over the previous twenty years, the cause for the expansion was to be found not within the civil service but outside it. The public should understand that civil servants were not policy-makers and did not initiate schemes, and so had not within their control the determination of the size of the civil service at any given time.

Mr Costelloe also commented on the matter of income tax which, he said, lay with intolerable harshness upon a section of the community already labouring under many oppressive disabilities. Members of the association were part of the salaried middle classes who paid for everything for themselves and for everybody else but got nothing in return. The position of single men and women was doubly inequitable since they suffered from discrimination in rates of pay as well as discrimination in rates of income tax.

Mr Costelloe went on to say that the association would continue with other organised groups of salaried workers to agitate for a radical revision of income tax law which would distribute the load of income tax in proportion to the individual's capacity to bear it.

The annual report for 1952/53 was written at a time when civil servants were anxiously awaiting the publication of the report of the Civil Service Arbitration Board on the general revision of pay claim that had been heard at the beginning of November. The scheme of conciliation and arbitration had not resumed effective working until October 1952, but nevertheless the minister insisted on delaying publication of the report and

In Public Service

indicating his attitude to the findings of the board until he was compelled to do so under the provisions of the scheme.

Addressing the 1953 annual general meeting, the new chairman, P. O'Muiri, referred at length to the negotiations that had led to the adoption of the revised arbitration scheme. He cited the strenuous efforts of the staff side to preserve in its original form the clause determining the government's action on the findings of an arbitration board. The Minister for Finance, he said, could not be prevailed upon to accept this view and pressed for the inclusion of the new clause 20(2) of the revised scheme, arguing that the amendment was an advantage to the staff side because, in order to save the public finances, the Minister for Finance would not be obliged to take the extreme step of going to the Dáil for the rejection of the findings of an arbitration board on a general revision of pay claim.

The exchequer protection clause, as the amendment came to be known, was, the minister said, merely a question of deferment of consideration of the full payment of an arbitration finding. He felt that the government would be bound to make provision in the following year for payment of the finding, assuming any kind of normal financial conditions. In response to an enquiry about whether the staff might take it that the minister did not wish to deprive the civil service of any part of an arbitration finding of this nature, the minister replied that this was indeed so unless the circumstances were exceptional.

Within a matter of months, the minister's use of this clause to modify an award for a general increase in pay was to cause a crisis in civil service industrial relations. (This event is covered elsewhere in this chapter.) The association's annual report for 1954/55 was able to record that the amount withheld on foot of the 1952 award had been paid on the change of government. The same report expressed satisfaction that 1955 would see the introduction of a permanent scheme of conciliation and arbitration for the civil service. The report also stated that staff organisations were fully alive to the merits of conciliation and arbitration and was glad to record that they were at one in their determination to see that the machinery functioned properly and efficiently.

1951-1969

Early in 1955 the Minister for Finance met the staff side and made two very important promises: first, to clear, as far as his department was concerned, all claims then listed for hearing at arbitration before the end of 1955 and, second, to meet the staff at the end of the year to discuss the functioning of the scheme during those twelve months.[1] All the claims then listed for arbitration were disposed of and the board also heard a number of claims listed later. The year was also notable for the fact that a claim for a general revision of civil service pay was approved by the general council, giving rise to hope that, in future years, conciliation would prove a better instrument for dealing with staff matters than it had been.

The chairman of the association, J. G. Doyle, speaking at the 1956 annual general meeting, referred to two matters of particular concern at the time. One was the claim for new salary scales for executive and higher executive officers, the other was the claim for a promotion scheme for the executive officer grade. These matters were discussed again the following year. In the course of his address to the 1957 annual general meeting, the chairman, H. O'Sullivan, said that it was a matter for regret that the general council had not disposed of the association's scheme for rationalising promotions to the higher executive officer grade. He referred to the continued favouring of the selection board system over the seniority system in certain influential quarters of the civil service. He went on to mention that 'the most recent attack on the seniority principle of the association's scheme was made by a contributor to the autumn issue of a publication called *Administration*, a publication not, alas, noted for its pro-executive bias.'[2]

In the course of the article, T. J. Barrington had maintained that the interview system was manifestly fair, reasonably acceptable and by and large efficient. He apparently referred to the fact that in 1932 the association had told the Brennan Commission that promotion should be on merit alone. The chairman asserted that at that time, and in the light of the information then available, the members came to conclusions that were not accepted in 1957. 'It must be remembered,' he said, 'that in the Executive grade, in view of the rigid method of recruitment, the material from which selection was made was of a uniformly high quality and differences of ability were largely marginal.'

The year 1956 will be remembered for legislation dealing exclusively with the civil service, the Civil Service Commissioners Act and the Civil Service Regulation Act. The association objected to sections of the latter relating to the readmission of widows, in particular to the possibility that they might be placed in a grade lower than that from which they had resigned on marriage, even when they were adjudged to be competent to be restored to their former grade.

The 1957 annual report devoted most space to the serious position in which staff organisations found themselves following the Minister for Finance's announcement of the government's intention not to pay any increase, however small, which the Civil Service Arbitration Board might award on the claim for an increase of more than 12 per cent in the cost of living. In view of the economic situation, the staff organisations had limited its claim to an increase of $7\frac{1}{2}$ per cent, subject to a minimum of 10 shillings per week where that sum would be greater than the $7\frac{1}{2}$ per cent increase. The report contended that it had always been a guiding principle of the conciliation and arbitration scheme that, while a claim was being processed, no public comment should be made by either party that might influence the eventual decision. It was to be feared that the Arbitration Board, in considering the claim, might feel stultified in its deliberations by the knowledge that the government could upset its just decision.

H. O'Sullivan, in the course of his address to the 1958 annual general meeting, reviewed the background against which the government's statement had been made. Early in 1957 the Minister for Industry and Commerce, Seán Lemass, had convened a meeting between the Provisional United Trades Union Organisation and the Federated Union of Employers, to seek a formula for a national wage agreement. The meeting had been convened in the face of the certainty that, arising out of increased living costs, largely traceable to the abolition of food subsidies, the 6th round of pay increases was on the way. The Irish Conference of Professional and Service Associations, to which the Executive and Higher Officers' Association was affiliated through the Civil Service Alliance, sought to be represented at these discussions, but was informed that the Minister for Industry and Commerce had refused to accede to this request. Becoming aware of the interpretations that the government sought to put on the agreement in the case of civil servants, the Provisional United Trades Union Organisation issued a letter repudiating the suggestion that the agreement could be so interpreted. Despite recording disagreement on the claim in December 1957, the general council went along with increases in April 1958.[3]

The year 1959 was notable, among other things, for the fact that it was the first time, since the introduction of conciliation and arbitration in the civil service, that the association had participated directly in the affairs of the staff panel of the general council. The altered relationship of the association to the panel took effect in June 1959 when the association ceased its indirect representation on the panel through the Civil Service Alliance.

The introduction of the reorganisation scheme for the civil service in July 1960 had a dislocating effect on a number of matters that otherwise would have occupied the association's time and attention. Matters such as the promotion scheme could not be decided finally pending clarification of the future of the executive grade. In 1961 the executive committee saw as its main task the preparation and prosecution of grade claims. In his address to the 1962 annual general meeting, the chairman, D. J. O'Driscoll, described the arbitration findings on the claims as representing an appreciable improvement in salary scales. He went on: 'However there still remains to be resolved the claims of our members for an improved incremental scale for Executive Officers and this most important issue will no doubt engage the urgent attention of the incoming Executive.'

The next most important issue for the association that year was the proposed promotion equalisation scheme. The chairman described this as a special challenge facing the association. Mr O'Driscoll said that, after a prolonged examination of possible methods, the association had now reached the point where it would be faced with taking a decision to launch a scheme which would have far-reaching effects on the promotion prospects of executive officers. The annual report for 1962/63 said that there had been two special general meetings during the year to discuss the promotion scheme, but despite all the activities the negotiations had not been concluded at the end of the year. The recruitment of administrative officers and the serious threat to the future of all members of the executive and higher executive grades by increased recruitment of such officers caused the executive committee in 1962 to submit claims for discussion at general council asking that the administrative officer grade be abolished and that, in the interim, the guarantee of promotion to the assistant principal grade after seven years be discontinued. The same year also saw a challenge to the association: it was suggested that redundant officers from the departmental grades of social welfare officer and social welfare supervisor be assigned to executive and higher executive posts. The executive committee made strong and continuous representations to the Department of Finance, pointing out the injustice of such an assignment and urging that no drastic steps be taken to absorb these officers into the general service grades. The committee maintained that it would be unfair to expect general service grades, which were not concerned with the reorganisation in the Department of Social Welfare, to bear the cost of the redundancy and that some of the cost should be taken up by the government, particularly since there would be considerable long-term savings to the administration. The committee considered that the fact that the proposals were not implemented was due in some measure to the association's strong action.

The annual general meeting, held on 23 February 1963, was in a position to consider a response from the executive committee to the government's recently published White Paper, *Closing the Gap*, whose purpose was to draw attention to the economic danger caused by the gap between incomes and productivity. The government sought the understanding and co-operation of all sections of the community in its efforts to close the gap and deemed it necessary that departments and state-sponsored organisations should not accede to any claims for increases in wages and salaries, or for changes in conditions of work having the same effect, which would arouse expectations of similar increases in other employments. The government did not envisage that conciliation and arbitration procedures should be put in suspense, but rather that the findings should be considered in relation to their possible reaction in other sections and, if necessary, not applied until this could be done without damaging the national economic interest. The executive committee's immediate response was to reject the serious implications evident in the White Paper. It considered it unfair that one section of the community should be forced into a position inferior to its counterparts in other employments and that no redress should be given at independent arbitration which could decide on the merits of a claim. While the White Paper asserted that the scheme of conciliation and arbitration was not suspended, it was obvious that, if the findings were subject to government direction, the scheme was one of conciliation and arbitration in name only.

The Irish Conference of Professional and Service Associations, of which the association was a constituent, was also loud in its condemnation of what it called the 'wages standstill'. The 1963/64 annual report referred to the White Paper and noted that, notwithstanding the effective standstill on wages and salaries, the staff of the ESB had secured an interim increase of 7 per cent and that later salary increases were awarded at conciliation and arbitration to the gardai and the primary teachers. In November 1963, in a letter to the Irish Congress of Trade Unions, the Taoiseach, Seán Lemass, announced that 'the gap to which the White Paper refers has since been virtually closed by reason of the continued expansion of the total national production during the present year.' The letter continued: 'In the confident expectation that the country's present rate of economic growth will be maintained and in conformity with the Government's policy that its benefits should be fairly distributed amongst the whole community, a further upward revision of wages and salaries might now be safely envisaged.' The Taoiseach called for a national agreement between representatives of employers and the workers on the scale of such increases and undertook that the government's policy would be to facilitate the application throughout the public services of whatever wage and salary increases were negotiated by agreement in relation to private employment.

In January 1964, agreement was reached between the Federated Union of Employers and other employers' organisations and the Irish Congress of Trade Unions for a national wage increase of up to 12 per cent on salaries of £1,500 or less per year, with a minimum of £1 per week for adult male workers. Special consideration was to be given to the portion of salaries over £1,500 per year. The agreement was for a period of two years, but a revised recommendation would not operate until a further six months had elapsed. Agreement on increases in the civil service was recorded on 4 February 1964, and provided for an increase of 12 per cent for all full-time civil servants with effect from three days before. The 12 per cent was effective up to £1,580, the maximum point of the grades within the conciliation and arbitration scheme. There was a minimum of £1 for adult male workers at age 21 or over, or where there was a specific age point of 21 years.

Many important projects begun in other years were brought to a conclusion in 1964. The introduction of the five-day week, the status increase for executive officers[4] and the implementation of the scheme for promotion to higher executive officer are three that are worthy of mention. Outstanding at the end of the year was the status claim for higher executive officers, the delay in the conclusion of which, the association asserted, served to focus attention on the protracted delays that had become an inherent part of the way the scheme of conciliation and arbitration was being administered. The arbitrator's finding was not given until 15 March 1965.[5]

The issue of decentralisation first came to the fore in 1964. The chairman, F. J. Woods, in his address to the 1965 annual general meeting, posed the question 'Are Civil Servants considered as human beings at all or just insensitive robots?' He was referring to what he termed 'so-called decentralisation, by which apparently is meant the movement willy nilly of Departments or parts of Departments to remote provincial centres.'

Parliamentary questions have elicited that a decision in principle has been taken to decentralise some Departments. The civil servants have been told that they will be consulted at the appropriate time. Here we feel we have not only the right but the duty to protest in no uncertain terms. Administration is our business and it is clear to us that the best, cheapest and most efficient administration in our circumstances is a centralised one near to the seat of Government. If the decentralisation is undertaken not in the interests of efficiency but as a social experiment or a means of reviving a depressed area,

1951-1969

can anyone imagine anything less likely to succeed than importing a number of reluctant and dissatisfied civil servants who have been suddenly uprooted from the only place where they want to live and work.

In 1965 the association introduced its own orphans' pension scheme in conjunction with the Law Union and Rock Insurance Company Limited. Some 388 members joined the scheme.

On 15 October 1965, the government announced that it intended to seek the authority of the Houses of the Oireachtas for the setting up of a tribunal to consider pay levels of the basic clerical grades in the civil service, the local service and the main state-sponsored bodies, such as Aer Lingus, Bord na Móna, Córas Iompair Éireann and the ESB.[6] The Minister for Finance, Jack Lynch, said that 'for some time past the Government have been concerned at the serious implications for the economy of the apparently unending series of pay increases occurring between or independent of agreed national increases in pay.' He declared that this would be the first occasion when all these grades would have their pay rates examined simultaneously by an authoritative body in the light of all available material. In the minister's view, the findings of a responsible body of this kind obviously would receive the closest attention from all those who were responsible for the fixing of pay rates in individual employments. The motion in the Dáil was carried by 89 to 17, the Labour Party voting against. Part of the motion required the tribunal to inquire and report on the absolute levels of pay for the grades mentioned as the basis for the application of any future general increase in pay.

The ICTU expressed great concern about the proposal and rejected any suggestion of a government standstill on the conceding of claims to the particular workers. The Congress also drew attention to the fact that the then existing pay levels of the categories of workers mentioned had been settled by an independent arbitrator. In no case had they been resolved as a result of strike action. The chairman of the Executive and Higher Executive Officers' Association, F. J. Woods, referred to the tribunal in the course of his address to the 1966 annual general meeting. He deplored the fact that the setting up of

131

In Public Service

the tribunal meant that a 'wage-freeze' was confined to the public sector and that the tribunal was to set absolute levels of pay for the clerical grades in the public sector, especially in a period of economic depression:

In discussions which the Civil Service Staff Panel had with the Minister for Finance in connection with the Tribunal, a fact emerged which may be more important in the long run than the setting up of the Tribunal itself. The Minister said that it was his ultimate aim to have an Arbitration system for the public sector as a whole under the umbrella of the Labour Court. This matter, insofar as it would result in a fundamental change from the system of conciliation and arbitration we now have, is a very important one as far as the Association is concerned. One of the main faults which we have found with the civil service conciliation and arbitration scheme is that there have been such long delays in finalising claims under the Scheme. This has sometimes resulted in civil servants obtaining increases obtained earlier by outside bodies and often giving outside bodies and the general public the incorrect impression that civil servants are getting something extra. In actual fact, civil servants suffer from the long periods which they have to wait to catch up on outside bodies. If then, the civil service, with its multitude of different grades, is included in one arbitration system with the local authorities and semi-state bodies, is it not going to result in even more prolonged delays?

The tribunal called for evidence from the association and referred to the executive officers in its findings. Its report was issued in May 1966 but caused the association little concern. Indeed, the 1966/67 annual report stated: 'The Tribunal's findings fully justified the statements frequently made by civil service staff associations that they have no fear whatsoever of having the duties and conditions of the grades which they represent subjected to the closest scrutiny in comparisons with outside employments.'

The same year also saw positive steps being taken to implement proposals to bring civil servants, as well as other parts of the public sector, under the umbrella of the Labour Court. Proposals for the amendment of the Industrial Relations Acts and the Trade Unions Acts were drafted and sent for consideration to the ICTU. The association's annual report described the proposals as being very wide and drastic, but it understood that they had been modified following discussions between the Congress and officials of the Department of Labour. The report stated that the main proposal for the civil service was that the Labour Court would take over the function of the arbitrator in the conciliation and arbitration scheme.

The application of the 10th round of pay increases to the civil service brought the association into disagreement with the remainder of the staff side. When efforts to renew the National Wage Recommendation (9th Round) failed in December 1965, the ICTU called a special delegate congress which adopted the following executive council resolution:

> Conscious of the needs of the low paid workers, Congress recommends that trade unions should strive to secure wage increases at this time of not more than 20 shillings per week for their members with effect from such date as it may be possible to secure in each instance.[7]

The government was later to accept the ICTU policy as a fact. The question of making a general pay claim for the whole civil service was discussed at a staff panel meeting on 21 March 1966. The association proposed that a claim for a general increase of 10 per cent, with a minimum of £1 per week, should be submitted on behalf of all grades comprehended by the scheme. The grades catered for by the association were specifically excluded from the claim at the association's request. The staff panel's claim resulted in a settlement of £1 a week for male married officers and 15 shillings a week for females and unmarried males. There was a ceiling of £1,200 to the award and there were special arrangements for juveniles and part-time workers.[8] When negotiations on the staff panel claim were completed, the association lodged claims for an increase of 12 per cent to compensate for the increase in the cost-of-living on behalf of executive officers and higher executive officers. In the course of discussion at the general council, the association argued that the ICTU was composed mainly of industrial workers, to whom the £1 per week meant an average increase of 8 or 9 per cent. The claims eventually were dealt with at the Arbitration Board and the outcome was described in the 1967/68 annual report as 'unsatisfactory'.[9]

In Public Service

The Association's claims for a 12% increase to compensate the Executive grades for an increase in the cost-of-living since 1 February, 1964 were rejected at conciliation and arbitration. The only increase which the civil service has received as a compensation for the over 16% increase in the cost-of-living since February, 1964, is the £1 per week increase — and this only up to a ceiling of £1,200. When one remembers that the £1 per week formula was envisaged originally as an interim increase for the year 1966, and that no further increase has since been obtained, it seems that the organisations representing certain workers in this country have been brainwashed into accepting the inevitability of the real value of their members' pay scales being eroded with no compensation for the erosion. This Association at least challenged the £1 per week formula and strove to maintain the real value of its members' pay scales.

In November 1967, the Taoiseach announced that the government had decided to transfer the Department of Lands to Castlebar and the Department of Education to Athlone. A meeting of the staff panel's general purposes committee took place on 20 November at which it was decided to ask for discussions with the Department of Finance to seek clarification of the whole matter of decentralisation before deciding a future policy. The association's chairman, K. J. Nolan, speaking at the 1967 annual general meeting, also referred to the establishment of the Public Services Organisation Review Group, which was later to take up much of the time of the executive committee. The 1968/69 annual report referred to the new scheme for pensions for widows and orphans of civil servants. It described the scheme as being the greatest change in the superannuation code of the civil service since the first Superannuation Act of 1834:

It is well worth realising that, if the Association had achieved nothing for the members during the year but the Widows and Orphans Pension Scheme, it would have secured an improvement in conditions of such magnitude that the year 1968/69 would have been a year well worth recalling.

The association applied for affiliation to the Irish Congress of Trade Unions following a motion adopted at the 1969 annual general meeting. It was accepted into affiliation from 1 April 1969. The report of the Public Services Organisation Review

1951-1969

Group was published in September 1969. The 11th round pay award, which provided for a 9 per cent increase in pay with effect from 1 June 1968, terminated on 31 May 1969. The second phase of the agreement provided for an increase of 4 per cent up to £1,800, with a minimum increase of £65 per year.

ASSOCIATION ORGANISATION

The increased activity of the association during the 1950s and 60s reflected a growing membership and an increased income. Membership and income on 31 December of five separate years was as follows:

Year	Membership	Income £s
1951	891	2,256
1959	941	2,809
1961	1,195	3,021
1964	1,278	3,657
1969	1,538	8,864

Four general secretaries served the association during the period:

Ben O'Quigley (S. B. O'Coigligh), who resigned in January 1961.
Miss Dympna Headon, who resigned in 1964.
Michael Magner, from the Office of Revenue Commissioners, who resigned in 1968.
Daniel Murphy, from the Department of Transport and Power, who was appointed in 1968 and who still serves as general secretary.

At the quarterly meeting of the council in September 1956, the three advocates who presented the claims for new scales for the executive officer and higher executive officer grades — J. G. Doyle, ex-chairman, M. Stanley, S. B. O'Coigligh, general secretary, and the two staff nominees on the board, T. C. Horgan, and H. Sullivan — were each presented with a cheque as a token of the association's appreciation of the work they had done during the arbitration proceedings. M. J. O'Driscoll, who made the presentation, said that a fund had been opened at the council's request and members of the association had subscribed to it. The recipients of the presentation individually replied and thanked the members not only for their generosity

In Public Service

but for their co-operation and assistance throughout the period of preparation; they also paid tribute to their colleagues on the claims sub-committee, who had given so much help and guidance in the preparation of the claims.

The general secretary, Senator J. B. O'Quigley, resigned from 27 January 1961, following the expiration of three months' notice. The newly appointed general secretary, Miss Dympna Headen, in her first contribution to the *Civil Service Review*, recalled the words from *Hamlet* quoted by Senator O'Quigley in his first editorial of January 1949:

> When sorrows come, they come not single spies,
> But in battalions.

Miss Headen commented: 'This continues to be the case. The period of transition is never-ending in the life of an Association. I am, however, aware that there are many active and generous members who have given their experience and time to building this Association into a strong and effective body. I am deeply conscious of the responsibilities which I have been called upon to bear and I rely on the co-operation and criticism of every member to help me to carry out these responsibilities.' A special general meeting was held on 9 April 1962 to consider a resolution recommended by a majority of the executive committee that it be given the authority to conclude an agreement on certain proposals put forward by the official side concerning interdepartmental promotion schemes. A majority voted in favour of the motion, but it failed to get the necessary two-third's majority. According to the association's rules, a motion certified by the standing orders committee as being a matter of major policy required a two-third's majority to be implemented immediately. If that was not obtained, the rules provided that the motion could not be implemented for three months. A further special general meeting was held on 30 April 1962, but the decision remained unchanged. At the 1962 annual general meeting, two motions were passed requesting the executive committee to consider the setting up of a study group where members could discuss matters of importance and interest. The committee considered these motions and concluded that, since there was sufficient scope for all members to acquaint themselves with the association's policies and problems, a study

1951-1969

group would be merely a duplication of activity that would bypass the proper channels of organisation. Since the principal organ of the association was the branch, the executive considered that it would be useful to hold a meeting of all branch officers where an informal discussion on association matters could take place. At the meeting, the chairman, S. R. Stratton, addressed the officers on the history and structure of the conciliation and arbitration scheme; F. J. Woods spoke on the association's external affiliations and also on the role of the branch treasurer. The meeting was not well attended, and was not representative of the more junior branch officers. At the 1963 annual council meeting, the elections to the executive committee were, for the first time, by means of the single transferable vote system. The report of the meeting stated that it was only to be expected that, in its first year of operation, the pattern of the voting could not easily be predicted, but the general conclusion was that this system had produced a fair result and that each department had secured a reasonably correct representation in proportion to the number of its members.

In his address to the 1964 annual general meeting, S. R. Stratton stressed the need to bring members of the executive grades to what he termed 'an adequate starting line' since the principle of the application of a national wage policy had been accepted. He emphasised the necessity for the civil service to put itself in a competitive position with outside employment, to recruit well-qualified school-leavers by raising the starting point and reducing the incremental span of the executive officer scale. The *Civil Service Review* of March 1964 welcomed the appointment of Michael Magner from the Office of the Revenue Commissioners as the new general secretary. Dympna Headen had resigned to become a third secretary in the Department of Foreign Affairs. The *Review* stated that, although Michael Magner's experience of association affairs was short in years, it was very wide; Mr Magner had been active as an officer in his own branch and his voice had been heard regularly at council and general meetings. Good wishes for his success as general secretary were extended and he was assured of the members' full co-operation.

The 1964 annual general meeting adopted two resolutions: (a) directing the incoming executive committee to examine the

In Public Service

advantages of affiliation to the Irish Congress of Trade Unions, and (b) that the executive committee should determine whether it would be advantageous for the association to become a registered trade union or a branch of a registered trade union. The general secretary, writing in the *Civil Service Review* in February 1965, stated that the executive committee had considered these two resolutions carefully. However, because a report on the matter would be made available to members before the annual general meeting, the executive committee had decided that the association should not seek affiliation to the Congress at that time, and that in the circumstances then prevailing it should not become a registered trade union or a branch of a registered trade union. The chairman, K. J. Nolan, in his address to the 1967 annual general meeting, referred to the minister's proposal to have one arbitration system for the public service as a whole: 'Our present Scheme of Conciliation and Arbitration might not be a perfect one, but it gives civil servants the long sought right of negotiating with their employer at conciliation and of having an independent arbitrator in the event of disagreement. This was a right civil servants would not wish to surrender.' He went on to say that the minister's idea would not be an improvement and that the association's interest would be better served under the civil service scheme.

At the next year's annual general meeting, K. J. Nolan referred to the civil service's poor public image. He said that the civil service had been subjected to many attacks, some anonymous, in the public press and these had caused no small amount of irritation among civil servants. The most frustrating aspect of the displeasure was that civil servants did not have the right to defend themselves in the public arena. These attacks had convinced him that the civil service needed a proper public relations service.

The March/April 1968 issue of the *Civil Service Review* contained the final contribution from Michael Magner, who had resigned from his position as general secretary on his appointment to a post in the Department of Finance. Mr Magner said that he had very much enjoyed his term of office and was leaving regretfully. He had received excellent assistance and encouragement from the members. He went on to write that if there was one thing that he had learned in his years as general secretary, it was that it was unreasonable to expect to make spectacular gains overnight and that it was the true role of a staff association to make progress steadily in achieving better conditions for its members. Micheal Magner was succeeded as general secretary by Daniel Murphy.

The 1969/70 annual report marked the first occasion on which it was published separately from the *Civil Service Review*. This report noted the deaths of Senator Ben O'Quigley and Paddy Murray, former general secretary and chairman respectively. It also marked the retirement of May O'Doherty, who had been chairman of the association for 1958-1960. As a token of the association's appreciation of her outstanding service, the executive committee held a reception in October 1969. It was attended by members and former officers of the association, staff panel and representatives of other civil service organisations and members of the official side.

CIVIL SERVICE GENERAL COUNCIL STAFF PANEL

Liam Ó Muirgheasa, who had been chairman of the panel since its inception, tendered his resignation in May 1954, following his promotion to the grade of assistant principal.[10] In his final statement to the panel, he said that the five years during which he had the honour of being chairman of the panel had been the most critical years in civil service affairs since the establishment of the state. The service had seen the birth of arbitration and had looked after its early development. There had been times when things had not gone as smoothly as everyone would wish, but he believed that they had done their part and had laid the early structure reasonably well.

There was only one nomination for the post of chairman and J. C. Horgan was appointed. In February 1961, Mr Horgan tendered his resignation on his promotion to senior examiner in the Estate Duty Office.[11] This grade was outside the scope of the scheme of conciliation and arbitration. W. J. Farrell, who recently had retired as general secretary of the Civil Service Clerical Association, was proposed as chairman by the Staff Officers' Association and the Irish Post Office Engineering

In Public Service

Union. D. N. Clarke, Revenue Group and general secretary of Comhaltas Cana, was proposed by the Post Office Workers' Union and the Revenue Group. H. Sullivan of the Executive and Higher Officers' Association was proposed by the association delegates, and E. J. Murphy was proposed by the Civil Service Alliance. Mr Farrell, who was not present at the meeting, informed the chairman that he wished to withdraw from the election if he did not have the support of the general service organisations. However, Mr Dooney of the IPOEU was not prepared to withdraw his proposal. The result of the ballot was: Clarke 11 votes, Farrell 8 votes, Murphy 2 votes, and Sullivan 2 votes. Mr Farrell's name was then withdrawn. The second ballot as follows: Clarke 17 votes, Sullivan 4 votes, Murphy 2 votes.

On 3 July 1961, Mr Clarke resigned the chairmanship because of his promotion to a grade outside the scope of the scheme of conciliation and arbitration. The following were nominated to fill the post of chairman:[12]

W. J. Farrell, proposed by the Post Office Workers' Union, the Irish Post Office Engineering Union and the Federation of Government Employees.
T. McMahon, proposed by the Civil Service Clerical Association.
E. J. Murphy was proposed but withdrew.

In the ballot, W. J. Farrell received 20 votes and T. McMahon 4 votes.

Mr Farrell then joined the meeting and took the chair, saying that he was greatly honoured by his election. He regretted D. N. Clarke's departure from the staff side activities and felt sure that all the representatives present thought likewise.

At the panel's annual general meeting on 16 December 1965, Mr Farrell announced that he would not be going forward for re-election. He was then a member of the Executive and Higher Officers' Association and the annual report paid tribute to his excellent chairmanship. His long experience and considerable ability were a great asset to staff sides at meetings of the general council, at which he acted as principal staff representative. Moreover, he had acted on several arbitration boards, including the boards that had heard the pay claims of executive and higher executive officers in 1961 and the higher executive officer claim in 1965.

Harry Nally of the Revenue Group was unanimously elected chairman of the panel. He had been chairman of the revenue staff panel for a number of years, as well as being the representative of the revenue group on the general council staff panel. In 1969 both the chairman and secretary of the panel resigned. P. Breathnach had been secretary to the panel since 1951 and was a higher executive officer in the Office of the Revenue Commissioners. On the proposition of D. Murphy, seconded by P. Connick, the panel appointed Miss Maureen Donnellan as secretary with effect from 16 April 1969. She had been secretary to the Revenue Group of Associations and to the Revenue departmental staff side.

At the annual general meeting of the panel, S. Hollingsworth, Post Office Controlling Officers' Association, and C. Devine, Civil Service Clerical Association, were proposed to fill the post of chairman. The result of the ballot was Mr Hollingsworth 17 votes, Mr Devine 3 votes.[13]

HIGH COURT ACTION — 1963

An action taken in the High Court in 1963 on behalf of the Civil Service Clerical Association was of profound importance for the workings of the conciliation and arbitration scheme and for the relationships between the various affiliates to the general council staff panel. The Executive and Higher Officers' Association was not a party to the dispute, but the general secretary was called as a witness. The case arose in the following circumstances.

In 1959 and 1960 discussions about the reorganisation of the grades of writing assistants, shorthand typists and typists took place in the general council; agreed recommendations were made by it and were accepted by the Minister for Finance. The terms of the reorganisation were set out in circular 3/60. Its purpose was 'to secure less dispersal of effort and thus to promote efficiency in the discharge of public business and ultimately a reduction in number'. The new grade of clerk/typist was an all-female grade and a merger of the grades of

In Public Service

writing assistant, shorthand/typist and typist. This grade had an upper duties test, whereby a serving writing assistant or typist or an officer recruited directly as clerk/typist could not proceed beyond a certain point unless she was certified by the head of the department as fully capable of discharging the highest duties of the clerk/typist grade. The upper duties test was to be a searching one, based normally on performance of the highest duties for at least six months.

In April 1961 a claim for an increase in pay on behalf of clerical officers in the civil service was granted after negotiations under the scheme of conciliation and arbitration, and the Civil Service Clerical Association then prepared a pay claim on behalf of the clerk/typists. At the time, claims for increases in remuneration, known as the 8th round, were being made. The claim on behalf of the clerk/typists did not contain any reference to the barrier points or to the date from which the increases in pay were to operate. Justice Kenny, in his judgment, stated that he was satisfied that the omission of any reference to the barrier points was inadvertent and that it was assumed by the general secretary and the officers of the association that the barrier points would be raised by an amount corresponding to the percentage increase in remuneration which would be granted in the claim.[14] The claim, which was approved by the staff panel and placed on the agenda for a general council meeting, had as its basis:

(a) The ratio of the clerk/typist scale to clerical officer scale.
(b) Rates paid for comparable employment outside the service.
(c) The severely limited promotion prospects.

Justice Kenny set out the features in the working of the scheme of conciliation and arbitration which had developed out of practice and were accepted because they were convenient. Such practices might not be strictly in conformity with the terms of the scheme.

(a) The staff panel had 25 members and since it had to deal with a great amount of business, a general purposes committee was formed consisting of one representative from each organisation. This committee dealt with most of the business of the staff panel but did so only when there was unanimity. If an unanimous decision could not be made, the matter was sent forward to the panel.

(b) Although paragraph 15(2) of the scheme provided that the staff representatives to attend meetings of the council were to be selected by the members of the staff panel, so that one team of representatives would be elected to deal with all matters coming before the council, a convenient practice grew up by which different staff representatives were appointed to act with the principal staff representatives for each claim. Thus, those most competent to put forward and argue each claim were appointed to the council. Moreover, the appointment of staff representatives for each claim was not dealt with by the staff panel or by the general purposes committee, but by the staff side secretary. If, however, the claim was being made by two associations, then a mixed team representing them, together with the principal staff representative, was appointed.

(c) The chairman of the staff panel usually acted as principal staff representative without selection as a staff representative, although in some cases, he was appointed by the general purposes committee or the staff panel as one of the staff representatives. Thus, on 11 December 1961, a minute of the staff panel stated that it had been agreed that the representatives to attend the meeting of the council (to conclude the agreement in regard to the operative date of pay settlements) would be the staff panel's chairman (principal staff representative) with others. A slightly revised claim on behalf of the clerk/typists was sent to the staff side secretary and, on 25 October 1961, three representatives of the Civil Service Clerical Association were appointed as the staff side representatives for the council's next meeting. At that meeting on 27 October, the general secretary presented the claim and said that its primary purpose was to maintain relativity with the clerical officers who had already got an increase. He was relying on the scales of salary paid in outside employments. The chairman of the council said that the official side was not in a position to make an offer and would examine the case.

Another meeting of the council was held on 18 December at which the official side made an offer. This offer was submitted and rejected at a meeting of the association on 2 January 1962. On 4 January the association sent to the panel secretary a new scale for clerk/typists upon which to record disagreement at a general council meeting. There was discussion on the new claim

In Public Service

at a council meeting on 17 January 1962, and at the end of it the chairman asked whether the staff side wished to record disagreement. The official side stated that, in order to avoid a counterclaim, it would be well for the staff side to expand its claim to make it clear that it was subject to the reorganisation scheme set out in Council Report 3/60 as regards liability to undergo the upper duties test before passing the barrier. The official side suggested that there could be a statement in the agreed report that the staff side were not seeking to have the position under the reorganisation scheme altered.

At a further meeting of the council on 19 January, the general secretary said that the staff side thought that any reference to reorganisation in the claim would be prejudicial to its case before the arbitration board and might preclude the representatives from saying things they would otherwise wish to say. On 25 January the general secretary wrote to the staff side secretary stating that his association did not see fit to change the terms of its claim on behalf of the clerk/typist grade and that it wished to have disagreement recorded on the claim forthwith. The council's chairman made it clear that if the claim did not make any reference to the reorganisation agreement, the official side would have to submit a counterclaim, which would indicate that any claim for a review of the clerk/typists' pay must be expressed so as to show that regard was being had to the remuneration structure of the grade expressed in the reorganisation scheme. At the council meeting on 16 February, disagreement was recorded on both claims. Subsequently, the panel and the association disagreed on the purpose of the clerk/typists' claim.

It transpired in the course of the court case that the Civil Service Clerical Association was not prepared to accept that its claim had to be expressed to show that regard was being had to the remuneration structure of the reorganisation scheme. Discussions at the panel and with the official side failed to achieve agreement on a report. A meeting of the panel was held on 30 May to hear a report on the proceedings of a meeting of the general purposes committee held the previous day and to take further decisions about the clerk/typist pay claim. The chairman of the panel gave a history of the claim.

1951-1969

A resolution was proposed and was carried by 17 votes to 6. It read:

This special meeting of the General Council Staff Panel held on 30 May, 1962, having considered a report of recent developments arising out of the hearing of a staff side claim for increased pay for the clerk/typist grade *Endorses* the actions and decisions of the General Purposes Committee of the Panel *Notes* disagreement on the claim was recorded on 16 February, 1962, when representatives of the Civil Service Clerical Association were present *Agrees* that sufficient time has been devoted to the problem by the staff side and that it is desirable to have the matter finalised at Conciliation at an early date so as to enable the General Council and the staff side to devote attention to other claims submitted by constituent organisations *Agrees* it is desirable that the claim should be brought to Arbitration without further delay *Instructs* the Officers of the Panel to seek an early meeting of the General Council for the specific purpose of allowing representatives of the staff side to conclude at conciliation level the staff side claim on behalf of Clerk/Typists and to agree a Council report of the conciliation proceedings, thereby ensuring that the way is clear to allow the claim to be referred to Arbitration.

When the motion had been adopted, the appointment of staff side representatives to attend the council meeting was discussed. Eight persons were nominated, including the general secretary of the Civil Service Clerical Association, who said he would have to consult his solicitor about the matter. The panel then decided that anyone who was appointed should give an undertaking not to obstruct the staff side in its efforts to have the resolution implemented. William Bell, Post Office Workers' Union, who had been nominated, said that he could give such an assurance but he explained that he had urgent business on 31 May and that he might not be able to attend the meeting; in such an event, Maurice Cosgrave would attend in his place and the meeting could have a similar assurance from him. All those nominated, except the general secretary of the Civil Service Clerical Association, gave a similar assurance. The panel then decided that only those nominated who had given the assurance would be appointed to the staff side representatives for the meeting.

In Public Service

The council meeting was held on 31 May. The official side representatives were Louis Fitzgerald, chairman; Seamus ÓConaill, Seamus Gaffey, William Smyth and Michael ÓCiagain as secretary, all of whom were defendants in the court case. The staff side representatives were William Farrell, Maurice Cosgrave, Edward Murphy, Patrick O'Shea, Malachy Dooney, Patrick Connick, Denis Harrington, Samuel Hollingsworth, Colm O'Sullivan and Patrick Breathnach as secretary, all of whom were defendants in the case. A discussion took place about the agreed report and agreement was reached on its terms. General Council Agreed Report Number 287 referred to the meeting. This report was later cancelled in the light of the court's finding. The plaintiffs, on behalf of the Civil Service Clerical Association, then began proceedings in which they claimed declarations that the agreed report should not incorporate any reference to issues, matters or discussions that arose or meetings of the general council which took place after the recording of disagreement on 16 February. They also sought that paragraphs 11, 12 and 13 of the agreed report should be deleted before the report was submitted to the Minister for Finance and an order declaring that the meetings of the council held on 29 and 31 May were invalid and of no legal effect; they also claimed an injunction to restrain the minister from requesting arbitration on the pay claim, pending the deletion of paragraphs 11, 12 and 13 of the report.

In his judgment, Justice Kenny decided the following:

1. The plaintiffs had referred to the scheme as 'a statutory scheme'.
   Judgment: The scheme is a contract and nothing more.
2. Part of the plaintiffs' case was that the meetings of the general council on 29 and 31 May were unlawful and invalid because the council could not consider or deal with any new matter of the clerk/typists' pay claim after 16 February 1962, when it was agreed to record disagreement.
   Judgment: The council has jurisdiction to discuss new aspects of a claim until the agreed report is made up, despite any agreement to record disagreement which may have been made before then. The arguments based on the contention that the council has not jurisdiction to do what it did on 31 May are incorrect.

3. The effect of an agreed report.

Judgment: The primary purpose of an agreed report is to inform the minister whether the council has made agreed recommendations on the claim before it or whether it has recorded disagreement, but it is also intended to be a statement of the substance of the discussions that have taken place at council meetings. It is an essential preliminary to Arbitration, for a claim cannot be referred to the Arbitration Board unless it is the subject of either recorded disagreement by the council or an agreed recommendation which has not been accepted by the minister. It is not, however, a decision or an award and for that reason the plaintiff's reliance on what was called 'natural justice' was misplaced.

The plaintiffs relied on two other irregularities. The first was that William Bell stated after his election that he might not be able to attend and that if he were not able to attend, Maurice Cosgrave would take his place. Mr Justice Kenny decided that there was no provision in the scheme for a substitute being appointed or acting for one of the staff representatives. Mr Cosgrave had not been elected as a staff representative and the legal rule expressed in the phrase 'delegatus non potest delegare' applied in the same way as it applied to a director of a company who could not appoint a substitute or alternative director unless there was provision for this in the company's articles of association. Therefore, Maurice Cosgrave's attendance at the meeting was not in accordance with the provisions of the scheme.

The second irregularity was that Martin Murtagh, general secretary of the Civil Service Clerical Association, had been debarred from election as a staff representative at the meeting of the panel on 30 May by being required to give the assurance referred to in the panel minutes. Mr Justice Kenny decided that the only qualifications for membership of the council were those in paragraph 17 of the scheme, which provided that all members of the council must be serving civil servants or staff association officials and it followed that any serving civil servant or staff association official who was proposed for selection as a staff representative was entitled to have his nomination voted on by members of panel. The scheme did not authorise the chairman of the staff panel to impose any condition on a candidate for selection and could not refuse to put his name before the meeting for selection because he would not give an undertaking. In the Justice's opinion, the refusal to put Mr Murtagh's name before the panel was not authorised by the scheme and was a breach of it. The plaintiffs had established that there were three irregularities in connection with the meetings on 30 and 31 May; the effect of these was that an agreed report issued from a meeting which had been constituted irregularly.

It followed that the so-called 'agreed' report was invalid and the last problem in the case was whether Mr Justice Kenny should declare that the document called an agreed report was not an agreed report for the purpose of the scheme. The making of such a declaration by the court was discretionary and it was vigorously contended that in the exercise of his discretion he should not make any declaration in favour of the plaintiffs. The Justice agreed that the Civil Service Clerical Association representative had tried to take advantage of the ambiguity of the pay claim to achieve another purpose and did lead the members of the staff panel to believe that the claim was a pay claim and no more. Moreover, he had consistently and deliberately refused to give unambiguous answers to questions about the relation of the pay claim to the barrier points and the upper duties test. The Justice expressed a belief that the Civil Service Clerical Association representative hoped to abolish the concept of barrier points and the upper duties test by that devious way. However, the scheme was a contract between the association represented by the plaintiffs and the Minister for Finance and the other associations that had signed it and, in his view, the plaintiffs were entitled to rely on the fact that the terms of the scheme had not been observed. Mr Justice Kenny stated:

I do not think that in the exercise of my discretion I am entitled to refuse relief when a breach of the Scheme which involves a breach of contract has been established. It may be that a declaration will not assist the members of the Association, it may be that it will put them in a worse position than they were in before but the plaintiffs represent the members of the Association and they have decided to ask for this relief. . . . If it does not assist the members of the

1951-1969

Association they will be the losers. I do not think that I am entitled to impose on them my ideas of what will suit their interests when their representatives have other ideas. Lastly, I cannot be certain that the staff panel will again elect the same representatives to attend a meeting of the Council and I cannot be certain that a meeting of the Council will produce the same agreed report.

The action against Mr Breathnach was dismissed since he was not a member of the staff side but attended the meeting as secretary. The Justice declared that the document headed 'Civil Service Conciliation and Arbitration Scheme General Council Report Number 287' was not an agreed report for the purposes of the scheme of 1955 and that the meeting of the general council held on 31 May 1962 was invalid.

The position of the Executive and Higher Officers' Association was set out on 24 May 1962 in a letter from the general secretary to the staff side secretary:

I am directed by my Executive Committee to refer to the position in regard to the report on the Conciliation proceedings on the grade claim for Clerk Typists submitted by the Civil Service Clerical Association, and to the projected meeting of the General Council to finalise the issue. The views of my Executive Committee were sought at a specially convened meeting on Wednesday, 23rd inst., and as a result of this meeting I am directed to inform you that it is the view of my Association that it would not wish to be included as a member of the Staff Side at the meeting of General Council, if, as it is understood, the Civil Service Clerical Association will not be represented at that meeting, and do not wish to be a party to any agreement arising out of that meeting. My Association considers that a report agreed on at the meeting without the consent of the Civil Service Clerical Association, the body primarily concerned, would not be a solution to the present difficulties.[15]

This letter was read out in court but, on the application of counsel for the Department of Finance officials, it was ruled to be inadmissible evidence because it was not relevant. The general secretary was summoned as a witness for the Civil Service Clerical Association.

The court's judgment was considered by the staff panel at a special meeting on 4 June 1963.[16] The chairman stated that 11 June had been tentatively fixed for the next meeting of the general council. He said it was for the panel to decide whether it would appoint one team of staff side representatives for the whole meeting to deal with all items, and he referred to the remarks of Mr Justice Kenny on this point. His Lordship had said, inter alia:

> Although paragraph 15(2) of the Scheme provided that the staff representatives to attend meetings of the Council were to be selected by the members of the staff panel so that one team of representatives would be elected to deal with all matters which came before the council, a convenient practice grew up by which different staff representatives were appointed to act with the Principal Staff Representative as the staff side representatives for each claim and it became usual to appoint four or five representatives from the association formulating the claim to act with the principal staff representative.

In the light of the comments of Mr Justice Kenny, the panel decided to appoint one team of representatives for the meeting on 11 June and to continue to do so in respect of future meetings unless and until the provision in paragraph 15(2) of the scheme was amended. This decision caused problems for the Executive and Higher Officers' Association, as was evident from the comments in the *Civil Service Review* of June and December 1963. In December the *Review* commented:

> In the June issue of the *Civil Service Review* reference was made to the procedure which has been adopted by the staff panel of electing five representatives to negotiate on all matters arising on the agenda of a General Council meeting regardless of whether the five members chosen represented the Association whose interests are involved or not. This Association thinks that this is an intolerable situation, which in the long run must lead to confusion and dissatisfaction, and may result in the so-called agreements which are reached at General Council being rejected by the members. At the meeting of the staff panel held on 4 June, 1963, this Association was one of three associations whose representatives were not elected to attend the General Council meeting of 11 June, although there were three items on the agenda in which the Association was immediately concerned.

The three items were:

1951-1969

1. Eligibility of inspectors of agents and senior inspectors of agents for promotion to general service grades of staff officer and executive officer respectively.
2. Claim for overtime for staff officers, executive officers and higher executive officers.
3. Claim for a five-day week.

The association wrote to the Department of Finance on the matter on 13 June 1963.[17] The department replied on 24 June as follows:

In reply, I am directed by the Minister for Finance to say that he does not consider it appropriate to comment on matters arising out of the discharge by the panel of staff representatives of their function under paragraph 15(2) of the Scheme of Conciliation and Arbitration. Copies of your letter and this reply have been sent to the General Council Staff Panel.

The association did propose an amendment to the scheme and this amendment was accepted by the staff panel. The association's annual report for 1964/65 sets out the discussions on the proposal as follows:

The purpose of the amendment was to restore the practice whereby claims made by each organisation on the staff panel could be prosecuted by a team composed of members of the particular organisation involved.

The official side accepted the amendment in principle but produced an alternative wording (to the amendment). The following amendments to the scheme were agreed at a general council meeting on 12 June 1964. Sub-paragraphs 15(2) and 35(2) were changed to read as follows:

The staff representatives to attend meetings of the Council will be selected by the members of the panel and may be varied at such times and in such manner as the members may determine, including the selection of different representatives to attend different parts of a meeting.

Paragraphs 18 and 38 were changed to read as follows:

The number of official representatives and of staff representatives to be appointed under sub-paragraph (2) of paragraph 15 (or 35) preceding may exceptionally be increased by agreement between both sides.

In Public Service

The *Civil Service Review* of January 1964 was able to record that the position of the number of representatives attending general council meetings had been varied for the meetings held on 30 January and 4 February 1964, at which a general pay claim was discussed. In addition to the principal staff representative and secretary, there were ten staff side representatives on both occasions, one from each of the organisations represented on the staff side.

SCHEME OF CONCILIATION AND ARBITRATION

The original scheme of conciliation and arbitration was to operate for one year, after which it would be subject to review. On 19 May 1951, the Department of Finance issued a circular letter to the staff associations, suspending the operation of the scheme from 31 May.[18] The staff panel contested this suspension, maintaining that the scheme should be allowed to operate until discussions had taken place about its revision. In reply to a request for an interview with the Minister for Finance, Seán MacEntee, to discuss the immediate resumption of the scheme, the Department of Finance stated that no useful purpose would be served by such an interview and requested that the staff side should put forward suggestions about how the scheme should be revised. The *Civil Service Review* commented: 'To our mind, apart from minor amendments designed to cut out delays in the working of the scheme, there should also be provision for the interpretation of the scheme, in case of disagreement, by an independent party — preferably the Chairman of the Arbitration Board.'

In the course of a letter to the Minister for Finance, dated 16 October 1951, the staff panel wrote:

As you are aware, the staff side proposals for the amendment of the original scheme were forwarded to the Department of Finance on 24 August last, but so far the Official Side's proposals have not been made known. The withdrawal of the original scheme of conciliation and arbitration from 31 May last has left the civil service staff organisations in a worse position than ever, since they have now no effective means at their disposal for making representations on behalf of their members.

A reply was received on 19 October as follows:

1951-1969

I am desired by the Minister for Finance to inform you that he hopes it will be possible to arrange almost immediately for the issue to the Staff Side of the list of amendments to the scheme proposed by the Official Side.

The decisive meeting on the amendments to the scheme took place on 21 March 1952. Opening the meeting, the minister said that the official side amendments were necessary in order that the public interest should be preserved and the essential prerogative of the government maintained. He was anxious to secure a practical working arrangement that would enable the best relations to exist between the government and its civil servants.

In response, Liam Ó Muirgheasa said that he wished to recount the fundamentals of the staff side objection to the three important amendments introduced by the official side. In regard to the amendment to clause 20 (the exchequer protection clause), the staff were convinced that the minister had adequate powers under the original provision. It was a cardinal principle of the original agreement that no authority less than Dáil Éireann had the right to set aside or modify an arbitration finding. The minister's amendment was a violation of the principle since it sought to introduce the minister's right to evade or modify an award of the board on a general pay claim. In regard to public agitation, Mr O'Muirgheasa agreed that the staff side had already accepted that agitation and conciliation could not go hand in hand. There was much common ground on this proposal and the staff side would accept an arrangement that prohibited resort to public agitation on claims that were sub judice or in any way under discussion within the framework of the conciliation and arbitration machinery. As regards political affiliation, the staff side view was that restrictive clauses should be withdrawn and the whole matter left to the good sense of the civil service staff organisations. However, they were not pressing that view and were prepared to accept the restrictions provided in the original scheme. They were opposed to the official side amendment which sought to introduce further irritating restrictions.

In his reply, the minister directed attention to paragraph 2 of the original scheme, which indicated that the introduction of the scheme did not imply that the government could surrender its liberty of action in the exercise of its constitutional authority and the discharge of its responsibilities in the public interest. The government of the day must necessarily be the judge of what is the public interest. It had accepted the principle of independent arbitration for the civil service, subject to certain safeguards. Having accepted that principle, it followed that it also accepted that awards made by the Arbitration Board should become effective in the ordinary course. There were, however, exceptional circumstances where the public interest might render it impossible to meet an award in the current financial year or to meet it in full.

On the amendment regarding political affiliation, the minister said that it appeared to him that this position had already been accepted by the staff side in the original scheme. He added that if he had been in office at the time of the inauguration of the scheme, he doubted if he would have agreed to allow any civil service staff organisation with political affiliations to participate in it. Participation in or association with politics by the civil service was very bad, for both the public and the civil service. Inevitably it would destroy the security of tenure of civil servants and bring in its train the spoils system. He admitted that some grounds could perhaps be made for exceptional treatment as regards the Post Office Workers' Union. Members of this association did not exercise the same influence on administration nor did they have access to confidential documents to the same extent as members of other civil service organisations. The official amendment expressed the considered viewpoint of the government in this regard. If there had not been a change of government in 1948, the action of the Civil Service Clerical Association in making a contribution towards the election expenses of a political party would have been taken notice of officially.

In dealing with the exchequer protection clause, Seán MacEntee said that a very difficult situation had been created during the trial year by the general pay finding and the consequences of this finding were lamentable for the public finances. The Minister for Finance, for the future, would have to be in a position to determine whether he could accept such an arbitration finding in the current year or not. The minister might not have the money available to meet the finding and it would be most undesirable that he should be called upon to go into debt in order to pay the increases. The amendment was an advantage for the staff in that, in order to save the public finances, the Minister for Finance would not be obliged to take the extreme step of going to the Dáil for the rejection of the finding. The amendment visualised that the minister would pay what he could during the current year and that there would be a contingent obligation to pay the balance in due course.

The minister added that if, following a general pay finding, it was found that it was not possible to meet it in full in the current year, he would be prepared to agree to allow the matter to be brought before the general council to afford the staff side representatives an opportunity to put forward their views on the proportion the minister proposed to pay. In conclusion, Seán MacEntee said that the exchequer protection clause was merely a question of deferment of consideration of the full payment of an arbitration finding. He felt that the government would be bound to make provision in the following year for payment of the finding, assuming any kind of normal financial conditions. In response to an inquiry about whether the staff might take it that the minister did not wish to deprive the civil service of any part of an arbitration finding of this nature, the minister replied that this was so, unless the circumstances were exceptional.

An agreement providing for the restoration of the conciliation and arbitration scheme was signed in the Department of Finance on 24 June 1952, by the Minister for Finance and by the following staff organisations: Post Office Workers' Union, Civil Service Alliance, Post Office Engineering Union, Government Employees Federation, Revenue Group Departmental Federation. At this time, recognition had been withdrawn from the Civil Service Clerical Association.

In his address to the council of the Civil Service Alliance in June 1952, the president, J. C. Horgan, defended the action of the alliance in signing the conciliation and arbitration scheme. He said that the absence of any machinery for making representations on their many grievances had created an intolerable state that could no longer be suffered; it was necessary, in a time when the cost of living was reaching new heights, that they should have some machinery to adjust their salaries to meet high prices. Civil servants knew only too well that every time-lag in the gaining of compensation for the increase in the cost of living had resulted in a lowering of their standard of living; they would lose their position relative to the rest of the community if they did not accept the best means at their disposal for the preservation of that position. Mr Horgan went on to say that, in a formal meeting on 21 March 1952, the minister had stated that the government had accepted the principle of independent arbitration for the civil service and that, having done so, it followed that it also accepted that awards should become effective. The alliance had accepted in good faith the minister's declaration and, entering the agreement on that understanding, would co-operate with their colleagues in the other staff organisations in ensuring that the scheme would work efficiently and smoothly.

On 26 March 1955, a new revised scheme was signed at Government Buildings by the Minister for Finance on behalf of the government and by the representatives of the staff side. It came into operation on 1 April. The scheme would continue in force unless it was terminated by six months' notice given by the Minister for Finance or by the panel of staff representatives of the general council in accordance with the provisions of paragraph 13(1) of the scheme. Although 78 amendments of the old scheme were proposed by the Minister for Finance, the new scheme did not differ radically in its main provisions from the old one. An important provision of the new scheme was that which enabled occasional amendments to be made to it on the proposal of the Minister for Finance or the staff panel of the general council. There was little alteration to the provision relating to political association by a recognised staff association save that, for the future, such political association had to be 'official' to incur the withdrawal of recognition. There were new provisions with regard to public agitation. Under the provisions of the old scheme, if a staff association sponsored or resorted to any form of public agitation, it was open to the Minister for Finance to withdraw recognition from the association. Recognition would not be withdrawn under the new scheme for public agitation in accordance with the provisions of sub-paragraph (2) i.e. non-arbitrable matters on which discussions at the general council or at a departmental council had concluded without agreement having been reached or, (b) a matter that had been the subject of a motion introduced and carried in Dáil Éireann. The terms of the new scheme were set out in Department of Finance circular 3/55. Present at the signing of the scheme were: G. Sweetman (Minister for Finance), L. M. Fitzgerald (chief establishment officer), J. C. Horgan (chairman, General Council Staff Side), M. Dooney (Post Office Engineering Union), W. J. Farrell (Civil Service Clerical Association), D. N. O'Cleirigh (Revenue Group of Departmental Associations), H. Sullivan (Civil Service Alliance), W. Bell (Post Office Workers' Union), C. O'Sullivan (Institute of Professional Civil Servants), C. J. Tunney (Post Office Clerical Association), P. Breathnach (secretary, Staff Side).

The following acted as chairmen of the arbitration board during the period covered by this chapter:

F. C. King BL	1950-1951
General Daniel McKenna	1952-1955
Judge J. C. Conroy	1955-1956
T. K. Liston SC	1956-1964
R. N. Cooke SC	1964-1968
S. Gannon SC	1968-1969

THE MCKENNA AWARD

In November 1946, the system of basic pay plus bonus was abolished and pay was consolidated on the basis of a cost-of-living index figure of 270 (base 1922 = 100). This is recorded as the first of general pay rounds. In November 1948, pay was revised on the basis of a cost-of-living index figure of 290. This is recorded as the second general pay round. The third general pay round in 1951 was the first occasion on which a general revision of civil servants pay was decided at the Arbitration Board.

The board consisted of F. C. King (chairman), L. M. Fitzgerald and S. McGamhna, nominated by the Minister for Finance, and L. O'Muirgheasa and W. Bell, nominated by the general council staff panel. Mr J. Dolan acted as secretary.

In Public Service

The following acted as advocates: for Minister for Finance, T. K. Whitaker, deputy assistant secretary, Department of Finance, and S. O'Conaill, principal officer, Department of Finance; for the general council staff panel, D. A. Morrissey, general secretary, Civil Service Clerical Association, T. O'Sullivan, Institute of Professional Civil Servants, and M. Dooney, Irish Post Office Engineering Union.

By a majority decision, the board decided to award the following increases in pay from 15 January 1951:

1. Officers on a yearly rate of pay of £200 or less — 15%
2. Officers on a yearly rate of pay exceeding £200 — 15% on the first £200 of such pay and 10% on the remainder.

Allowances in the nature of pay were to be increased by 7½ per cent.

On the resumed functioning of the conciliation and arbitration scheme in 1952, the general council staff panel decided to present a claim for compensation for the rise in the cost of living which had taken place since January 1951. It was calculated that the effect of the reduction of food subsidies, together with other increases, would have brought about an increase of 20 per cent in the cost of living by 5 July as compared with January 1951. A claim for a 20 per cent increase in pay at all levels of salary was submitted to the general council; the claim was discussed on 11 August 1952.[19] The official side indicated that the minister wished no increase to be granted and disagreement was recorded. The Arbitration Board heard the claim on 3 and 4 November 1952. The board consisted of General D. McKenna (chairman), S. O'Conaill and S. MacGamhna, representing the Minister for Finance; and L. O'Muirgheasa and W. Bell, representing the general council staff panel.

The official side advocates were J. J. McElligott, secretary, Department of Finance, T. K. Whitaker, deputy secretary, Department of Finance, and M. O'Brolchain, principal officer, Department of Finance. The staff advocates were W. Norton, TD, Post Office Workers' Union, J. B. O'Quigley, Civil Service Alliance, and M. Dooney, Irish Post Office Engineering Union.

1951-1969

By a majority decision, the board arrived at the following finding:

1. That the following increases should be granted by way of variation of the percentage additions awarded in 1951:

    (a) On the portion of remuneration (exclusive of the percentage additions referred to) at a rate of £200 a year or less, the existing addition of 15 per cent to be raised to 27½ per cent.

    (b) On the portion of remuneration (exclusive of the percentage additions referred to) at a rate exceeding £200 a year but not exceeding £965 a year, the existing addition of 10 per cent to be raised to 15 per cent.

2. That an increase of 5 per cent should be granted on the present gross amount of allowances in the nature of pay, other than children's allowances.

3. That the existing annual rate of children's allowances payable to married men whose remuneration is governed by differentiation on a marriage basis should be increased by £2.

4. That the foregoing increases should operate on and from 1 November 1952.

The report was dated 18 November 1952.

Three questions in connection with the report were asked in the Dáil on 10 December 1952. Declan Costello, William Norton and Liam Cosgrave wished to ascertain when it was proposed to publish the report and the action the government intended to take in the matter. The minister, Seán MacEntee, stated in reply:

The report of the Civil Service Arbitration Board dealing with the subject matter referred to in the questions was received on 18 November, 1952. Under the terms of the agreement concluded with the Civil Service staff associations, the Government is required to present to Dáil Éireann a report from the Chairman of the Board within three months of its receipt or, if at the expiration of the three months the Dáil is not sitting, then on the first day of the next sitting. No report is to be published before submission to Dáil Éireann. Prolonged investigation and consideration will be necessary before the Government is in a position to take a decision in this matter. The report cannot be submitted to Dáil Éireann until that decision has been taken.

In Public Service

On 12 January 1953, Liam O'Muirgheasa sought an interview with the Minister for Finance to tell him of the growing resentment and dismay at the unreasonable delay in informing the service about the findings of the board and the government's intentions. The chief establishment officer replied on 15 January, quoting paragraph 19, Part IV of the scheme, which set out the period of three months from receipt by the minister of a report before the report had to be presented to Dáil Éireann. The letter continued:

> That condition was specifically written into the agreement to lay emphasis on the fact that the Government's primary responsibility is to Dáil Éireann. As the purpose of the interview is, apparently, to secure publication of the findings of the Board before these can be submitted to the Dáil, the Minister is satisfied that no useful purpose would be served by receiving yourself and Mr. Bell. The Minister proposes to abide by the terms of the Agreement, as signed, and he considers that it would be quite improper for him to by-pass the Dáil by publishing the findings of the Board before he has acquainted the House of the contents of the Board's report.[20]

At a staff panel meeting on 19 February 1953, the staff side decided to seek an immediate interview with the Taoiseach to protest about the delay in granting increased wages and securing an assurance that the government would honour the award in full and with retrospective effect to 1 November 1952. The Taoiseach and the Minister for Finance met the staff side in the Dáil on 26 February 1953. The staff side were represented by L. O'Muirgreasa (chairman of the staff panel), W. Norton, TD, Post Office Workers' Union, M. Dooney, Irish Post Office Engineering Union, J. C. Horgan, Civil Service Alliance, M. Bird, Federation of Government Employees, L. Mannion, Institute of Professional Civil Servants, W. J. Farrell, Civil Service Clerical Association, R. N. Halliday, Revenue Group, and P. Breathnach, secretary of the staff panel.

They presented a strong case on the reasons why the government should honour the Arbitration Board award.[21] *The Postal Worker* of March 1953 commented on the meeting as follows:

> The interview with the Taoiseach and the Minister for Finance was most disappointing and it was difficult to imagine a more

1951-1969

unsatisfactory interview from the staff point of view. The Government made no effort to counter the morality and justice of the staff side case, beyond pleading Exchequer difficulties. The Taoiseach said he could give no assurance that the award of the Arbitration Board would be honoured in whole or in part, but the position would be further considered when the Budget was being framed in May next.[22]

Following this, the staff panel met and considered the whole position. It was decided to set up a special action committee to launch a campaign to protest against the government's attitude towards the arbitration award and to enlist public sympathy for the staff side's claim that the government, having been a party to the arbitration proceedings, was morally bound to implement the Arbitration Board's award. Parades and protest meetings were organised in a number of centres and were well attended by civil servants of all grades.

After a delay of almost six months, the Minister for Finance announced the government's decision on the arbitration award in his budget statement on 6 May 1953. He indicated that the government would not pay any increase in remuneration in respect of financial year 1952/53 and that the arbitration award would be given effect to only as from 1 April 1953. The Arbitration Board's report recommended that the increases should be granted from 1 November 1952, so the government's decision meant that it was withholding the increases for a period of 21 weeks. The government's decision was considered by the staff side and the following statement was issued to the press:

> The Minister's Budget statement in regard to the Civil Service Arbitration Board award will cause widespread disappointment and resentment throughout the public service. The Arbitration Board's award, effective from 1 November, was presented to the Government on the 18th November last. Having held up that award for six months the Government now propose to give effect to it only from 1 April, thus depriving thousands of lowly-paid Civil Servants of 21 weeks benefit which they badly needed. The hardship involved in this proposal is incalculable and can only be appreciated by those who have to suffer the loss.[23]

In Public Service

On 13 May 1953, the staff panel wrote to the Taoiseach requesting him to receive a small deputation to discuss the matter before the modifying motion was introduced in the Dáil. A reply, dated 19 May, stated inter alia:

> As the Government, following the most careful consideration of all the circumstances, have taken their decision in the matter, the nature of which was announced in the Budget statement of the Minister for Finance on the 6th inst, there would be no point in the Taoiseach's receiving a further deputation from the staff side of the Civil Service General Council.[24]

Subsequently, the Minister for Finance introduced the following motion in the Dáil:

> That Dáil Éireann approves of the action which, as indicated in his financial statement of May 1953, the Government propose to take in relation to the Report of the Civil Service Arbitration Board presented to Dáil Éireann on the 18th February 1953, namely to give effect to the findings of the Board subject to the modification that the increases shall operate with effect from 1st April 1953.

In the course of the Dáil debate on the budget statement, William Norton said:

> If this Government do not honour this award in full, then I hope it will not be many months until another Government is in office. If the Labour Party have any responsibility in that Government, we shall do our best to ensure whatever balance of this award is not paid by this Government will be honoured and paid by the next Government that controls the destinies of this House.[25]

Deputy Norton was followed by Patrick McGilligan on behalf of Fine Gael:

> I want to echo what Deputy Norton said. So far as I am concerned for the future, if I again become associated with any party that forms a Government in this State I will do it on the condition that whatever is not met of this Arbitration award by the present Government will be met by the Government I might help to form. We can give that assurance as Deputy Norton has given it on behalf of one Party, and if, say, the Inter-Party Government were to meet again, just as we did meet our promise with regard to the removal of certain penal taxation in the year 1948, we would honour it.

1951-1969

On 15 June 1954, the Minister for Finance in the second inter-party government, Gerard Sweetman, announced the government's intention to pay the outstanding amount due from 1 November 1952 to 31 March 1953 inclusive. When the supplementary estimate was moved in the Dáil, the vote was put and agreed.[26]

IRISH CONFERENCE OF PROFESSIONAL AND SERVICE ORGANISATIONS

M. P. Linehan of the Irish National Teachers' Organisation was president of the Irish Conference of Professional Associations in 1957. In his address to the annual conference, he stated that the organisation had come into being as the result of a meeting of various salaried groups held in Jury's Hotel in 1946, on the initiative of the ESB Salaried Staff Association.

In September 1958, representatives of the conference met the Taoiseach, Seán Lemass, to lay before him the problems of its members. Subsequent to this meeting, the conference submitted a memorandum to the government, expanding on its verbal submission.

Two groups of the community had not benefited from the increased prosperity; the salaried classes and those dependent on fixed incomes, the pensioners and the widows of members of these classes. The state had done nothing directly to benefit those groups as it had done in the case of agriculturalists, industrialists and wage earners.

The memorandum also dealt with conciliation and arbitration:

Conciliation and Arbitration machinery and Industrial Relations machinery are available to most groups of the salaried classes as well as to wage-earning classes to deal with their problems in the matter of remuneration, but there are various reasons why this machinery instead of improving the conditions of the salaried classes contributes in no small way to the worsening of these conditions. In the absence of a set of principles, decisions and awards are haphazard; they cause or continue anomalies; they leave claimants in a state of frustration and play their part in depressing the standards of salary workers. From the period of the first world war it has been generally accepted that only the lowly-paid suffer the full impact of rising living costs and that as incomes increase the proportion of such

In Public Service

incomes which suffer from the rising living costs is lessened. Through the acceptance of this idea arbitrators have acted on what was called the tapering policy and the implementation of that policy formed an integral part of the remuneration framework.

The memorandum cited the civil service cost-of-living bonus arrangement as an example of the tapering policy. In its reply, the government stated:

There is no foundation for the assumption that the conciliation machinery so recently made available has operated to the detriment of the main salaried classes represented by the conference; although the salaried classes have lost ground since 1939, it is possible that their conditions would have been less favourable were it not for the operation of the machinery which the conference criticises. In the civil service the conciliation and arbitration machinery was set up in response to protracted demands by staff associations; and the cost of settlements favourable to the staff which have been reached since the machinery commenced to operate exceeds £5 million a year, of which over £4 millions represents general pay increases on grounds of cost of living. These settlements have not been confined to wage earners.[27]

The *Civil Service Review* of May 1957 reminded members of the Executive and Higher Officers' Association that the conference was one of the bodies entitled to make nominations on the Labour Panel under the Seanad Electoral Act. Two of the nominees of the conference were successful in securing election — Senator Dominic F. Murphy of the Transport Salaried Staffs' Association and Senator J. B. O'Quigley. Senator O'Quigley was then the general secretary of the Executive and Higher Officers' Association. For many years the Civil Service Alliance was affiliated to the conference. In consequence of the Executive and Higher Officers' Association's withdrawal from the alliance, the association was no longer represented on the conference. The executive committee considered the matter and thought it would be desirable that the association should become a member of the conference, recommending this course to the council. The council agreed that the association should affiliate and this was done.[28] The association's annual report for 1960/61 stated that the conference represented 40,000 salaried workers.

1951-1969

AFFILIATION TO THE IRISH CONGRESS OF TRADE UNIONS

In December 1968, the general secretary of the Executive and Higher Officers' Association, Dan Murphy, submitted a memorandum to the executive committee on affiliation to the Irish Congress of Trade Unions. Such an affiliation had been considered in 1964/65 following a resolution adopted at the 1964 annual general meeting directing the executive committee to examine the advantages of affiliation. In the course of his memorandum, Dan Murphy set out the reasons why the association did not seek affiliation at the time:

(a) The association was affiliated to the Irish Conference of Professional and Service Associations and there was no point in affiliating to both bodies.

(b) The association might be restricted if it were affiliated to the Irish Congress of Trade Unions.

(c) A clash of interests might arise between the large mass of lower paid workers in the Congress and those of the association, which would be the highest paid affiliated group.

Mr Murphy set out some advantages which affiliation to Congress would confer on the association:

(a) Affiliation to Congress would confer a certain amount of prestige on the association because it would be more closely integrated with the trade union movement as a whole.

(b) The facilities and services of Congress's research department would be available to the association. Affiliation would mean that the officers of the association would be able to make many contacts in trade union circles which would be of benefit not only in securing the sympathetic understanding of other unions to the association's claims, but also in gaining the advice and experience of such people.

(c) So far as dual affiliation to the ICPSA and ICTU was concerned, it should be borne in mind that many organisations were affiliated to both bodies.

(d) There was no reason to believe that the association would be restricted in its activities if it were to affiliate to the Congress. The Congress laid down general lines of policy which each affiliate might accept or reject.

(e) If it were to become affiliated to Congress, the association would not represent the highest paid group in affiliation. Mr Murphy instanced the affiliation of the Medical Union, the workers in Aer Lingus, Guinness, ESB, Irish Shipping, Bord na Móna, local government, many of whom were higher paid than higher executive officers.

(f) The most important argument in favour of affiliation was that it would give the association a voice in the formulation of policy in Congress, which was the only organisation recognised as being the representative of persons who work for a living. The only manner in which the association could ensure that its interests were not overlooked was by becoming an affiliate of Congress.

At that time all the affiliates to the civil service general council staff panel were affiliated to the Congress except the Institute of Professional Civil Servants and the Executive and Higher Officers' Association. The general secretary's paper was discussed at a meeting of the executive committee held on 10 February 1969; with one dissension, it was agreed that the committee would put down the following motion for the annual general meeting: 'That this Association seek affiliation with the Irish Congress of Trade Unions.'

There was a similar motion from the Department of Education branch and a less positive motion from the Department of Transport and Power branch. The motion was adopted at the annual general meeting and, at a meeting of the executive committee on 14 April 1969, the general secretary announced that the association had been accepted into affiliation with Congress. The association had also been accepted into membership of the public services committee of Congress.

SCHEME OF PROMOTION TO HIGHER EXECUTIVE OFFICER

At its 15th meeting, on 28 July 1955, the general council discussed a scheme of promotion proposed by the Executive and Higher Officers' Association. Its primary objective was to establish seniority as the basic principle in the making of promotion from executive officer to higher executive officer and to establish the two corollaries of this principle, (1) the equalisation of prospects between one department or office and another, and (2) to ensure equality of opportunity in the matter

1951-1969

of promotion for all members of the executive officer grade. The scheme envisaged that promotions would be made in accordance with seniority. A list would be drawn up in each department or office on which officers suitable for promotion would be placed in order of their service seniority. When a vacancy in the higher executive officer grade arose in a department or office, the most senior officer on the list would be appointed. Only officers with the requisite period of service rendering them eligible for promotion to the higher executive officer grade would appear on the seniority list.

It was proposed that the period of service necessary to render an officer eligible for promotion to the higher executive officer grade be changed from seven years in the case of an open entrant to the executive officer grade and three years in the case of an entrant through the confined examination for the executive officer grade to twelve years in the case of the former and, in the case of the latter, the equivalent of twelve years' executive officer service, determined in accordance with a formula which the association had evolved after examining the periods of service of higher executive officers who were serving in January 1952. The period of eligibility of twelve years' executive officer service, which the staff side was proposing, was, they contended, a more realistic figure. From the statistics compiled from the higher executive officers serving in all departments or offices in January 1952, the following emerged:

(a) Five higher executive officers who had been recruited through the open executive officer examination were promoted before 1940, with an average of 14.7 years' service in the executive officer grade.

(b) Higher executive officers similarly recruited and promoted between 1940 and 1945 had an average of 9.7 years in the executive officer grade.

(c) One hundred and five higher executive officers similarly recruited and promoted since 1945 had an average of 11.8 years' service in the executive officer grade.

(d) With regard to higher executive officers whose entry to the executive officer grade was by means of the confined competition, seven were promoted before 1940, and they had an average of 13.1 years' pre-executive officer service, and an average of 7.9 years in the executive officer grade.

In Public Service

(e) Ninety-two promoted after 1945 had an average of 14.3 years' pre-executive officer service, and an average of 6.9 years in the executive officer grade.

The association submitted that, by increasing the period to twelve years, the period of eligibility would be more realistic. The figures showed that, taking the average of all the officers over the year, pre-executive officer service worked out as an equivalent of one-third the value of service in the executive officer grade. In the case of open entrants, the average worked out at 11.8 years, and the staff side said that twelve years, therefore, seemed to be the necessary period of service to render an officer eligible for promotion to the higher executive officer grade. By making three years' pre-executive officer service the equivalent of one year's service, and having regard to the twelve years' service then necessary to render a clerical officer eligible for confined competition to the executive officer grade, confined entrants and open entrants, generally speaking, would be on an equal footing as regards seniority after the confined entrant had three years' service in the executive officer grade. With regard to the equalising of promotion prospects between departments or offices, the staff side emphasised that the accidental placing of officers in departments from examinations should not be the determinant in the matter of promotion. It could well happen that an officer who got first place in an open executive officer competition would be assigned to a department in which the promotion rate was slow, while a colleague who got a much lower place might be assigned to a department in which the promotion rate was relatively fast. An all-service seniority list would help to remedy this inequality of opportunity.[29]

The official side responded on 14 June 1959,[30] observing that, although this was a staff side proposal regarding the future method of recruitment to the higher executive officer grade, the scheme omitted certain grades eligible for promotion to the higher executive officer grade. The staff side agreed that it was so and pointed out that, in the introduction to the proposed scheme in the memorandum of claim, this had been stated specifically. The promotion of other eligible grades was not provided for in the proposed scheme, but was a separate question. In answer to a question about how it was proposed to determine seniority in the case of first entry to the executive officer grade, the staff side said that what it had in mind was that seniority would be determined by length of previous service, if any. An officer who secured a high place in his examination, therefore, would be rated as junior to any officer who did less well at the same examination but who had longer service. He would also rank junior if his appointment happened to be delayed. The placing in the competition would be the determining factor only where two officers with either no previous service or with equal service entered the grade on the same day.

The official side could not subscribe to the staff side view on the question of determining seniority for purposes of promotion and the disregard of placing in competitions. Neither could it accept the proposition that all executive officers who had the minimum qualifications for promotion were necessarily equal in ability; experience showed marked differences in ability between officers of the same rank. In view of this and on general grounds, the staff side proposal, which, in the eyes of the official side, involved the replacement of merit by seniority in the selection of officers for promotion, was unacceptable.

The official side went on to say that it shared the staff side concern that there should be greater equalisation of promotion opportunities between departments. It was undoubtedly true that, under the methods then used, officers with very short service in one department might secure promotion, while officers at least equally worthy of promotion in other departments might have to wait a long time before an opportunity for promotion arose in their own department. The official side went on to say that it was anxious that the staff side's efforts towards improvement of the existing arrangements should bear fruit and suggested that, since both sides were as one on the question of greater equalisation of promotion opportunity, and because this problem existed independently of the seniority question, the staff side should consider the matter as a separate issue. The official side said that it would be glad to know if the staff side would favour a scheme under which: (a) departments that had only officers of short service in eligible grades would fill higher executive officer vacancies by way of selection board competition from among officers in eligible grades in all departments, only officers with a certain minimum service to be eligible, or (b) a proportion of all vacancies for higher executive officer would be filled by inter-departmental competition, it would also be for consideration whether the selection boards set up in accordance with such a scheme should be organised by the Department of Finance or by the Civil Service Commissioners.

The staff side members said that selection board procedure did not commend itself to them. This did not imply any reflection on the personnel constituting such boards. The fact was that the interview board system was by its nature unreliable. The relative capabilities of officers could not be assessed in the course of a short interview, during which the questions asked and the officer's response to them might have little bearing on his suitability for the post on offer. There was no uniformity in the subjects on which candidates were questioned. The report available to the board on candidate's performance on official duties could vary in value, depending on the outlook of a candidate's superior officer and the quality of the work on which he had been engaged. The official side said that it was prepared to listen to any suggestions the staff side might wish to advance for an improvement of the selection board system. They inquired whether, for example, if uniformity in methods of marking and a fuller and more standardised system of reporting on candidates was introduced, the system would commend itself. The staff side undertook to consider the matter. One point on which it sought information was the interview system of marking; the official side expressed its willingness to furnish information on this, if required.

The association's annual report for 1958/59 summarised the question as follows:

Prior to the Annual General Meeting last year, the Executive Committee had been considering against the background of the discussions which had taken place at General Council, the formulation of a revised promotion scheme. The Executive Committee considered that within the policy laid down it would be difficult to redraft a scheme. A resolution was, therefore, passed at the Annual General Meeting which, while maintaining that the Association's scheme based on seniority provided an equitable basis

1951-1969

for promotion, authorised the incoming Executive Committee as an interim measure to discuss a scheme for the equalisation of promotion opportunities as between departments at the General Council. The Executive Committee entered upon its task early in the year but at that time, arising out of the announcement by the Minister for Finance in his Budget statement that certain reorganisation proposals affecting the grading structure of the Civil Service were under active consideration, the Executive postponed further consideration of the scheme pending the publication of these proposals. The proposals were not available by the middle of the year. The Executive, therefore, decided to take up again consideration of the promotion scheme and much time was spent . . . in discussing the matter during the year. In an effort to ascertain the extent to which the views of the Association and those of the Department of Finance coincided on the main aspects of a new scheme, informal discussions were held under the aegis of the General Council Staff Panel. These talks are of a purely explanatory character, and in those circumstances it would not be proper to say anything about them in this report. As a result of the talk, however, the Executive Committee feel that there are good grounds for stating that substantial progress in the formulation of a new scheme should be made in the not too distant future.

The *Civil Service Review* of June 1961 commented that the absence from the limelight of the interdepartmental promotion equalisation scheme might have led many members to think that the question had become dormant. In fact, there had been continuous though slow progress, and the scheme was again being considered by the general council. The matter was not finalised at general council until 13 November 1964. Agreement was recorded in General Council Report No. 344.

The scheme of promotion to higher executive officer began on 1 January 1965, almost ten years from the date of the first discussion at general council. The agreement was subject to review after one year.

INSTITUTE OF PUBLIC ADMINISTRATION

The *Civil Service Review* of April 1957 reported that the Association of Higher Civil Servants had invited other service and local government associations to a meeting to discuss the need for, and the possibility of establishing, an Institute of

In Public Service

Public Administration. There appeared to be a wide measure of agreement and a committee was set up from the various bodies to explore the matter further.

The objects of such an institute were stated to be:

(i) to promote the study and practice of public administration.

(ii) to enable members to improve their knowledge of the theory and practice of public administration and to provide a forum for the views of the members.

(iii) to foster the common educational and ethical interests of the public service and to act as a spokesman for such interests.

(iv) with these objects in view, to hold discussions, debates, and lectures, to publish a journal, to provide a library for members and to establish and maintain contact with similar institutions in other countries.

(v) to act as liaison between the universities and the public service in order to advance the study of public administration.

The *Civil Service Review* of May 1957 reported that a number of meetings had taken place and that a representative of the association had attended as observer. The broad basis of the institute had been worked out tentatively and it was proposed to hold a further meeting to ascertain the general views of the bodies that had attended meetings on the institute's constitution and financial provisions. It seemed to the executive committee that the cost of affiliation would be about £100 per annum. Members of the association joining the institute as individual members would be entitled, if the association were a corporate member, to join at half the subscription rate payable by individual members, which had been tentatively fixed at two guineas (full) per annum. The *Review* went on to say that the executive committee in due course would consider whether it would recommend to the association that it join the institute as a corporate member. However, it appeared to them that a decision of a special general meeting would be necessary to decide on such a course.

When the institute's constitution was finally approved by the drafting committee, the executive examined it and decided to recommend to a special general meeting that the association become a corporate member. The council endorsed this decision and a motion to approve the association's membership of the

1951-1969

institute was put down for a special general meeting on 28 November 1957. Because of the small attendance at that meeting, it was decided that the association's membership be determined by a ballot of members. The result of the ballot, published in the *Civil Service Review* of March 1958, showed 367 for affiliation and 245 against. The *Review* posed a question about the mentality of the 300 or so members who could not give a simple yes or no to the question. The *Civil Service Review* of January 1958 devoted a considerable amount of space to the publication of a symposium on possible membership of the institute. The contributors were H. Sullivan, chairman of the association, Ms May O'Doherty, Seán O'Donnell and N. Murphy, the association's treasurer. Messrs Sullivan and O'Donnell supported affiliation and Mr Murphy and Miss O'Doherty were opposed. Ms O'Doherty maintained that the association, as a trades union, was founded in order that members should enjoy proper conditions of work, adequate opportunities of promotion and just wages. Since members did not enjoy any or all of these things, the association should mind its own business and spend its funds on the management of that business. As individual members, they spent their time and money on pursuits, academic and otherwise, without resort to association funds. Why, therefore, make an exception of the institute? Ms O'Doherty went on to say: 'Membership of the Institute will afford pleasant educational opportunities and stimulating discussion in an agreeable "clubby" atmosphere, but the improvement of public administration is an inside job and will never be achieved by armchair academicians.' Miss O'Doherty was elected as chairman of the association at the 1958 annual general meeting and, as such, was appointed as the association's representative to the institute and was co-opted to its executive. She commented on her position in the May 1958 issue of the *Review*:

Ironical, no doubt, since my views as expressed in the symposium are that the subsidisation of scientific management is not a function of our trade union. Nevertheless for better or worse, we are in, and as we have paid our annual subscription of £100, and while that is so, it is my intention, as a representative, to do my best to ensure that we do participate in as full a manner as possible.

In Public Service

The same issue of the *Review* commented that only 42 members had joined the institute even at the reduced rate. A special general meeting of the association on 27 November 1959 decided to discontinue membership of the institute from that date. The initial disagreement with the institute arose from a decision of its executive committee to censure Miss O'Doherty for publishing information concerning the proceedings of the institute's executive committee, sub-committees and council. The association endorsed the entitlement of Miss O'Doherty to inform the members of institute proceedings.

FIVE-DAY WEEK

Agreement was reached on the introduction of a five-day week for civil servants at a meeting of the general council on 12 June 1964. The arrangements necessary for its introduction were agreed as follows:

1. Hours of attendance
   The hours of attendance shall be: 9.15 a.m. to 5.30 p.m. Mondays to Thursdays, 9.15 a.m. to 5.15 p.m. Fridays.
2. Privilege days
   It is agreed that the existing privilege days at Easter and Christmas will be continued.
3. Saturday attendance
   Where an officer is required to work a full Saturday morning, i.e. 9.15 a.m. to 1.00 p.m., he shall be allowed a full day's leave in lieu. Where an officer is allowed to work for part of a Saturday morning, he will be allowed time off in lieu at the rate of time plus a quarter, or, if the officer is a member of an overtime grade, he may, if he elects, be paid at the rate of time plus a quarter in respect of the attendance given.

REORGANISATION OF CERTAIN GENERAL SERVICE GRADES

In his budget speech of 8 May 1957 the Minister for Finance said:

The Existing Civil Service structure seems too elaborate for our needs. The grading system is, to my mind, unduly complex. I intend that these matters will be examined and radical changes made which will, I believe, ultimately produce worthwhile economies.

When the views of the heads of departments had been received and discussed, the official side sent a memorandum on the proposed reorganisation to the staff side on 15 December 1958. The Finance proposals concerned in the main the clerical and sub-clerical grades and the grades of staff officer. They envisaged that recruitment to the grade of clerical officer would be stopped and that, as vacancies in the clerical officer grade arose, they would be allocated to the new grade of clerk-typist who would be in receipt of an extended scale. Arrangements would also be made for the integration of typing grades into the new structure. The staff officer III would remain as a grade, as would the so-called 'purified' clerical officer grade. The staff officer II grade would be merged in the executive officer grade, while the grades of staff officer I and higher staff officer would be abolished. Some of the higher staff officer posts were regraded as higher executive officer posts. The Finance proposals went on:

It is intended to examine further the relation of present practice to the level of performance appropriate to the Executive grades and, accordingly, no proposals concerning these grades are being put forward at the moment.

The chairman and secretary of the Executive and Higher Officers' Association met Seamus O'Conaill of the Department of Finance on 19 March 1958.[31] He was asked to amplify the reference to the proposals on the future of the executive grades. Mr O'Conaill stated there were instances when the executive grades, in particular the higher executive officer grade, were not doing as much as they were capable of doing and as they were intended to do. There was a body of opinion that felt that the higher executive officer grade should assume a great deal more responsibility than it had been carrying. The association representatives pointed out to Mr O'Conaill that the blame for this situation was not attributable to the officers in the higher executive officer grade but to the administration of departments which determined the work and duties to be discharged by these officers. The representatives went on to say that a resolution had been passed at the 1957 annual general meeting, requesting the executive committee to make arrangements for maintaining and improving the high level of efficiency in the civil service. The representatives then pointed out that a good deal of disquiet existed about the position of the executive grades in the present civil service structure. Mr O'Conaill said it was not intended to alter radically the executive officer — higher executive officer — assistant principal officer grading, and that, with minor improvements, this structure should be maintained. The association representatives then discussed the merging of the staff officer II grade with that of executive officer and the disappearance of the staff officer I and higher staff officer posts. It was pointed out that the introduction of staff officers II into the executive officer grade would mean more competition for higher executive officer posts. Seamus O'Conaill thought that the bulk of higher staff officer posts might be regraded as higher executive officer posts, but there was no fixed policy in regard to regrading these grades. The question of the seniority of the regraded staff officer II was also raised.

The association representatives finally dealt with the administrative officer grade and pointed out that, in modern times, the necessity for recruiting to this grade did not exist. Mr O'Conaill adhered to the Finance view about the need for this grade but, according to the report to the association's council, certain of his observations gave some hope that a solution to the administrative officer problem might be reached. At a special meeting of the council, Michael Stanley, a member of the executive committee, stated that the Civil Service Clerical Association was in favour of assimilating the higher quality clerical officer posts, estimated as between 400 and 600 in number, into the executive officer grade. The Civil Service Clerical Association, he said, contemplated that assimilation would take place over a number of years and would be effected by means of a confined competition to fill the requisite number of posts as they arose. The remaining clerical officers during the transition period would still have their chances by confined competition to the executive officer grade and by departmental promotion.

At this meeting the general secretary said that the executive committee had considered the discussion at the general purposes

1951-1969

committee (of the staff panel) and had decided (i) to resist the assimilation of the staff officers III to the executive officer grade; (ii) to recommend the retention of the staff officer III grade as providing an outlet for the new clerical assistant grade; and (iii) to resist the regrading of the 400-600 clerical officer posts and, in lieu of this proposal, to recommend the regrading of staff officer I and higher staff officer posts to higher executive officer posts.

At the quarterly meeting of the council on 23 June 1959, the general secretary said that, following the special meeting of the council to consider the reorganisation of the general service grades, there had been a meeting of the general purposes committee at which, in addition to ordinary members, a second representative of the association was allowed to be present. The chairman and he had attended with Mr Stanley on behalf of the association. At that meeting the Civil Service Clerical Association had put forward a proposal that the clerical officer grade be abolished and that, over a period, the average and below average clerical duties be delegated to writing assistants who would, from the start, be put on an extended scale, and that the duties which were above average and which they estimated involved 500-600 posts, should be regraded as executive officer duties, these posts to be filled by competition by the remaining clerical officers in the grade.

It was essential to the Civil Service Clerical Association proposal that all writing assistants should be put on an extended scale. The Staff Officers' Association reiterated its proposal for the absorption of the staff officer III and staff officer II grades into the executive officer grade, and staff officer I and higher staff officers to be regraded as higher executive officers. The association representatives objected to both these proposals for a variety of reasons. It was pointed out that the introduction of twice the number of new executive officers would swamp the promotion prospects of existing officers. The inclusion of work in the executive officer grade, hitherto demarcated as clerical work, would result in the lowering of the standard of the grade which, in turn, would be followed by the lowering of the scales. The representatives pointed out that the Department of Finance maintained that higher executive officers had not realised the standard of work expected of them. If the standard of the executive officer was lowered, the Department of Finance might seek to reduce the higher executive officer scales, with a consequent loss to those who would be promoted in the future. The lowering of the standard of the executive officer grade would provide the Department of Finance with an argument for justifying the recruitment of administrative officers. The meeting agreed that the association representatives should pursue its policy of seeking to preserve the grading structure. At a meeting of the general council staff panel, held on 16 July 1959, the following resolution was adopted:

That this Panel, whilst not in favour of the proposals as drafted, would be prepared to co-operate in a re-organisation of General Service Grades involving a new structure consisting of Clerical Assistant, Executive Officer and Grades above Executive Officer as at present, provided that outlets for existing Departmental and General Service grades are maintained or improved, and that Official Side agreement would be forthcoming to assimilation of serving Writing Assistants and Typing grades to the Clerical Assistant Grade and of Staff Officer Grades II and III and an agreed number of clerical officer posts to the Executive Officer grade, of Staff Officers I and Higher Staff Officers to the Higher Executive Officer grade and subject to agreement on a suitable salary scale for Clerical Assistants. It is also to be understood that such re-organisation would be without prejudice to the rights and conditions of service of Grades not comprehended in the present proposals.

The content of this resolution was reported by the chairman, Miss O'Doherty, to a meeting of the executive committee of the Executive and Higher Officers' Association on 17 July 1959. The general secretary reported on the proceedings of a meeting of the general council held that same day. He said that the panel's policy, as expressed in the resolution, was said by its chairman to represent the united viewpoint of the staff side. He had been perturbed by this misrepresentation of the position, but had not wished to intervene to make a correction because of the staff panel's rigid attitude about the representation of minority views at general council. The executive committee decided to write in the first instance to the chairman of the panel, asking for a correction so that the association would be seen to have exhausted all remedies within the scheme and if, as was likely, correction was not forthcoming, a panel meeting would be summoned; if that did not produce the desired results, the committee would write to the Department of Finance, setting out its views. It was also decided to establish a sub-committee to examine both the Finance and staff side proposals and to consider what amendments could be made to either proposal in order to harmonise them with the association's view, and to consider proposals for the association's scheme on reorganisation and also the means by which the proposals objectionable to the association might be countered.

At a meeting of the executive committee on 17 August 1959, the general secretary gave a report of the proceedings of the special meeting of the panel convened to discuss the misrepresentation of the panel's decision on the reorganisation proposals, made at the meeting of the general council. He said that the panel had decided by a vote of 12 to 3 not to take any action on the complaint. The committee agreed to write to the Department of Finance; the letter would refer to the meeting of the general council and the statement that was made, asserting that it was not correct that the decision represented a united viewpoint, and also informing the department that the association had sought to have the panel correct this matter, but that the panel had declined. It would also be further stated that the executive committee felt constrained to state that the association did not support the panel's proposals. It was further agreed to write another letter to the Department of Finance some days after the first letter. This letter would seek exploratory talks on the matter. The sub-committee set up by the executive committee at its meeting of 17 July concluded its considerations on 25 August 1958, and reported as follows:

Outline of Scheme of Reorganisation for Certain General Service Grades

Hereunder is a possible scheme of reorganisation for the General Service Grades:
1. Retain existing HEO grade and absorb into it (a) all HSO posts (33) and all SO I posts (46). New Establishment, 425 + 33 + 46 = 504.
2. Retain Existing EO Grade and absorb into it all SO II posts (111). New Establishment, 685 + 111 = 796.

3. Retain existing SO III grade and increase the present establishment by the 400 to 600 higher clerical posts. New Establishment, 518 + 400 − 600 = 918 − 1,118.
4. Regrade remaining CO work as Clerical Assistant work. Establishment of new grade would be present number of W.As, 1,773 + 2,410 − 2,210 = 4,183 − 3,983. The standard of recruitment to the Clerical Assistant grade should be that of the Intermediate Certificate and the grade should be open to both sexes.
5. *Promotion*
    (a) To EO grade — Competition to EO grade to be from the expanded SO III grade and to be effected (i) by means of the confined competition as at present with an increase in the number of posts available for competition and (ii) by Departmental promotion to a certain proportion of posts.
    (b) SO III grade to be filled by promotion of (i) Clerical Assistants, and (ii) other grades at present eligible for promotion to the Clerical Officer grade.
    (c) HEO grade to be recruited from the EO grade. The AO grade should be abolished and AO posts merged in the HEO grade.
6. The terms of assimilation of one grade into another and the means by which the 400 to 600 COs be selected to be the subject of specific discussions and the scales for the new Clerical Assistant grade to be agreed or in default to be settled by the Arbitration Board.

25th August, 1959

The report, presented to a special meeting of the council of the association held on 3 September 1959, was adopted with the following addendum:

In relation to Higher Staff Officer and Staff Officer I posts, the considerations which govern the promotion of members of these grades to the Higher Executive Officer grades be maintained as at present.[32]

A further amendment deleted the word 'competition' in the first line of paragraph 5(a) and the word 'promotion' was substituted. The council then decided that the general secretary should write to the Department of Finance, stating that the association had views on the reorganisation, and that it would be glad of an opportunity to discuss the proposals with the department, and that no other disclosure on the proposals should be made to any other body. There was one dissension from a member of the council who favoured informing the general staff side of the proposals.

At the meeting of the executive committee on 28 September 1959, the general secretary reported on the meeting of the staff panel a week earlier at which the association's position in relation to the reorganisation proposals had been discussed. He said that a motion by the Staff Officers' Association, that the Department of Finance be told the actual voting at the panel on the panel's proposals for reorganising, was withdrawn after a discussion, in the course of which both the alliance and himself had supported the Staff Officers' Association proposal. When the panel came to select the staff side to attend the next meeting of the general council at which the reorganisation proposals would be discussed, Malachy Dooney (Post Office Engineering Union) proposed that the association not be permitted to attend because of the attitude the general secretary had adopted at the July meeting, and the subsequent action of the association in writing to the Department of Finance. The panel so decided. It was reported to the executive committee that no replies to the letters sent to the Department of Finance in connection with the reorganisation had been received. It was decided to write requesting a reply to both letters.[33] The letters did not receive replies. The outcome of the discussions at general council were reported in the 1960 annual report:

At the date of the last General Meeting, the Association was somewhat uncertain as to the course the re-organisation proposals were taking. This uncertainty arose from a decision of the Staff Panel to exclude the Association from representation at General Council Meetings because of certain differences between the Association and other constituents of the Panel. In the first two months of the year, little appeared to be taking place, but at the end of March the Executive Committee received from the Chairman of the General Council Staff Panel, Mr J. C. Horgan, a detailed report of the latest developments which had crystallised into a scheme which eventually formed the basis of the re-organisation scheme that took effect on 1 July last. This revised scheme resulted from the deliberations of a sub-committee of the General Council which had been formed, with the concurrence of the Panel in December, with a view to seeing if common ground on any points could be found. The Association was not represented on the committee but it had been agreed that nothing touching its interests would be discussed in its absence. The revised proposals as far as they impinged on the Association's interest were a good deal less objectionable than were the original proposals. At a special meeting of the Council in mid-April, these proposals which at the time had been reduced to writing were considered by the Council. The Executive Committee endeavoured to have the proposals further amended and in this their efforts were not unfruitful. The scheme was eventually agreed at the General Council at a meeting held on 14 April 1960.

The agreed recommendations were embodied in Finance circular 3/60; the relevant General Council report was numbered 216.

MAY O'DOHERTY AND THE EQUAL PAY INCIDENT

May O'Doherty was elected chairman of the Executive and Higher Officers' Association in 1958. Events later that year resulted in an attempt to remove her from the chairmanship and, more seriously, to cause a split in the Civil Service Clerical Association and the setting up of a breakaway Clerical Officers' Union. This situation arose from a request by the Executive and Higher Officers' Association that the staff panel should forward to the Department of Finance a claim for the abolition of the limit on the number of children's allowances payable to officers on marriage-differentiated scales of pay. The panel's general purposes committee considered the claim but deferred action upon it on the grounds that it would cut across a claim for equal pay for equal work for men and women submitted by the Post Office Workers' Union.

At a later meeting of the general purposes committee, the Post Office Workers' Union claim was considered and the Civil Service Clerical Association put forward a suggestion that a claim for the abolition of marriage-differentiated scales should be considered as a preliminary to the pursuit of the claim for equal pay for equal work. The grounds upon which the Civil Service Clerical Association representative put forward his suggestion were that the differentiation in pay between single and married men in certain circumstances was incompatible

1951-1969

with the principle of equal pay for equal work and, in fact, obscured sex-differentiation in those grades. It was therefore argued that it might be advisable to try to remove marriage-differentiation before attempting to obtain equal pay for equal work. The Civil Service Clerical Association's suggestion envisaged that married men then entitled to children's allowances would retain them, but single men would be given the option of either remaining on the single scale, with an entitlement to children's allowances in the event of marriage, or being placed on the new male scale. The general purposes committee decided that this proposal should be reported to the staff panel for examination. This decision was made on 6 June 1958, and the matter was deferred at a panel meeting held on 26 June.[34] The executive committee of the Executive and Higher Officers' Association received the following correspondence, dated 4 July, from the Women Civil Servants' Advisory Board:

Dear Sir, Your organisation caters for grades in which women are employed and you accept their subscriptions.

On behalf of those members, my Board requests me to forward to you a copy of a resolution passed by a mass meeting of Women Civil Servants in the Round Room, Mansion House, on 4 July, 1958. Further action pends your reply within one month.

Yours sincerely,
Sheila Twohig
Honorary Secretary

The resolution read as follows:

Women Civil Servants' Advisory Board Meeting,
Round Room, Mansion House
Friday, July 5th, 1958

Women Civil Servants assembled in mass meeting protest against the action of the General Purposes Committee of the Civil Service Staff Panel in dictating policy to our staff organisations by causing to appear on the Agenda of the Staff Panel Meeting of 26 June, 1958, an item:
'Proposal that a claim be submitted for abolition of marriage differentiation in pay scales.'
We protest against the proposal itself since it is directly opposed to the interests of members. We hold our Organisations responsible

In Public Service

and, since they are represented on the General Purposes Committee, we demand that justice be served and order re-established by:
(1) The deletion of the item from the agenda
(2) The assurance that the interests of members will be loyally served
(3) The restoration to its original status of the Panel of Staff Representatives, and the restoration of proper function and authority to Staff Associations.

We give our organisation one month to meet our demands and we withhold subscriptions in the meantime.

This letter was considered by the executive committee on 14 July. It was decided to mark it 'Read' and to take no action on it. Ms O'Doherty was actively involved in the organisation of the Mansion House meeting and in the July issue of *Civil Service Review* set out reasons for her participation in that meeting in an article entitled 'Realities':

The Minister for Finance set up a scheme for Conciliation and Arbitration. Under that scheme the top level on the Staff Side was a panel of Staff Representatives. It functioned at top level for some years, but now we find that, although each Constituent group pays anything from £20 to £40 per seat on the panel, it is now a back seat. A sub-committee composed mainly of the General Secretaries of the constituent groups with the Chairman and Secretary of the Panel — eleven men — now run the show, and the Staff Panel goes on stage quarterly or on call if one of the Eleven rings the bell. These Eleven men do not arrive from outerspace; they are flesh and blood civil servants, receiving members' cash to serve members. This Association formulated a claim for an extension of Children's Allowances and forwarded it to the Panel two years ago. Enquiry re its fate met the attitude that the claim cut across a claim for equal pay for equal work entered by the Post Office Workers' Union since 1951. 'Considerable discussion' on this claim ended in a suggestion by the General Secretary of the Civil Service Clerical Association that a claim be submitted for the abolition of marriage differentiated scales, and resulted in a proposal that such a claim be submitted, appearing on the Staff Panel agenda for 26 June. All associations with women members are represented on the Sub-Committee which brought forth this proposal. The cycle is now complete. With upwards of a dozen claims from Staff Organisations waiting for attention, the Sub-Committee suggests a claim and proposes it to the Panel. This Association's claim for the abolition of children's allowances becomes a proposed claim which implies the

1951-1969

abolition of Children's Allowances. The Post Office Workers' Union claim for equal pay for equal work for men and women becomes a proposal to claim equal pay for men and the substitution of one inequality for another inequality!! Associations exist for the benefit of members. General Secretaries appointed by members exist for the service of members. Resolutions on policy come from the floor of the house at members' level and claims are formulated according to policy by the Association and sent up to the Panel which exists solely on behalf of Associations' members. No 'claim for the abolition of marriage differentiation in pay scales' has been forwarded to the Staff Panel by any Association. There are several Staff Associations catering for grades in which there is not marriage differentiation and the members are paid solely on a sex basis and there is not equal pay for equal work for those members. There is nothing to prevent any organisation now, nor indeed for the past 35 years of the existence of the Irish Civil Service has there been anything to prevent any organisation, from seeking Equal Pay for Equal Work.

Ms O'Doherty then set out her views on the nature of equality:

The only possible equality there can be is the rate for the job paid to men and women, married, single and widowed and children's allowances paid to married and widowed officers with children.

Arising out of the meeting of women civil servants, the association's executive committee considered the position of the presiding chairman, in view of the resolution passed at the meeting. The majority of members felt that the chairman's activities in connection with the campaign conducted by the Women Civil Servants' Advisory Board were detrimental to the interests of the association and that she should be removed from the chairmanship in view of her failure to disassociate herself from these activities.

A Special General Meeting of the Association was held on 28 July, 1958. Some 200 members attended. The Executive Committee proposed the following motions: 'That in the opinion of the majority of the Executive Committee, the activities of the Chairman in connection with the recent campaign conducted by the Women Civil Servants' Advisory Board are detrimental to the interests of the Association, and as she has refused to disassociate herself from these activities, the Executive Committee recommends that she be removed from the Chairmanship of the Association.

In Public Service

The motion was discussed for about four hours. When the chairman had replied, a vote was taken. There were 62 votes in favour of the motion, and 138 against.[35]

The item dealing with marriage-differentiated scales was on the agenda of the meeting of the general council staff panel held on 22 September 1958. On a motion from the representative of the Civil Service Clerical Association, the panel agreed to defer the item. The chairman, J. C. Horgan, stated that it would not appear on the agenda of the panel again until some organisation brought it forward.

DECENTRALISATION

The question of decentralisation of the civil service dominated the affairs of the association and the staff panel during the latter part of the 1960s. The matter was mentioned in the *Civil Service Review* in October 1964 when the general secretary reported:

> Reports of a proposed decentralisation, whether or not without foundation, certainly have an immediate effect on any staff likely to be concerned. The lack of certainty and the sometimes conflicting rumours proved very frustrating in the recent occurrences so that it became apparent that the first essential as far as any proposed decentralisation is concerned is that there should be adequate consultation with the Staff Side.

Some more definite information came to hand in time to be reported in the association's 1964/65 annual report:

> The question of decentralisation of the Civil Service assumed an amount of topicality during the year, and in a reply to a recent Dáil Question it was admitted that the Government had accepted in principle that the Civil Service should be decentralised and that an inter-departmental committee was investigating the practicalities of the matter.

The question was put down by Brendan Corish, who asked the Minister for Finance: 'What plans the Government have under consideration for moving Civil Service Departments out of Dublin to provincial centres; and if he will state at exactly what stage of progress each of any such plans is.'

1951-1969

Dr James Ryan, Minister for Finance, replied: 'It has been decided in principle that certain Government Offices should be transferred from Dublin. The various practical problems involved in implementing this decision are at present being examined by a Committee.' Dr Ryan went on to say that no department has been specifically selected.

The association's annual report stated that the question of adequate consultation with the staff side before any decentralisation would take place had been the subject of correspondence between the staff panel and the Department of Finance. At the 1965 annual general meeting, the following motion, proposed by the executive committee, was carried by a large majority:

That this Association is opposed to the decentralisation of Public Services as adding to the cost of government and causing unnecessary hardship among Civil Servants.

The general secretary reported in the *Civil Service Review* of October/November 1967 that the government had announced that it intended to decentralise two departments. He stated:

The two Departments are the Department of Lands and the Department of Education and it is intended to transfer them to Castlebar and Athlone respectively. The Taoiseach made the announcement through the Government Information Bureau on Friday, 16 November, 1967. On the previous Monday, the Minister for Finance informed the Chairman of the Staff Panel, Mr H. Nally, and Panel's Secretary, Mr P. Breathnach, of the decision. The Staff Side was not consulted at all before a decision was made despite the fact that it had on several occasions asked to be consulted before any decision was taken.

In the course of his statement in the Dáil, the Taoiseach said:

The decentralisation of as much of the Administration and the commerce and industry of the country as possible is an essential part of the programme of the present Government and its predecessors. In coming to this decision they have been influenced by a number of important national considerations, the principal one being the necessity to take whatever action is possible to redress the imbalance of population in the country. . . . It will take a number of years to give effect to the decision and during this period there will be full consultation and liaison with the staff organisations.

In Public Service

A special general meeting of the members of all the organisations attached to the Department of Lands staff panel was held in the Adelaide Hall, Dublin, on 14 December 1967. It was attended by the chairman of the staff panel, H. Nally, and by the general secretaries of the Institute of Professional Civil Servants, the Civil Service Clerical Association and the Executive and Higher Officers' Association. The meeting expressed its opposition to the proposed transfer of the Department of Lands to Castlebar.

Decentralisation was discussed at length at the association's quarterly council meeting on 13 December. The delegates expressed their sympathy with members of the departments immediately concerned with the matter and promised every assistance and support. It was acknowledged that it was a matter affecting all departments and not just the two departments immediately concerned.

The February 1968 issue of the *Civil Service Review* revealed that civil servants had received a new shock when they read the Sunday papers on 4 February. The general secretary commented:

> They could hardly believe their eyes when they read that the Minister for Lands, Mr O'Morain, had told reporters on the previous evening that the Department of the Gaeltacht was to be moved to the West. The fact that Mr O'Morain had in November last informed the press of the Government decision to transfer the Department of Lands and Education to Castlebar and Athlone before the Taoiseach made a similar announcement through the Government Information Bureau was enough to convince most people that the Government had taken a decision to move the Department of the Gaeltacht and that once again Mr O'Morain had beaten the Cabinet to the draw in making the announcement.

The reactions of civil servants to Michael O'Morain's announcement were summed up in a fair and reasonable manner in a report in the *Evening Herald* on 5 February:

> The announcement by Mr O'Morain has shocked civil servants. They have been having discussions on the whole question of transferring Government Departments to the West and the news of another Department going without consultation with them had added fuel to the smouldering fires of resentment over the

Government's attitude. Many civil servants were today taking the announcement of Mr O'Morain without having consulted the Staff Panel as an indication that the earlier protests about the other two Departments were not getting much attention from the Government.

When the report appeared, the chairman of the staff panel, H. Nally, immediately sought a meeting with the Minister for Finance, Charles Haughey. The meeting took place on 6 February and the staff representatives consisted of the general secretaries of the Civil Service Clerical Association, the Institute of Professional Civil Servants and the Executive and Higher Officers' Association. After the meeting, the following statement was issued through the Government Information Bureau:

> The Minister for Finance received a deputation from the Staff Panel of the Civil Service General Council today to discuss recent reports about the decentralisation of the Department of the Gaeltacht. The Minister gave an assurance to the deputation that no final decision to transfer from Dublin any Department, other than the Department of Education and Lands, the transfer of which had already been announced, had been made or would be made by the Government without prior consultation with representatives of the Staff Panel.[36]

Subsequent discussions at the general council culminated in the issue of General Council Report No. 451, which stressed the voluntary nature of transfer arising from decentralisation.

PUBLIC SERVICES ORGANISATION REVIEW GROUP

The appointment of the Public Services Organisation Review Group was announced on 21 September 1966:

> As foreshadowed in his budget speech on 9 March last, the Minister for Finance has set up a group with the following mandate: 'Having regard to the growing responsibilities of Government to examine and report on the organisation of the Departments of State at the higher levels, including the appropriate distribution of functions as between both Departments themselves and Departments and other bodies.'

The expression 'higher levels' referred to grades, administrative and professional, not covered by conciliation and arbitration machinery, i.e. above higher executive officer.

In Public Service

The members of the group were: Liam St J. Devlin, (Chairman), Lieutenant General Sir Geoffrey Thompson, Professor P. Leahy, T. J. Barrington, J. F. Dempsey, Dr Thekla J. Beere, and L. M. Fitzgerald. Peter Gaffey acted as secretary.

On the assumption that the review group would concern itself with such matters as recruitment and promotion as part of the organisation of the civil service, the Executive and Higher Officers' Association decided to make a submission to the group. In fact the association made two submissions — written and oral. The letter referred extensively to the matter of decentralisation. Set out in the following pages is an outline of the written submission and notes on the oral submission.

The group did not report until September 1969, and the association's reaction to the report will be dealt with in the next chapter.

Outline of Submission to Public Services Organisation Review Group
1. *Organisation of the Civil Service in Relation to the Executive Grades Position of the Executive Grades in the Civil Service.*
    The Executive grades form part of the mainstream of general service grades in the civil service. The duties on which they are engaged form a large portion of the administrative work of the Government Departments. The Executive Officer grade is the most important grade in the civil service, as the standard of the entrants to that grade will largely decide the standard of the officers who will occupy the majority of higher posts in the civil service. The Executive grades are thus pivotal grades in the civil service.

    Recruitment:
    It is important that a high level of recruitment be maintained. The complacency in this matter which existed in less competitive years must now be discarded. Incentives to join the civil service must be improved under the various headings hereunder, e.g. remuneration, promotion, public relations. The Executive Officer grade must be made so attractive that it can compete with not alone other employments at Leaving Certificate level but also with Universities. The inordinate length of the Executive Office scale is an important factor in this regard.

    Promotion:
    Promotion prospects are becoming increasingly important. Some years ago, when there was a scarcity of salaried jobs, school-leavers were not inclined to look beyond the rate of pay at the

entry grade when deciding on their future. Nowadays in more affluent times, with a wide choice of careers open to them, including careers after going to University (with an increased number of scholarships) they are inclined to be more far-sighted. Promotion prospects should be stressed when recruiting. (This is already done at Administrative Officer level.) A clear picture of equitable promotion prospects should be presented. The wording of a U.N. Covenant, adopted by the General Assembly in December 1966, seems to sum up admirably: 'Equal opportunity for everyone to be promoted in his employment to an appropriate higher level, subject to no considerations other than those of seniority and competence.' If it could be shown to successful Executive Officer candidates that on the basis of seniority and competence — taking into account the average length of service in the Executive Officer grade and the intermediate grades — that they could reasonably expect to be promoted to the grade of Principal in the civil service, it would make a career in the civil service appear to be very attractive and would certainly put a job as an Executive Officer in a very competitive position in relation to outside employments, both at Leaving Certificate and University level.

The U.N. Covenant, which was subscribed to by this country, summarises the Association's views on the principles of promotions and we contend that these principles are the best ones, not alone from the point of view of equity and justice but also from the point of view of efficiency. The Association strongly feels that promotion to all general service grades in the civil service should be exclusively from general service grades. We feel that this is important from a point of view of efficiency and as far as good organisation is concerned.

Remuneration:

We feel that the remuneration of civil servants should be of a sufficiently high level to attract the best type of recruit to the civil service. In equity, the rate of pay of any civil service grade should be at least as high as that obtainable in outside comparable grades engaged on the same level of work. In addition, as an incentive to join the civil service and to counteract some of the disadvantages of being a civil servant, we feel that something in addition to the outside comparable rate should be paid. In this respect, we feel that if, for example, one decides on a career as an administrator, that the highest field and the most important one in which one can work is in the administration of one's country. The importance of having the best men in this particular field is stressed, and one way of attaining this end is by having the best rates of remuneration in this field. We feel, also, that certain disadvantages of entering the civil service, such as having one's individual efforts, however brilliant, covered in a cloak of anonymity and of having one's civil rights impaired, should be offset by extra remuneration to counteract unattractiveness which these disadvantages impart to a job in the civil service. The civil service superannuation code which was at one time considered to be very favourable in comparison with outside schemes, has now been overtaken by many outside superannuation schemes. This must affect recruitment. There are many more aspects of civil service remuneration on which the Association has strong views, but realising that the Group's mandate does not include the subject of remuneration, we are referring only to certain important aspects of the matter which we consider to affect recruitment to the civil service.

Training:
The Association is very concerned that adequate training should be given to civil servants. The Executive Committee has produced a Report on Training for the Executive grades in the civil service and it is proposed to include this Report as part of the Association's submission to the Group.

Public Relations:
The Association is concerned at the poor image of the civil service which is presented to the public. It is also most concerned at the large number of attacks on the civil service — some of which seem to be part of a deliberate and organised campaign — which are allowed to go unanswered. The Association would favour the setting up of Public Relations Officers in each Government Department and a central Public Relations Section to deal with publicity on the civil service as a whole.

2. *Civil Service Grades:*
The Association considers that the present grading structure in the civil service is more or less adequate — now that recruitment to the Clerical Officer grade has been resumed — with the exception of the grade of Administrative Officer, which the Association thinks is unnecessary and should be abolished. The reason for this contention by the Association will be advanced in the Association's submission.
One of the dangers of a grade such as Administrative Officer grade is that it tends to create a gap between grades up to

1951-1969

Higher Executive Officer level and those above that grade. This is particularly true in the Department of Finance. The Association thinks that any such gap is a false one and is opposed to the creation of any such gap. We would point out that the vast majority of the people who at present fill the higher posts in the civil service were recruited at Executive Officer level or lower.

3. *Organisation (General):*
   The Association contends that Departments are often inhibited from logical expansion (e.g. on taking on new work as a result of new legislation) on an organisational basis because of anticipated public or political opposition. This often results in the organisational structure becoming overloaded and lines of demarcation becoming blurred. For instance, a Department performing a new service because of new legislation which might wish to set up a new section within the Department to do this, might have to spread the new work over existing sections because of anticipated public or political opposition to the setting up of a new section.

4. *Financial Fluidity:*
   The lack of financial fluidity for a Department to spend money on not alone additional staff to improve its organisation but also on modern aids to doing its work is, we think, an obstacle to the improved efficiency of the organisation of a Department. We appreciate the role of the Department of Finance in civil service expenditure, but think that Departments should be given a certain amount of financial fluidity to enable them to improve the staffing organisation of their Departments and to obtain modern aids, such as computers and business machines and to spend money on public relations.

5. *Personalities:*
   We feel that the extent to which the difficulties mentioned at 3 and 4 above militate against a particular Department, may depend to a large extent on the personalities of the permanent heads of the Department and the Minister in charge of a Department. Observation of the rate of success of some Departments in relation to others have led us to this conclusion. We think that this problem should be overcome in some way.

In Public Service
PUBLIC SERVICES ORGANISATION REVIEW GROUP

Oral Submission by the Executive and Higher Executive Officers' Association — 3 March 1968

1. The representatives of the Executive and Higher Executive Officers' Association, Messrs. Maher, Nolan, Tucker and Magner were heard by the Group on 1 March 1968.
2. The Association representatives said that, since they had made their written submission, a new issue had been raised by the Government announcement on decentralisation involving the transfer of two Departments to the country. This was a major organisational change and they were surprised that it should have been announced while the Group were sitting. Everything in the Association's written submission is affected by the proposed transfer and the Group cannot report without taking account of the proposal. Recruitment to the Civil Service will be adversely affected. A census taken by the staff associations in the Department of Lands showed that 30% of the staff will resign rather than move. Only 5% said they would go voluntarily, 45% would volunteer to go on promotion and 50% will not go on any terms. Even the locals won't go and now the Civil Service Commission are trying to divert Mayo candidates to Lands and the Roscommon/Westmeath candidates to Education, but they just refuse appointment. The Government have acted unilaterally; even the Department of Finance don't seem to have been consulted and the whole approach makes a farce of management/staff relations. A properly phased, scientifically thought-out decentralisation might work but the present proposals will break the morale of the Civil Service. Already morale has gone in Lands and Forestry where the only prospect is Castlebar. The Association would like the group to do two things:
    1) If it can, the Group should conduct a detailed examination of decentralisation and report on the question or, if it feels it cannot, it should recommend that some other group be set up to examine the problem, and

1951-1969

2) should draw attention to the bad effect on morale of the breach of good staff relations in the shock announcement of decentralisation.

3. Recruitment will be futher affected by decentralisation and there are recruitment difficulties at the moment. Up to the immediate post-war period, the Civil Service was able to get all the talent it required because the choice of career was narrow. Now the leaving certificate holder has a choice of a variety of State Sponsored bodies and of a growing number of University scholarships. The Civil Service must now compete for staff and it cannot do so if it offers the completely unrealistic and lengthy incremental scale it offers to the Executive Officer recruitment grade. The Service has benefited in the past from 'economic conscription' but those days are gone and it must shorten the Executive Officers' incremental span if it is to compete with other employments. The second impediment to civil service recruitment is the bad public image. Most of the public and school leavers have no idea of what working in the Civil Service means. The Civil Service administers the country and is not merely a company or a State sponsored body and working in the Civil Service should provide an interesting and satisfying career.

4. Placement of recruits in the Civil Service is completely haphazard. Allocation should be more scientific. Preferences and aptitudes should be ascertained and more choice allowed to people in the type of work to which they are assigned. This should not be carried as far as involving complete departmentalisation but is desirable to avoid having the square peg in the round hole so common in the Service under the present absence of a system. People should be given a variety of posts during their early careers. Now the only person who gets transferred is the man whom people are trying to get rid of. Planned development of potential through a system of job rotation is essential. People came in at very much the same level and the differences in their development after a few years may be in part personal but are in a large measure the results of the differences in the work on which they have been

In Public Service

engaged. The Association has no policy on mobility in general; they incline to the view that there is a lot of the work of Departments which requires a degree of specialisation but they do feel that if the Government want mobility in the Civil Service, they should operate it in an equitable manner. Mobility at the top might be preferable to mobility at the lower levels. In Britain, an Assistant Secretary knows that he will never be Secretary of the Department in which he is serving.

5. The Association believe that promotion should be based on seniority subject to competence with the occasional exception for the man of extraordinary ability. Merit is linked with seniority and competence, and experience is part of competence. Promotion by merit means that merit must be measured and there is no reliable method of doing this. Apart from this the Association believe that people should get promotion within a reasonable time. The rat-race is bad both for the individual and for the Civil Service. It should not be necessary for an officer to have to spend his spare time reading up all sorts of irrelevant things to answer interview board questions. Promotion on the results of annual assessment might have possibilities if there were a uniform standard of assessment. One benefit of a good system of assessment would be that it would give better contact between the individual and the Personnel Officer; the passed over man would know why he was passed over and everyone would get a chance to correct his faults.

6. The big problem facing the Association is the extension in the recruitment of Administrative Officers. In the 1950s, 4 or 5 Administrative Officers were recruited each year and some 50-75% of those were serving Executive Officers. This year 29 candidates were called — the highest number ever — and the proportion of graduates who were successful has greatly increased; it would appear that the competition has been slanted in favour of the graduates. Traditionally, the Association has been opposed to the recruitment of graduates as Administrative Officers. Graduate entry at Administrative Officer level had a historical origin in the necessity to replace the large block of higher officers who left after the Treaty but the system has remained after the

reason had ceased. The Association realises that there must be some graduate entry; professional posts will always be filled by graduates and some graduates will be required in the General Service. These should enter as Executive Officers at a suitable point on the Executive Officer scale which would have to be made sufficiently attractive. Their promotion prospects would have to be spelled out and they would progress if they were good enough. The recruitment in one year of 29 Administrative Officers with a guarantee of promotion in seven years will mean that, unless they are promoted to specialised posts, all avenues of promotion will be closed to Higher Executive Officers. The position could well be reached in the General Service which has been reached on the professional and technical side where non-graduate technicians cannot rise above the lowest professional level open to graduates. In such circumstances, it would be impossible to recruit Executive Officers of the standard now required.

7. There is a place for the Professional in the Civil Service but it is not on the administrative side. In Administration only the Administrator has the experience and the objectivity to take in the broad picture; the engineer for example will take the narrow engineering view. In any event, the Professionals have their own promotion structures up to Assistant Secretary level. They are the best people for those posts just as people who are in administration all their lives are best for the top administrative posts.

8. The Association felt that their written submission covered the rest of their views. An improvement in accommodation and a more rapid filling of vacancies were two areas for attention. They would again emphasise the need for an objective review of decentralisation.

9. The Group thanked the Association for their submission.

V

1970-1990

The organisation which in 1970 operated under the rubric of the Civil Service Executive and Higher Officers' Association changed titles during the period covered by this chapter as follows:

1973 Civil Service Executive Association
1975 Civil Service Executive Union
1987 Public Service Executive Union

It should be noted that between 1970 and 1978 the policy-making body was the annual general meeting. The first annual delegate conference took place in 1979.

Tom Maher presided at the 1970 annual general meeting. In his address he said that the 11th round of pay increases would expire on 31 March 1970 and that the public service would need to prepare itself for negotiation on the 12th round. The round negotiated in the private sector represented the largest single round of increases since the war and the government's proposal for public pay increases did not come near these amounts. The public sector would not accept limitations that were exclusive to it. It would not accept discrimination against itself which forced it to fall behind in pay vis-à-vis comparable employments. Tom Maher went on to speak on the Devlin report. This was the first major examination of state machinery for some forty years. The government's view on the report's recommendations was awaited with interest. The central recommendation of the report provided for the creation of a separate department to manage the public service. The establishment of a Department of the Public Service was an effort to alleviate the tension within the Department of Finance between the personnel function and the budget function.

A union delegation at one of the many ICTU conferences to consider national pay discussions. The delegation here, in 1981, is (left to right of middle row): Dan Murphy, Garry Sweeney, John Daly, Seán Ó Conail, Michael Foster, Carmel Foley and Con Ó Donnchú. Behind Dan Murphy is P.J. O'Grady, a former union treasurer, but here representing the Association of Higher Civil Servants.

Presentation to Garry Sweeney by the Post Office General Branch on his retirement in 1983.

Some of the officers and executive committee at an annual delegate conference in the mid-1980s.

Delegates at an annual delegate conference in the 1980s.

Dan Murphy (general secretary) and Dave Thomas (president 1988-90) deep in conversation at the 1987 annual delegate conference.

Eoin Faherty addresses the annual delegate conference.

Tom Carew addresses the 1987 annual delegate conference.

Presentation to Bernie Gray in 1988 on her election as worker director in Telecom Eireann. From left to right: Tom McKevitt, Dave Thomas, Pat Taylor (chairman, Telecom Branch), Bernie Gray, and Willie McIntosh.

Executive committee members Madeline Curry, Martin Hanevy and Dermot Ryan at the 1988 conference.

Telecom delegates listen to a debate at the 1988 annual delegate conference.

Seán Ó Conail is presented with honorary life membership of the union at the 1989 conference. Dan Murphy (general secretary), Dave Thomas (president), Seán Ó Conail and Nancy Ó Conail.

The union's seminar on equality has become a major annual event. (1989)

The 1990 executive committee and officers. Standing l-r: Philip Crosby, Seán Beades, Peg O'Connor, Martin Diskin, Louie Glancy, Gerry Phelan, Brenda Feeney, Rory O'Connor, Brendan Shanahan, Nessan O'Leary, Martin Hanevy, Peter Ryan, Declan Bourke, Tony Nolan, Tom McCann, Eoin Faherty. Seated l-r: Billy Hannigan (A.G.S.), Martin McDonald (A.G.S.), Tom McKevitt (D.G.S.), Dan Murphy (G.S.), Willie McIntosh (president), Tom Carew (vice-president), Tom Geraghty (A.G.S.), Madeline Curry. Not pictured: Liam Hogan and Breifne O'Reilly.

Seven Union Presidents 1978-90 l-r: Joe Smyth (1978-79), John Daly (1979-81), Seán Ó Conail (1981-83), Con Ó Donnchú (1983-84), Noel Doyle (1984-86), Eoin Faherty (1986-88), Dave Thomas (1988-90).

However, it seemed that the proposed Department of the Public Service would have the same minister as the Department of Finance. Tom Maher submitted that conflicts between the personnel and budgetary functions would continue and he referred to the situation in Britain before the acceptance of the Fulton report recommendations when there had been a separate division for personnel and finance within the Treasury. The British situation had not worked and there was no reason to believe that the proposals of the Devlin group would work either. In Tom Maher's opinion, it was essential that the government should agree to the creation of a separate ministerial post of cabinet rank that would be responsible for the proposed Department of the Public Service. Without this, the personnel function would continue to flounder and the recommendations of the Devlin report were unlikely to be given real consideration.

Des Hickey presided at the 1971 annual general meeting. In his address, he referred to the fact that civil servants were now almost unique in being a group of white collar workers who had not taken industrial action. The reason for this lay in the conciliation and arbitration machinery which enabled disputes to be settled and which was operated by the staff side in a spirit of co-operation and determination to settle all difficulties peacefully. He recalled the difficulties of 1970 when the government had decided to abrogate its agreement with the public service but, after persuasion, had agreed to let the agreement run its course. Provisions for grade claims were an integral part of that agreement and the government was not living up to its commitments in regard to them. The government was not working the conciliation part of the scheme since it had refused to discuss the claim for an increase in pay, for the grades represented by the association, on its merits. This was in stark contrast to the government's recommendation on how the conciliation procedures of the Labour Court should be used by employers and workers outside the civil service. Des Hickey went on to say that the government's abuse of the negotiating machinery possibly might provoke a mood of revolt among civil servants, a loss of faith in the principle of free collective bargaining and a demand for industrial action as a means of settling disputes. It was to be hoped that industrial action would be avoided but, if it were not, the fault would not be with the staff side.

Des Hickey again presided at the 1972 annual general meeting. In his address he dealt with the structure and organisation of the civil service and the challenges that change presented to the association. According to the Devlin report, he said, there were 1,000 grades in the civil service. Many of these grades hardly could be justified. The existence of so many grades operating side by side gave rise to frustrations and misunderstandings among staff. Ireland's prospective partners in the European Community had a different civil service structure, and the British civil service, which was most like Ireland's, was changing. Increasing contacts between Irish civil servants and representatives of other countries probably would highlight the difficulties of the present civil service structure.

Des Hickey said that the pressure for change in the Irish civil service was very strong. The association could decide to resist change or to influence a newly constituted civil service. Resistance to change was a fruitless exercise and in the long run would not be in the best interests of members since it was doomed to failure. On the other hand, the association's logical course was to accept the necessity for change and attempt to protect the interest of its members. Changes would have to be acceptable to the civil service trade union movement. However, the forthcoming changes would present many challenges and difficulties for the association and it was imperative that members, activists, the executive committee and officers all realized the extent of the problems.

Richard Gillespie, in his address to the 1973 annual general meeting, spoke of the responsibilities of trade unions and in particular of the role of the association. He said that few people asked themselves what the actual functions of trade unions were, but unless members really understood the purpose, they would not be in a position to carry out the functions. A fairly common view of a trade union was that it was a sort of slot machine where you put in your few shillings and you got out a few pounds. Essentially this was a view of activities that would suggest that trade unions were very similar to an insurance company. This, however, was not really what a trade union was. To understand what it was, it was necessary to examine that phrase 'the association'. Members tended to use the expression as if they were referring to something outside themselves. 'The association' meant an association of people. The work, the ideals and the strength of the association lay in its members. There was no restriction on the things that the association could deal with. Again there was a feeling that association activities were confined to pay and conditions of employment. This was not so. In fact, there was no limit to the activities of the association, except the limit imposed by the members themselves.

Richard Gillespie, in his address to the 1974 annual general meeting, dealt mainly with national wage agreements. The question we must ask ourselves, he stated, was why trade unions should support the principle of national agreements. He made no apology for saying that in the first instance the association should ask: What is in it for us? Is there a better alternative? One of the strongest arguments made by those who opposed national agreements in principle was that it took away the traditional and sacred right of the trade unions to negotiate wages and conditions through collective bargaining. Collective bargaining, if it meant anything, was the strengthening of the bargaining power of individual workers by their coming together as a body to pursue their claims for better pay and conditions. Mr Gillespie submitted that the combined power of all the unions in the ICTU was the strongest possible instrument for collective bargaining. National agreements enabled unions working together to arrive at a settlement that was reasonably fair to all workers. It enabled them to make better provision for the lower paid and for those whose bargaining power was weaker. Another argument in support of the principle of national agreements was that they enabled the whole trade union movement to exert a powerful influence on the institutions of state responsible for price control and taxation. Employers also played their part. Prices had to be geared to keeping profits at a reasonable minimum and, to ensure that, government action should be firmer and more widespread that it had been hitherto. The association had accepted the principle of national agreements from the beginning, but this must not be seen as the association's permanent policy. The public service was the hardest hit by the inequitable tax system and the association

In Public Service

was anxiously awaiting the government's proposals on tax reform, Richard Gillespie said. The association's future attitude to national wage agreements would be determined on the merits of these proposals.

Ms Nabla McGinley presided at the 1975 annual general meeting. She remarked that, within three months, the association had had three chairmen — Richard Gillespie, who had been succeeded by Eddie Mortimer in April, whom she in turn had succeeded in June. Ms McGinley spoke to the members about their role and image. Pay was assumed to be the major interest of members and they had done fairly well in recent years. Because of the national wage agreements, they had been getting increases at much the same time as outside organisations, without having to wait until a standard had been set and then enduring long months of separate negotiations. In the matter of direct negotiations, too, members had not done badly. Within the previous twelve months they had got a 5 per cent increase under the anomalies clause of the national wage agreement. Nevertheless, Ms McGinley was perturbed by the tone adopted by the Minister for Finance in his budget speech. He had pointed out that, under the agreement, the average wage and salary earner would receive, in one year, increases totalling about 30 per cent of his original pay. The cost in the public sector would be about £90 million annually. He was proceeding on the basis that all concerned with the negotiation and settlement of income increases in 1975 would appreciate the gravity of the crisis facing the country and would show the moderation that was essential if they were to protect employment and living standards. Ms McGinley maintained that the necessary expertise and skills to improve the efficiency of the service were available. She said that comparatively few got the chance of professional training, university courses, courses in accountancy, economics, business studies and management. It was not good enough to say that this sort of expertise must be imported. The civil service had always had a bad public image.

This image was being fostered, possibly unintentionally, by their employer. While we did not want elitist groups, Ms McGinley said, we wanted those who directly served the public to be given the opportunity to acquire extra skills and to add to their expertise.

Nabla McGinley also presided at the 1976 annual general meeting. In the course of her address, she dealt with fair play for public servants — equal pay and trade union unity.

She said that it was not unusual for public servants to come under attack in times of economic recession. The attacks now were being orchestrated by government ministers. The public service was being misrepresented as overstaffed and as having a higher level of pay than the work justified. The management services division of the Department of the Public Service conducted a rigid examination of the numbers and grading of staff required to administer government policy. Such expansion of staff as had taken place in the civil service had been the direct result of various government policies which required the co-operation of staff to make them work. She instanced two cases: the Social Welfare Programme and the National Manpower Service.

Both would have been impossible to administer but for the provision of staff. Those who decried the present number of civil servants had a responsibility to indicate which civil servants were not necessary, said Ms McGinley, and also a responsibility to specify which government policies or which laws passed by the Oireachtas should cease to be administered. Civil servants were entitled to expect their employer to defend them in the face of attack. She reiterated the association's view that there should be a separate Minister for the Public Service, who would have full responsibility for the public service only.

On the matter of equal pay, Ms McGinley said that, along with other civil service unions, the association lodged a claim for equal pay for equal work in 1969. Equal pay was identified as an 'increase in the basic rate of pay of unmarried men or women to the married or male rate'. The government's decision to pay single men and single women on a lower scale than that paid to married officers was outrageous, she said. The married rate was the rate for the job. She demanded the full implementation of equal pay for equal work from 31 December 1975.

Speaking on trade union unity, Ms McGinley said that there seemed to be a campaign afoot that had the effect of dividing

In Public Service

the trade union movement and setting worker against worker. This was noticeable in the references to public service pay being met out of taxation and increases in such pay giving rise to higher taxation. It was essential that the trade union movement should not allow this divisiveness to grow. The only way forward for the movement was through united action on behalf of all workers in both the private and public sectors.

Ms McGinley was again in the chair when the 1977 annual general meeting was convened. In her address she returned again to the campaign against public servants and referred to a debate that had taken place at the Ard Fheis of one of the political parties. Two items in this debate had a direct application to the association's members. One sought to place an embargo on the employment of married women while single women were unemployed. That motion was defeated because it was discriminatory. However, there was no mention of discrimination when the other motion was being discussed. That motion called for the compulsory early retirement of public servants in order to provide jobs for school-leavers. That motion had passed without comment from the party's spokesman on Labour. Could these people not understand — or did they not accept — that we are members of the same community? Ms McGinley asked. That we have the same worries and responsibilities? That we have homes to keep and children to educate? And, indeed, that some had children who were unemployed? Widescale discrimination against a section of the community was not going to cure the evil of unemployment. The lack of charity displayed in the motion was saddening and it was frightening in its implications for trade unionists.

Ms McGinley then dealt with equal pay. She stated that a year had passed since an outrageous decision had been taken to introduce a new form of discrimination, based on one's marital status. The matter was under consideration within the European Community and members could rest assured that the association would not relent in its determination to have the chicanery exposed. It was obvious from the number and wording of motions on the agenda that members supported the executive committee's actions. On the subject of national pay agreements, Ms McGinley recalled that a special delegate conference of the ICTU had recently decided to accept the terms of a draft national pay agreement. The association's delegates had voted in favour.

The association had been in favour of that form of pay settlement since 1970. It had obvious attractions in that members got the same terms as everybody else and at the same time. Some members at the meeting had not been in the service when it had been necessary to wait to see the pattern of awards in other employments: this could take up to twelve months and then another six months or so of negotiations. What the trade union movement must do now, Ms McGinley argued, was to think out whether or not this type of agreement was suitable for or even relevant to present-day needs and thinking. There had been an effort to broaden the form and scope of negotiations. The tripartite conference, a preliminary to the pay negotiations, did not work because the government did not participate as government. What should have emerged from the negotiations was given in the form of a threat; either accept the terms of the pay agreement or there would be no money for the relief of the unemployed and not only would there be no tax reliefs, but there would be an increase in taxation. In the chairman's opinion, we should define what we want not in terms of pay alone, but in terms of society because no group lives in isolation. It was no longer enough to react. It would be difficult because there was a certain distrust, a reluctance to participate without evidence of commitment from the other parties. It would require a united movement and the active participation of all members. For better or worse, society was changing and members must be involved in shaping that change.

In 1978 James P. O'Brien presided at what proved to be the last general meeting of the union. He spoke on pay and taxation, health acts, appointments to the civil service and equal pay. He said that the following year would see discussions on the union's claim to secure an increase in pay for the executive grades. The members had been concerned at the erosion in differentials between those grades and other employments over the past years. James O'Brien spoke of the necessity to maintain substantial differentials between one grade and another in recognition of the different levels of work. In the absence of such differentials, people would refuse to accept promotion.

In Public Service

There must be proper reward for initiative and responsibility. He went on to welcome some increases in personal allowances for income tax purposes. In that section of his address dealing with the health acts, he said that those whose incomes were below the limit for social insurance were covered automatically for limited eligibility purposes under the health acts. Those whose incomes went over that limit could continue their cover by becoming voluntary contributors for social insurance purposes. With the abolition of the income limit, the voluntary contribution category disappeared. However, a new separate income limit had been introduced for health act cover. Those who had existing rights as voluntary contributors in 1974 were allowed to maintain these rights, but those who had gone over the income limit since 1974 had no means of securing health act cover. That situation was a scandal and a discriminatory scandal, too, since the income limit applied only to non-manual workers. The chairman expressed surprise and considerable disappointment at the government's reaction to ICTU representations in the matter.

With regard to equal pay, James O'Brien stated that the previous year had seen the elimination of pay discrimination based on sex or marital status. However, the effective date was 1 July 1977. The correct date in equity was 31 December 1975, the date provided for in the Anti-Discrimination (Pay) Act 1974. The union would continue to support a court case on behalf of a member to secure full retrospection to the correct date.

In 1979 Joseph Smyth presided and welcomed delegates to the first ever annual delegate conference of the union. He said that at the beginning of the year the executive comittee had decided to set up a number of standing sub-committees. Foremost among these was a sub-committee on pay, which rapidly had come to the conclusion that the principle to which the union had always adhered for deciding the remuneration of members — the principle of fair comparison — was the proper one. Yet there were enormous difficulties associated with implementing that principle.

(a) What was the work of the civil service grade?

(b) What grade(s) in outside employment was engaged on similar work?
(c) What were the pay and labour cost conditions of employment of the civil service grade and the outside grade(s).

Joseph Smyth maintained that they must devise a means of getting over the difficulties. The way in which the British civil service had got over the problem was the obvious one: they had established a system that independently assessed the facts. The Pay Research Unit provided independent factual information on the pay and conditions of outside grades that were comparable with civil service grades. When the unit had prepared its report for a particular group of civil servants, it was made available to the parties. At that stage the real negotiations would commence so that agreement could be reached on the rates of pay for the civil service grades. The executive committee had decided to seek the introduction of a system of pay determination based on pay research. With regard to the problem of income tax, Joseph Smyth accepted that a form of taxation was necessary to ensure a fair and equitable distribution of resources throughout the community. The poor, the underprivileged and those unable to care for themselves should be aided out of the public purse. It was accepted that the exchequer should fund schemes for the social and economic advancement of the people as a whole. What was opposed was inequality. The lack of fair play between different sections of the community was unacceptable.

The official side had been concerned during the year about the introduction of a scheme of all-grade, service-wide promotion for the filling of posts in the higher civil service, i.e. assistant principal and upwards and departmental, professional and technical equivalents. The executive committee had decided to indicate to the official side that the union would be prepared to negotiate to produce a system of interdepartmental and cross-grade promotion into the higher civil service between groups that effectively could perform each other's promotional posts. They were not prepared to agree to a system of promotion where some of the promotion posts to which members aspired would be filled by people in groups whose own promotional posts were effectively not open to union members. They would also be telling the official side that any negotiated system would be subject to the approval of the union's membership.

John Daly, who presided in 1980, said that a 30 per cent increase in pay had been claimed, based on fair comparison, and had been lodged at the general council. He also announced that the executive committee had recommended against a claim based on productivity bargaining and that the official side proposals on all-grade service-wide promotion had been rejected. The previous twelve months had seen a substantial increase in the union's membership and he particularly welcomed the members of grades who had recently joined the union — administrative officers, third secretaries and district court clerks. With the influx of new grades, the character of the union was changing. He believed that they should now have a fresh look at their methods of attempting to achieve their aim of trade union rationalisation within the civil service. Points of real concern to the union were the relatively low polls in the ballots on major issues during previous months and the disappointing attendance at two special delegate conferences.

John Daly again presided at the 1981 conference. He drew attention to the result of the arbitration on the union grade claims: an award of 7 per cent and $8\frac{1}{2}$ per cent at the maximum of the HEO and EO scales, plus a reduction of one point in each of the scales. There were consequent increases in the pay of the other grades represented by the union. He commented on the executive committee's decision to lodge a claim for a further increase in the pay of the grades represented by the union. Mr Daly said that, in his view, it was not a new claim but rather an attempt to deal with important and far-reaching difficulties that had arisen in the context of:

(a) the arbitrator's report on the pay claim
(b) increases in the pay of certain other groups within the public service.

It was evident from the arbitration report that the increases awarded were limited by recommendations made in the Devlin report on pay in the higher public service. John Daly maintained that they must not accept that the pay of members could be determined by the use of a report of a review body to which they had had no access. Attacks on the civil service had continued. Such attacks were not limited to pay; pensions and other conditions of employment had been cited as creating a sort of elitist status for the civil servant. The chairman did not consider that members should react to every criticism levelled at them. What they should do was to demonstrate clearly that it was in the interest of every citizen, of all sectors of the community, that the civil service was as efficient as it could possibly be. To achieve this efficiency, there had to be a fair and just reward for effort. More and more the community expected the government to develop and expand its role in economic and social services. On the other hand, there was a demand for a reduction in government expenditure. A balance had to be struck. It was for the government to suggest how that balance could be achieved.

Seán Ó Conail presided in 1982. The conciliation and arbitration scheme, he said, had stood the test of time and had succeeded in securing the confidence of the civil service. It had had to face many strains in the previous year. In the special budget of July 1981, the government had placed an embargo on realistic negotiations under the scheme. Ministers had made statements suggesting that there was something fundamentally wrong with the negotiating system in the public service. There had been suggestions from the Commission on Industrial Relations that the scheme should be scrapped in favour of access to the Labour Court. Seán Ó Conail was not saying that the scheme could not be improved; far from it. He felt strongly that the scheme must be improved and updated if it was to continue to work effectively. The previous year had seen the ending — at least for some time — of the series of national wage agreements that had started in 1970. This presented the public sector unions with a dilemma. They had decided that their interests lay in seeking to negotiate a reasonably acceptable level of settlement covering the year 1982 in advance of the government's budget, which would have the effect of providing for general increases in pay and for a means of resuming negotiations on other cost-increasing claims, as against the embargo introduced in the previous July. The outcome of the negotiations had been recommended by the negotiators, the

In Public Service

public service committee of ICTU and the executive committees of most of the unions, including the CSEU. The recommendations were made without any great degree of enthusiasm, but it was believed that negotiated arrangements were the best that could have been obtained. The executive committee had undertaken to process a claim for grade increases and this claim was awaiting arbitration.

With regard to staffing levels, Seán Ó Conail stated that the union had been deeply concerned about arbitrary measures taken by the government in the budget of July 1981 and in the abortive January budget to restrict staffing numbers in the civil service. The union had opposed these restrictions. In the course of the year, the attacks on the civil service had continued. Civil servants were depicted as paper-pushers, drones, underworked and overpaid. Mr Ó Conail made it clear that the civil service had nothing to be ashamed of and nothing to be afraid of.

Seán Ó Conail again presided in 1983. In his address he said that public expenditure was not some abstract concept unrelated to the ordinary citizen. It was necessary to provide citizens with social and economic services as well as with defence, police and legal services. Expenditure on the main social services — health, education and social welfare — was related to the need to attempt to maintain a civilised society. We should not have a situation where health care was provided only if a person could afford it; where access to education was restricted to an even greater extent, and where the elderly, the widowed, the unemployed, disabled or invalided were required to exist at even lower levels of income.

In order to provide these services, the government had to effect direct income maintenance payments, purchase goods and services, make grants and employ people. The pay of public servants was determined on well-settled principles that had been accepted as meeting two fundamental tests — fairness to the taxpayer as employer and fairness to the public servant as employee. There were frequent assertions that public service pensions were too costly. The actual cost was 2.4 per cent of total government expenditure, or 6.6 per cent of public service pay. Since December 1981, the policy followed by the government was that two vacancies in every three were not filled. This had considerably reduced the number of civil servants.

Mr Ó Conail spoke finally about taxation, contending that the burden of taxation affected the members of the union as much as any other citizen. Members naturally felt very strongly on the issue, but there was no point in reacting to it in a simple-minded way. He said that people had two separate and distinct concerns about taxation. One was the inequity of the system. The Irish Congress of Trade Unions, in its submission to the government, had identified a large number of issues that needed to be dealt with in order to curb evasion and avoidance. The government should respond positively to the submission and ensure that there could be a degree of social harmony in the community since the PAYE sector would not and could not accept the continuation of the inequities, evasions and avoidances in the present system. The other concern was the level of taxation. The trade union movement recognised that the burden of taxation could not be reduced unless public expenditure was cut significantly. Any reduction in public expenditure necessarily would involve cuts in public services and in employment in the service.

Con Ó Donnchu presided at the annual delegate conference in 1984. He was a member of the customs and excise branch of the union and a former president of Comhaltas Cana, which amalgamated with the CSEU in 1979. He opened his address by saying that the fact that he was addressing the conference as president marked an important milestone in the union's history. When, some years before, Comhaltas Cana had taken the bold step of seeking amalgamation with the CSEU, he was aware that each organisation had to place enormous reliance on its collective judgment of the situation and in the good faith of the other party in the negotiations. This entailed certain risks for the CSEU since, to many people, the customs and excise fraternity was an unknown quantity. From the Comhaltas point of view, there was a known loss of autonomy, a possible loss of identity and a decided risk of being submerged in the larger body.

Con Ó Donnchu said that all the new branches that had joined the union as a result of amalgamations were making a definite, measurable and positive contribution. The union was

In Public Service

now stronger as a result of its increased and more diverse membership. He believed that the union should continue carefully along the road of amalgamation and create one strong voice to speak for all within the service.

Mr Ó Donnchu then spoke of the proposed reform of the public service. He mentioned that the Minister for the Public Service had spoken of his plans on a number of occasions. The union had made a submission to the minister on the question of changes. It had been assured that consultation would take place before changes were made. Members welcomed the opportunity to discuss such changes if they had the effect of improving the service to the public and if they made the service a better place in which to work. Con Ó Donnchu pointed out that the majority of the changes had come about as a result of action by the union, rather than through any management enlightenment.

Noel Doyle presided at the 7th annual delegate conference of the union in 1985. He said that the combination of effective pay cuts, the embargo on the appointments to vacated posts, the drying up of promotion opportunities, the uncertainty over new promotion procedures and the hostility of their political masters had done serious damage to civil service morale. This damage had led to a growing apathy. The government's delaying tactics over the reappointment of the chairman of the Arbitration Board were a serious attack on the whole scheme of conciliation and arbitration. Without an independent arbitrator, there would be no scheme. Without the scheme, there would be no agreed procedure for negotiations. Without agreed procedures, there would be industrial relations anarchy.

Speaking on equality, Mr Doyle said that, with the removal of the marriage bar in 1974 and the passing of equality legislation in 1977, the number of women in middle and higher level posts in the civil service was expected to increase. The expectations had not been fulfilled. Men still held a disproportionate number of posts at all save the clerical level.

On the issue of Irish bonus marks, Noel Doyle said that, with the increased use of competitions for the filling of posts at higher levels, the issue of Irish bonus marks became more important. The government had stated that its aim was to get the best person for the job and yet it maintained a system that deliberately distorted the results of competitions. The bonus marks system was claimed to be a measure that was generally supportive of the Irish language. Mr Doyle believed the opposite was true. The bonus mark system bred a cynicism about the language that had become ingrained in the civil service.

Trade union rationalisation had been the union's policy for many years. Rationalisation led to greater strength because both human and financial resources were pooled. More time could be spent on the union's real job — safeguarding and promoting the legitimate interests of members, rather than in disputes between unions. It was easier to resolve disputes between people within the same organisation than between groups in different organisations.

Noel Doyle again presided the next year. He said that the union had come through a bruising encounter with the government over the reappointment of the arbitrator. The service-wide decision to strike had finally brought the government to its senses. In 1984 the threat of a strike had been sufficient to have the arbitrator reappointed. In 1985 they had to carry out the threat and 15 October was a day that would go down in the annals of not only the CSEU but of the trade union movement generally. The entire public service had come out in opposition to the government's interference with the agreed negotiation machinery and its derisory pay proposals. The union had engaged in the first all-out strike in its history and had showed that it could take decisive action when its vital and legitimate interests were threatened. The scheme of temporary clerical trainees was a cynical abuse of young people. Ideally, it should have given people a sound training and experience in administrative work, which undoubtedly would have enhanced a person's job prospects. However, when the trainees were first recruited, no resources were made available to train them properly. There was not even a plan about how they should be trained. Pressure from all the civil service unions brought about some formal training, but even that level of training was totally inadequate. In practice the scheme was merely a device to employ cheap labour to plug gaps caused by the job embargo.

In Public Service

The scheme of job-sharing was welcomed by the union and was recommended to members where circumstances warranted. However, the recruitment of people to job-sharing posts was a practice that they vehemently opposed. It was one thing for two people in full-time employment to decide, after proper consideration of all the facts, that job-sharing was suitable for them. It was quite different to tell a school-leaver that he or she could have half a job or nothing.

Noel Doyle said that the executive committee had again examined the issue of the under-representation of women in the higher civil service i.e. assistant principal and above. Although women constituted approximately one-third of the higher executive officer grade, their number at assistant principal level was nothing like that. In 1981 approximately 17 per cent of the assistant principal grade were women and this had increased to 19 per cent in 1984. This was still a long way from the 33 per cent expected.

Finally, Mr Doyle announced that the move to new premises at 30 Merrion Square would take place in the summer. The building was large enough for the union's current needs and had sufficient extra space to cover expectations for the future. The increased level of subscription, introduced to finance the purchase of the new premises, would cease from January 1987.

Eoin Faherty presided in 1987. He began by stating that, in the budget, the government had indicated that it was making no provision for a further general increase in public service pay, despite the fact that the 25th pay round had expired during the year. The government had indicated also that no special increases in pay or in any other conditions would be met. This indicated that the government was not prepared to allow public servants to be paid at rates comparable to other employees and that it intended to breach the agreement which provided that claims could be processed. The union grade claim was one such claim. In the previous six years the civil service had been reduced in size significantly. Thousands fewer people were employed in the civil service than at the start of the decade. The methods chosen by the government to produce these reductions had varied from completely arbitrary arrangements for filling only a proportion of vacancies to the ultimate decision not to fill vacant posts. In effect, there was a

1970-1990

continuous decline in the level of service to the public, a continuous decline in the number of job opportunities for young people and a sharp decline in morale in the civil service as the prospect of promotion became progressively more remote. Eoin Faherty stressed that the union would continue to further a policy of trade union rationalisation and he hoped that in the not too distant future it would see a greater emphasis on a united trade union structure within the civil service. The union had made a significant contribution to the formulation of equality guidelines. It was dismayed at the government's attitude to the claim for creche facilities.

The official side had to realise that the scheme of lateral mobility would be a failure unless it actively pursued the right of executive officers to be involved in the staff exchanges.

Mr Faherty said, in conclusion, that it was some twenty years since the ICTU had first raised the issue of civil rights for civil servants. The government's response had been almost entirely negative. The union had supported the efforts of those employed in Government Communications Headquarters in Britain to maintain their right to remain members of free trade unions.

Eoin Faherty again presided at the 1988 conference. He said that the programme for national recovery, which was the culmination of discussions between the social partners, contained a series of commitments by the government that were vital for the country as a whole and for employees in the public sector and members of the union in particular. It included specific provisions for pay increases over a three-year period, but even more important was the commitment to maintain arbitration and to provide a means for dealing with the arbitration finding on the union wage claim. The programme also contained a commitment to tax reform and to specific job creation in matters such as marine, tourism, forestry and telecommunications.

The union continued its efforts to promote full and effective equality for men and women. The equality guidelines agreed in 1986 were being monitored by a joint management/union committee. Agreement had been reached with the Department of Finance on the provision of an education/counselling programme for breast and cervical cancers. The union's special

In Public Service

training course for women members proved successful and it was intended to continue with such courses.

Mr Faherty said that the government had decided to extend the terms of the scheme of early retirement offered earlier to health service workers to employees in the public service who were working in offices with surplus staff. It was later decided to widen the scope of the early retirement scheme to staff in the public service who were over fifty. The result had been:

- posts that fell vacant were not being filled
- work levels were not falling, with the result that a diminishing number of staff were expected to carry out increased workloads
- there were no career prospects for members, with the result that morale had reached an all-time low
- no compensation was being paid for redistributed work among staff at the same level or assigned to lower grade staff
- despite trenchant opposition from the unions, only a small number of posts were being filled and less than half of these were being filled in the normal way.

The remainder and all posts arising as a consequence would be filled by the redeployment of staff in the civil service and exchequer-funded agencies where there were redundancies.

The executive committee had decided on a comprehensive five-point plan of action to meet that situation:

1. Members were not to take on extra or higher duties except under protest and pending discussions between management and the local branch. If no solution was found, members could be instructed to refuse to carry out those duties. Industrial action by members of the branch could follow disciplinary action by management.
2. A comprehensive survey to establish the precise impact of the reduction in staff on workloads of members and services to the public, ministers and elected representatives.
3. A joint approach to the Department of Finance by all the unions in the civil service with a view to securing agreement on a planned approach to a restoration of the normal filling of vacant posts.
4. A concerted media campaign to project and promote the extent of the problems facing members because of government policies.

5. A broad approach by the unions in the civil service on the filling of posts by redeployment of redundant staff with a view to securing an assurance that the arrangements being implemented despite union opposition were exceptional and had a limited lifespan.

Dave Thomas presided at the eleventh annual delegate conference in 1989. He said that the single most noticeable feature of the year had been the lack of morale in the civil service and he considered that this absence of morale was due to the following:

1. The arbitrator's postponement of the 1987 pay award.
2. The continued embargo on the filling of vacant posts.
3. The redeployment of redundant personnel from state-funded agencies.
4. The effects of early retirement on staff levels.
5. The government's chaotic approach to the decentralisation programme.

Mr Thomas stated that, while the government had got great mileage out of the effects on the economy of the Programme for National Recovery, this could not have been achieved without the co-operation of the trade unions, particularly the public service unions. Indeed, many felt that the programme had been carried out on the backs of the public service, which had paid dearly in terms of pay and conditions of service. Nonetheless, the unions supported the programme because they believed that it was the only possible agreement that would work in the prevailing circumstances. They had shown that they were willing and able to reach sensible and intelligent compromises in the interests of themselves and the rest of Irish society. They then expected the government to show its commitment to the programme.

Mr Thomas went on to refer to the statement of the Minister for Finance that he intended to discuss with the ICTU the extension of PRSI in the public service. He said that public servants paid 8.16 per cent of pay for pensions and that the result of full PRSI would mean that public servants would have two pensions instead of one and that the exchequer would have to contribute about £200 million a year extra to the

In Public Service

Social Insurance Fund. Public servants would be forced to pay exorbitant contributions for benefits that they neither sought nor needed. Mr Thomas expressed pleasure at being in a position to announce that the members of the Irish Customs and Excise Union had decided to amalgamate with the PSEU. He extended a warm welcome to the union's general secretary, Martin McDonald, who would become an assistant general secretary of the PSEU, to Dick Beamish, president, Joe Keane, vice-president, and Declan Burke, deputy general secretary of the ICEU, who would become officers and members of the national committee of the new Customs and Excise Group, which would be the largest branch of the union.

EQUALITY

The Commission on the Status of Women was established by the government on 31 March 1970, with the following terms of reference:

To examine and report on the status of women in Irish society, to make recommendations on the steps necessary to ensure participation of women on equal terms and conditions with men in the political, social, cultural and economic life of the country and to indicate the implications generally — including the estimated cost — of such recommendations.

The Commission was chaired by Dr Thekla J. Beere, former secretary of the Department of Transport and Power. On 16 June 1970, the Minister for Finance requested the commission to prepare, as soon as possible, an interim report dealing with the question of equal pay, with particular reference to the public sector. An interim report on equal pay was presented to the Minister for Finance in August 1971 and was published two months later.

In 1969 the Civil Service General Council Staff Panel and the Association of Higher Civil Servants agreed on a claim for equal pay. The government decided not to concede the claim but to defer a decision, pending a report from the Commission on the Status of Women. The association, along with many other organisations, objected to this, but asked the commission to examine the matter as soon as possible. The association made a detailed written submission to the commission.

The Interim Report of the Commission on Equal Pay recommended as follows:

(a) Equal pay should be accepted and implemented.
(b) All women on sex-differentiated pay should be brought on to the man's pay.
(c) All people on 'single' scales that were differentiated on a marriage basis should be brought on to the 'married man's' pay.
(d) Equal pay should be introduced on a phased basis.
(e) The phasing should be annual increases in the women/single pay of 5 per cent of corresponding man/married pay.
(f) All phasing should be completed by 31 December 1977.
(g) The commencement date for phasing should be decided by the Employer-Labour Conference on its review of the national agreement.

The executive committee of the association decided to accept the commission's recommendation. It considered that the most pressing issues were securing acceptance of the principles of the report and ensuring that the phasing would begin as soon as possible. To this end, the executive committee was keen that the government should accept the report in principle and sought to ensure this through the ICTU.

The question of the employment of married women was discussed at the 1971 annual general meeting when the following motion was adopted:

That the Annual General Meeting favours the removal of the ban on the employment of married women subject to the negotiation of satisfactory conditions — an indispensable condition being the implementation of the claim for Equal Pay for Equal Work — and instructs the Executive Committee to draft proposals on the details of the matter to be submitted to a future General Meeting of the Association.

A special general meeting on 27 June 1972 adopted the following as association policy on the employment of married women:

(a) *Legislation*
The legislative prohibition on the employment of married

In Public Service

women in the Civil Service Regulation Act, 1956 should be removed.

(b) *Conditions of service*
Conditions of service of existing staff, requiring them to resign on marriage, should be removed. New staff should not have such a requirement in their conditions of service.

(c) *Circumstances in which married women could be employed*
   (i) A woman who is in the public service and who becomes married should not be required to resign on her marriage.
   (ii) A married woman should not be debarred from competing for a post in the civil service provided she fulfils the other requirements of age, competence, and so on.
   (iii) A woman should have the right to take special leave without pay and to resume duty as set out in (d) below.
   (iv) Married women who were civil servants until their resignation on marriage (on or after 1 January 1972) should have the right to return to the civil service in their former grade on the basis of a quota of the vacancies in the grade, such quota to be agreed in respect of each individual grade over the whole service. The order of return would be determined by the seniority of the women before their resignation.

(d) *Circumstances of return of a woman to the civil service*
A woman who at the time of marriage is employed in the civil service should have the right to take special leave without pay on marriage or on the birth or adoption of a child. She would not be paid or receive superannuation credit for the period she was on such special leave. On return to the civil service from such leave, a married woman would have the right to return to her own grade.

(e) *Marriage gratuity*
   (i) A marriage gratuity should be payable as before to any woman who resigns from the civil service on marriage.
   (ii) A marriage gratuity should be payable to any woman who resigns from the civil service within one year after marriage or on the birth or adoption of the first child after marriage. Such gratuity should be based on pre-marriage service and current rates of pay.
   (iii) A marriage gratuity should not be payable to a woman who is on special leave as defined in (d) above.
   (iv) If a married woman returns to the civil service sometime after her resignation and has already been paid a gratuity, she should have the following options:

(1) Repay the marriage gratuity immediately and be entitled to a full pension (based on actual service).
(2) Repay the marriage gratuity over a period of years and be entitled to a full pension (based on actual service).
(3) Repay the marriage gratuity by deduction from her retirement lump sum where payable.
(4) Do not repay the marriage gratuity and be entitled to a pension based on actual service exclusive of the service in respect of which she was paid the marriage gratuity, i.e. a maximum deduction of 12 years from actual service.

The arrangements set out above were to have effect from the date of the first phase of equal pay.

The Civil Service General Council Staff Panel, at a meeting on 18 January 1973, adopted the following as policy:

(a) The staff side is not opposed to the abolition of the marriage bar.
(b) The staff side feels that the marriage bar should be abolished on the effective date of the legislation abolishing the bar but not before 1 June 1973 (the date of the first phase on equal pay).
(c) The staff side feels that married women who resign on marriage before the date in (b) should have no rights to return to the civil service other than by open competition.
(d) Married women should not be afforded special leave without pay for reasons other than maternity leave.
(e) A married woman should be entitled to maternity leave.
(f) Marriage gratuities would be payable to a woman who resigns on marriage within two years or on the birth or adoption of the first child after her marriage. Only pre-marriage service would count towards the reckoning of the marriage gratuity.
(g) A woman who leaves the civil service having taken a marriage gratuity and who returns would have a choice of:
  (i) Repaying her marriage gratuity and being allowed to reckon her pre-marriage service for superannuation purposes.
  (ii) Not repaying her marriage gratuity and not being allowed to reckon her pre-marriage service for superannuation.
(h) Married women who are presently employed on a contract with a daily fee payment should not have their contracts renewed on the expiry of the current contracts. There should be no new contracts.

In Public Service

The ban on employment of married women was abolished in July 1973. Discussions on consequential changes covered such matters as maternity leave and marriage gratuities.

Discussions on the 14th round of the national pay agreement in 1972 took into account the findings of the Commission on the Status of Women. The essential feature of the agreement for members of the association was the provision that enabled discussions to take place on claims for reducing the differential between the married and single or male and female scales by $17\frac{1}{2}$ per cent of the difference between those scales with effect from 1 June 1973. The terms of the agreement were implemented throughout the civil service. As a result of strong pressure from the Irish Congress of Trade Unions, the government decided to provide by law for full equal pay not later than 31 December 1975. This was provided for in the Anti-Discrimination Pay Act 1974. It was a considerable improvement on the corresponding date in 1977 that had been recommended by the Commission on the Status of Women. The 1974 national agreement made provision for a minimum equal pay increase of $33\frac{1}{3}$ per cent of the difference between scales for men and for women. The agreement also provided for trade unions and employers in individual employments to negotiate alternative arrangements for the introduction of equal pay. Operating under this clause of the national agreement, the staff side and the official side negotiated an equal pay increase of 50 per cent of the difference between the scales, to take effect from 1 December 1974.

On 17 December 1975, in the course of a Dáil debate on the adjournment, the Taoiseach, Liam Cosgrave, announced that the government had decided to amend the Anti-Discrimination (Pay) Act 1974 to provide for the position of industries that would experience unemployment as a result of the implementation of equal pay. He said that the Minister for Finance and the Public Service, Richie Ryan, would be meeting the public service unions to discuss equal pay in the public sector. On 19 December 1975, the executive council of the ICTU issued a statement expressing shock at the government's blatant repudiation of its repeated assurances that equal pay would operate from 1 January 1976, and of its obligations under the EC directive on pay discrimination against women. On 23

1970-1990

December 1975, a meeting was arranged between the Minister for the Public Service and the public services committee of the Irish Congress of Trade Unions. The union's general secretary and deputy general secretary were present. At a prior meeting of the committee the following statement had been agreed:

> The Public Services Committee of the Irish Congress of Trade Unions met today, 23rd December, 1975, to consider the invitation of the Minister for the Public Service to meet him to discuss equal pay. The Committee decided to meet the Minister and to make it clear to him that the Committee could not deviate from the policy of the Irish Congress of Trade Unions on equal pay and would not acquiesce to any proposal to amend the existing legislation or agree to any proposal to defer the final step towards the implementation of equal pay as provided for under existing legislation. The Committee also decided to inform the Minister that further discussion on this issue would not serve any useful purpose.

At the meeting with Richie Ryan, he asked for the public services committee to agree to a deferment of equal pay in the public service. He was told that the committee would not agree to any such deferment and that further discussions would serve no useful purpose. The committee asked Mr Ryan to bring the committee's views to the attention of the government with a view to getting it to reverse its decision and implement equal pay in the public service as from 31 December, as was provided for in the 1974 act. Subsequently, a considerable volume of public agitation developed against the government's proposal. This included a mass meeting in the Mansion House in Dublin on 15 January 1976. The meeting was organised by a group of trade unionists and members of women's organisations, assisted by the union's chairman, general secretary and deputy general secretary. The meeting was chaired by Matt Griffin of the Irish National Teachers' Organisation, then president of the ICTU. The speakers were Barry Desmond, TD, Senator Evelyn Owens, Leas-Chathaoirleach of the Senate, Senator Mary Robinson, Sylvia Meehan, John Carroll, vice-president of the ICTU, Donal Nevin, assistant general secretary of the ICTU, and Dan Murphy, general secretary of the union. Councillor Ruairi Quinn deputised for the lord mayor.

In Public Service

On 21 January 1976, the government issued the following statement:

On 23 December last, the Minister for the Public Service, Mr Richie Ryan, T.D., met the Public Services Committee of the Irish Congress of Trade Unions and asked them to agree, in the prevailing economic and financial stringencies, to enter into discussions on modifications on the progress towards equal pay. Regrettably, the Committee declined to participate in such discussions. In the circumstances, the Government has come to the following decisions affecting the Public Service. The Government has decided to implement the abolition of sex discrimination in Public Service pay from the beginning of 1976. Arising out of this decision, all single women will be paid the same as single men. All married women will be paid the same as married men. A widow will be paid the same as a widower. . . .

On the following day the Irish Congress of Trade Unions issued the following statement:

The Officers of Congress condemn the astonishing decision announced by the Government not to implement equal pay in the public service and to amend the Anti-Discrimination (Pay) Act in regard to equal pay in the private sector. The Government in removing sex discrimination in the public service had introduced new pay discrimination as between single and married women and between married women and single men. That is blatantly in conflict with the acceptance by the Government of the Report of the Commission on the Status of Women and of its commitment under successive National Pay Agreements which specifically included under the implementation of equal pay, the abolition of marriage-differential rates. The introduction of pay discrimination in the form now proposed by the government is entirely unacceptable to trade unions and Congress. Congress wishes to make it quite clear that it will remain wholly opposed to the Government's proposals and will make formal representations to the EEC Commission against the government's attempt to maintain pay discrimination in the public and private sectors.

A meeting of the executive council of the ICTU on 30 January 1976 decided to make a formal complaint to the EC Commission, alleging that the Irish government had breached Community law.

1970-1990

At a meeting of the public services committee on 2 February 1976, the question of industrial action was discussed, but it became clear that there would not be general support for such action. The committee then decided to accept an invitation from the minister to meet him. The meeting between Richie Ryan and representatives of the public services committee took place on 22 March. The committee advanced the view that full equal pay (including the abolition of marriage differentiation) should operate from 31 December 1975. The minister indicated that the government considered that its decision of 21 January 1976 (to place the married person on the married man scale in the case of marriage differentiated categories) complied with EC obligations. The ICTU complaint to the EC about marriage differentiation had placed the view on test. The minister said that the government remained dedicated to the implementation of equal pay but did not see that this was immediately possible without further taxation or further borrowing — neither of which was acceptable. The government would give equal pay priority attention when the economic and budgetary situation improved. The union's executive committee, at a meeting on 26 April 1976, considered an opinion that had been received from Donal Barrington SC. The opinion envisaged that the union might finance an action by a member against the Minister for the Public Service seeking a declaration that she was underpaid in accordance with the terms of the 1974 Anti-Discrimination (Pay) Act. It was agreed that the union should indemnify an executive officer against the costs she might incur in taking a case in the courts. It was agreed that the woman who would take the action should be a person who had come into marriage differentiated rates of pay from a competition, other than the competitions by which single men had come into marriage differentiation. It was expected that the case would come up for hearing during 1977. Meanwhile, the ICTU received a letter, dated 24 June 1976, from J. Degombe, director general for Social Affairs in the EC Commission:

I should like to refer to my letter of 17 March, 1976, acknowledging yours of 23 February, 1976, addressed to Mr. President F. X. Ortoli with which was enclosed an official complaint

In Public Service

by the Irish Congress of Trade Unions against the Irish Government, which, in your opinion, is not respecting the principle of equal pay in the Public Service. In my acknowledgement, I informed you that the matter was being examined but this has, however, taken longer than anticipated. The delay is due to special circumstances which, as you are aware, arose on the one hand from the Irish Government's application — which the Commission rejected — for authorisation to derogate, pursuant to Article 135 of the Act of Accession, from the rules of equal pay between men and women, and on the other hand, from the importance and relevance of the pending judgement of the Court of Justice of the European Communities in case 43/75 (Gabrielle Defreune v. S .A. Sabena). My Department and the Legal Service of the Commission have carefully studied the situation as described by you and I have requested the Irish Authorities for their observations. I shall naturally keep you informed on developments in this matter.

The election manifesto of the national coalition government for the June 1977 general election stated:

To complete the process of removing discrimination against women, equal pay, including the elimination of the marriage differential, will be brought into effect in two stages — the first retrospectively from 1 January last and the second during 1978.

Subsequently, Richie Ryan, in a statement published on 13 June (three days before the election) said:

. . . that arrangements are being made for the immediate payment back to 1 January, 1977, of half the remaining difference between married and single rates under the marriage-differentiated salary system in the Public Service. This means that, by the end of this month, up to 80% of the original differential will have been eliminated. On 31 December, 1977, the balance will be removed so that the system of marriage differentiation will be brought to an end. Equal pay will then have been achieved in the Public service within the time scale recommended by the Commission on the Status of Women.

The public services committee issued its own statement on 14 June, asserting that the government statement that equal pay would be introduced during 1977 was unacceptable. It reiterated its view that full equal pay (including the payment of married and single people on the same rates) was outstanding as from 31 December 1975.

1970-1990

The general election led to a change of government, and the assistant general secretary of Congress, Donal Nevin, wrote to the new Minister for the Public Service, George Colley, seeking an early indication from the new Fianna Fáil government that it proposed to implement equal pay fully in the public service with effect from 31 December 1975. The minister replied through his private secretary on 27 July:

The Tánaiste and the Minister for the Public Service, Mr. George Colley, T.D., has asked me to refer further to your letter of 11 July, 1977, about equal pay in the Public Service. The Tánaiste has announced that the government, in fulfilment of the commitment in relation to equal pay, given before they took office, have decided to eliminate the system of marriage differentiation in public service pay scales with effect from 1 July, 1977. Instructions for payment are being issued. In regard to the broader question raised in your letter the Tánaiste has asked me to say that in present circumstances it would not be possible for the Government to enter into any further commitments in this area.

The executive council of Congress considered the letter on 29 July and issued a statement rejecting the government's position and seeking an urgent meeting with the Tánaiste in the hope that the question of equal pay in the public service could be resolved on the basis of justice and principle and without recourse to the courts.

It was not until 20 April 1978 that George Colley met representatives of Congress. Representing Congress were Donal Nevin and C. Devine, general secretary of the Teachers' Union of Ireland and Dan Murphy, general secretary of the union. They urged the minister to agree to pay the arrears of equal pay in the period 31 December 1975 to 30 June 1977 (full equal pay having been introduced unilaterally from 1 July 1977) and he agreed to consider the representations.

In September 1978, the Department of the Public Service notified Congress that the Tánaiste had authorised them to enter into discussions with a view to seeing the possibility of negotiating proposals on the outstanding problems on the subject of marriage-differentiation. A number of meetings took place between representatives of the executive council and the Department of the Public Service. The Congress representatives were again Donal Nevin and C. Devine, G. Quigley, general secretary of the INTO and Dan Murphy, the union's general secretary. On 13 October the following agreed proposal emerged from the discussions:

Each person who served in the period 31 December 1975 to 30 June 1977, in a position the pay scales for which were, up to 1 July 1977, differentiated on a marriage basis will be paid a gratuity equivalent to the amount of additional scale salary which he would have received in that period if marriage-differentiation had been eliminated on 31 December 1975. The amount due in respect of each person involved will be calculated, divided into three equal instalments annually, the first payment being made on 1 July 1979.

The agreement also included proposals in respect of children's allowances, marriage lump sums, superannuation and widows' allowances. It was agreed that the High Court action, due for hearing on 2 November 1978, would not proceed and that Congress would withdraw its complaint to the EC Commission.

During 1979/80 the union lodged claims for the following:

(a) indefinite special leave for family circumstances
(b) creche facilities
(c) an increase in maternity leave
(d) leave associated with adoption.

Following the coming into operation of the Maternity Protection Act, which provided for a statutory scheme of paid maternity leave, a claim was lodged at general council for an increase of two weeks in the maternity leave allowance, from 12 to 14 weeks. Agreement was eventually reached. The details of the arrangements applicable to women civil servants going on maternity leave were set out in Department of Public Service circular 27/81. The claim for special leave for family purposes was deferred for further consideration pending the publication of the report to the Minister for Labour of the Working Party on Child Care Facilities for Working Parents.

The union's 1982 annual delegate conference discussed the possibility of paternity leave. The executive committee carried out an examination of the position in respect of comparable grades in other employments and concluded that no case could be made for paternity leave.

1970-1990

In 1983 the official side made proposals on the matter of job-sharing, but the executive committee expressed grave reservations about some aspects of them. The union decided to support the principle of job-sharing, subject to the negotiation of satisfactory conditions. In November the staff panel entered into discussions with the official side without prior commitment and on the basis that any scheme of job-sharing should only be introduced after union-management agreement. In the following year the union established a special sub-committee on family and equality issues. Its members for 1984/85 were: Robin Hanon, Brenda Feeney, Paul Murphy, Pauline Jones, Colin Stokes and the union officers. A general council sub-committee was set up to review employment opportunities. The long-standing claim for indefinite special leave for family commitments culminated in an agreement at general council on 18 April 1984 on the scheme of career breaks for civil servants. (Agreed report 1011 refers.) In accordance with a motion passed at the 1984 annual delegate conference, the union conducted a survey of male members in June 1984, to establish the extent to which they would avail of a scheme of paid paternity leave. The survey showed the average number of days taken in connection with birth at 7.29. The claim for ten days' paternity leave was being discussed at the Working Party on Child Care facilities.

With regard to creche facilities, the official side undertook to carry out an examination of the facilities operated in other employments. In May 1986, the Minister for the Public Service, Ruairi Quinn, announced the setting up of a creche facility that would be jointly open to staff of the Department of Labour and AnCO, the Industrial Training Authority. The staff side was concerned about this development because it was clear that the terms and costs of operating the creche mainly had been settled in discussions between the Federated Workers' Union of Ireland and AnCO, with the danger that the resultant terms would be imposed on the civil service and, secondly, because negotiations were still in progress at general council on the claim for the whole civil service. Accordingly, the secretary of the staff side wrote to the minister seeking a meeting with him to discuss the provision of creche facilities generally in the civil service, and the manner of the announcement of the setting up of a creche in the Department of Labour. The minister replied as follows:

> I refer to your letter concerning the provision of creche facilities in the Civil Service. As you may be aware, I have directed that a feasibility study be carried out on the provision of creche facilites in the Department of Labour/AnCO. As this is still in progress it would not be appropriate for me to enter into discussions on this matter at this stage.

The first union seminar on equality was held in 1984. Its purpose was to inform branch representatives of the action being taken by the executive committee on various issues to do with family and equality, and to hear suggestions from the delegates as to how matters might be improved. Arising from a motion adopted at the 1985 annual delegate conference, the union had discussions with the Civil Service Training Centre with a view to ensuring that equality issues were covered on all general management training courses which were provided for members of the union and higher grades. The official side undertook to include equality matters in the new course on personnel management which would cover all the management grades from assistant secretary downwards. It also undertook to speak to departmental training officers about the courses run internally, with a view to including equality issues where appropriate, and would make it clear to the Institute of Public Administration, which organised certain 'skills' training for the civil service, that equality issues should be included in such courses as manpower planning. The union also asked that a specific individual be nominated in each government department/office, to be responsible for:

(1) The review and evaluation of progress towards equality of opportunity for women in the civil service.
(2) The annual reporting of progress.

Early in 1985 the union met representatives of the Department of the Public Service and the Civil Service Commission. The union asked for an arrangement to ensure that:

(a) Interview boards were composed of a proper balance of men and women.

1970-1990

(b) Members of the boards were properly trained in objective interviewing.

(c) Equal treatment would be afforded to all candidates who appear before the boards.

(d) Questions that had a discriminatory connection would not be asked at interviews.

The official side agreed to issue guidelines to departments. These would be in conformity with the staff side's request, except that (a) would say 'where possible' and (b) would exempt from training people who had built up expertise in interviewing. They would consult with the Civil Service Training Centre before issuing guidelines.

The union issued a leaflet on sexual harassment and held its first training course for women members in conjunction with the ICTU in April 1985. The course was attended by eighteen women members from twelve branches.

In 1986 the official side issued a statement on equal opportunities policy and guidelines for the civil service. The statement covered equal opportunity policy, encouragement of equality, the Employment Equality Agency's code of practice for the elimination of discrimination on the basis of sex or marital status, recruitment, placement and mobility, training, promotion, combining work and domestic responsibilities, the use of non-discriminatory language, sexual harassment and provision for the monitoring of the policy.

UNION ORGANISATION

The following were officials of the union:

General secretary	Daniel Murphy	
Deputy general secretary	Garry Sweeney retired 30 October 1983	Post created at 1971 AGM
	Tom McKevitt from 1 November 1983	

In Public Service

Assistant general secretary   Brian Fitzpatrick   post created at 1975 annual conference (July 1975 - May 1977)
John Daly (May 1977 - July 1978)
Michael Foster (July 1978 - December 1983)
Tom Geraghty (December 1983 to date)
Bill Hannigan July 1987 to date (this is a new post)
Martin McDonald (on ICEU merger)

The membership of the association on 31 December 1969 stood at 1,538. Ten years later, the membership had risen to over 4,000, and with the application of the agreement on transfer of engagements with the Irish Customs and Excise Union, the membership at 31 December 1989 exceeded 5,000. The actual membership in 1988 represented 94 per cent of the potential membership. The increase in the membership is reflected in the development of the union's organisation.

The annual general meeting held on 23 February 1971 amended the association's rules to permit the appointment of a deputy general secretary. When the meeting resumed on 23 March, the chairman announced that the executive committee had appointed Garry Sweeney from the Department of Agriculture branch to the post. The association discontinued its affiliation to the Irish Conference of Professional and Service Associations and concentrated its representations on the wider issues through the Irish Congress of Trade Unions.

At the 1972 ICTU conference in Galway, the general secretary was elected to the executive council of Congress for the first time. In continuation of its interest in the wide trade union movement, the association affiliated to the Dublin Trades Union Council in 1974 and in the same year affiliated to the Irish Labour History Society. It already had affiliated to the People's College, the trade union Adult Education Association. The 1975 annual general meeting approved the creation of the

1970-1990

post of assistant general secretary. Brian Fitzpatrick, an executive officer in the Department of Labour, was appointed to the post from 1 July 1975.

About this time the association moved into new accommodation at 109 Lower Baggot Street. Then commenced the organisation of schemes that were to provide benefits to members. The original scheme administered by the union — family income benefit scheme — ceased to have relevance with the advent of the Civil Service Widows and Children Scheme, later the Spouses and Children's Scheme. The series of new schemes included the income continuance plan, motor insurance, loan facilities, house insurance, discount scheme and a scheme of additional voluntary contributions for superannuation purposes. At this time, too, the union commenced its programme of education courses for branch officers. The 1975 annual general meeting considered motions advocating the deduction of subscriptions from salary. One of these motions, submitted by the executive committee, was adopted. The arrangements under which civil service trade union subscriptions could be deducted were agreed with the Department of Finance.

The council of the union ceased to exist at the end of 1978 and from 1 January 1979 was replaced by the advisory and organisation committee.

During 1979 the membership of the union increased to over 4,000 with the addition of administrative officers, third secretaries, district court clerks and higher officers of Customs and Excise from Comhaltas Cana. The social welfare officers entered into membership on 1 January 1981.

In the late 1970s unions in the public service became concerned that, as exempted bodies under the Trade Union Act, they did not enjoy the protection of the 1906 Trade Disputes Act. The act provided protection for members, officials, executive committees and for union funds in the event of a trade dispute. The act was defined as involving 'workmen'. The expression was interpreted by the courts to mean that the act applied only in circumstances where the employees were employed by a person engaged in a profit or loss concern. This excluded the public service. The government made a commitment under the terms of the 1980 National Understanding to amend the 1906 act so as to extend its protection to those workers excluded from its scope. The executive committee decided to explore the possibility of securing a negotiation licence which was necessary to comply with the conditions set out in the trade union acts. It was also necessary to become a registered trade union with the Registrar of Friendly Societies. Following correspondence with the registrar, the required amendments to rules were adopted at the 1983 annual delegate conference. An application for a negotiation licence was granted in the high court in May 1984. The decision to secure a negotiation licence became of special importance when the union decided to represent members who had transferred to the new semi-state bodies and companies. The decision to represent these transferred members posed a problem relating to the possibility of recognition being extended to non-civil service unions to represent civil servants.

Following discussions, the de facto position emerged that the official side was prepared to continue to recognise unions as representing civil servants, even though their membership extended beyond the civil service. All the unions that had recognition on behalf of grades in the former Department of Posts and Telegraphs were granted recognition by the boards of An Post and Telecom Eireann in respect of the same grades. This precedent was followed in the cases of further transfers of civil service staff to non-civil service bodies. During 1985/86 the executive committee considered the position in respect of the union at official level. They noted that, while the membership of the union had increased by 70 per cent since 1975 and although the scope of the union's field of organisation had risen significantly in that time, there had been no increase in the number of officials employed full-time by the union. The executive committee decided that the union's entire organisation — in so far as it related to the pressure placed at head office — needed to be thoroughly examined. A report based on this examination was to be made to the 1987 annual delegate conference. It was decided in the meantime to establish a temporary position of negotiating/organising official for a period of eighteen months. At the end of that period it was envisaged that the report to 1987 conference would have resulted in changes in the organisation of the union that would render another official unnecessary, or if not, another post of assistant general secretary would be considered. The executive committee decided to appoint Billy Hannigan to the temporary position and he took up duty on 6 January 1986. The 1987 conference decided to create an additional post of assistant general secretary and Mr Hannigan was appointed to it.

In October 1981, a special delegate conference of the union was convened for the express purpose of amending Rule 10(a) of the rules of the union. The executive committee hoped that the amendment, if adopted, would greatly assist the union in purchasing, as an investment, bigger and better office accommodation. The motion to amend the rules did not receive the necessary two-third's majority. The rule was subsequently amended in October 1982. The new rule provided that 25 per cent of all subscriptions should be placed in a separate premises account to accumulate capital to acquire premises to be owned by the unions. In 1983 the union left 109 Lower Baggot Street and secured an interest in the leasehold of 41 Upper Mount Street.

In November 1986 the union ceased to rent the premises in Upper Mount Street. The purchase of new premises at 30 Merrion Square had been completed in September 1986, and the union took up occupation at its present premises on 1 November.

The 1987 annual delegate conference adopted a new rule to provide for the granting of honorary life membership of the union; not more that one such award was to be made in any one year. The executive committee decided that the first person to be honoured under the rule would be the former deputy general secretary of the union, Garry Sweeney. A formal presentation was made at the 1988 annual delegate conference. At the 1989 conference Seán O'Conail, a former president of the union, was presented with a certificate of honorary life membership.

TRADE UNION RATIONALISATION

At the beginning of the twentieth century there were less than 50,000 trade unionists in the whole of Ireland. Since then the number has multiplied tenfold. There were about 500,000 members of the 70 unions in the Republic of Ireland in 1984.

In Public Service

The level of unionisation at about 55 per cent of all employees, although higher than in most EC member states, is somewhat less than three out of five employees. The remaining 40 per cent of employees, about 300,000 men and women, who are unorganised, are for the most part in small industrial and service industries in the private sector, widely dispersed geographically and, because of the nature of the employments, difficult to organise.

EFFORTS AT RATIONALISATION

As early as 1921 the Irish Congress of Trade Unions had a long debate about trade union structure. In the period 1936-39 when the Irish trade union structure was thoroughly debated in the Irish Trade Union Congress, a commission, especially created for that purpose, came out with the proposal that in order to combat union multiplicity, unions should amalgamate on the basis of industrial unions organisation. An attempt by government to impose rationalisation on trade unions by way of legislation in the 1941 Trade Union Act was declared unconstitutional. Shortly after the reunification of the two congresses in 1959, the executive council of the Irish Congress of Trade Unions set up a sub-committee with the following terms of reference:

To consider and report on the organisation of the Irish trade union movement, its structure and the relationship between unions, and to make recommendations concerning future policy with reference to the improvement of the organisation of the movement, its structure and relationship between unions.

The sub-committee recommended the setting up of a body to hear complaints from members of unions and suggested that industrial committees be established that would be concerned with the regulation within industries of inter-union relations. The executive committee of the ICTU later proposed that a committee of trade union organisation should be constituted.

The 1962 annual delegate conference of the ICTU adopted a motion to that effect. In 1963 this committee informed unions that it desired 'to encourage unions catering for similar categories of workers to consider amalgamation' and that

1970-1990

voluntary steps in this direction would be a valuable contribution to the emergence of a more orderly and efficient movement. The committee made a recommendation to the 1963 annual delegate conference of the ICTU concerning the protection of the income and conditions of officials of amalgamating unions. Speaking to the conference on the committee's report, James Larkin stated that the problem that was basic to the whole movement was that 'in some way or other we will bring into existence a more effective, rational and intelligent system of organisation.' He referred in his speech to the establishment of an appeals board which the committee saw as a means of making more rapid and effective progress in trade union organisation and structure.

THE SCHREGLE REPORT

In 1974 it was agreed between the Irish Congress of Trade Unions and the International Labour Organisation that the latter would undertake a survey of the trade union movement in Ireland. Joannes Schregle, chief of the Industrial Relations and Labour Administration Department of the ILO, was entrusted with the task. In a memorandum submitted to the ICTU in 1975 Mr Schregle stated:

Any preparatory move towards a new trade union structure will, sooner or later, lead to a discussion on what union members would gain, in terms of services, from a new structure. Any rationalisation of unions will eventually be judged by the criterion of efficiency, and its support will depend on prospects of improved services. Such discussion must take place against the background of clear and undisputed facts.

Mr Schregle continued:

Irish trade union leadership must be very circumspect so as to make sure that it is followed by the rank and file membership. Individual union members are primarily concerned about their own security of employment, security of income, improvement of working and living standards and, in a general way, improved position at their work place in their enterprise, in their industry and in the Irish economy at large. They will approve changes in the trade union structure only to the extent to which they expect them to be better suited to the attainment of these objectives.

Schregle, however, did comment that trade union history and trade union purpose were not normally considered to consist in improving the conditions of a few privileged at the expense of many less privileged, but rather to promote the lot of the workers in general in a spirit of solidarity, with special emphasis on improving the conditions of low-wage groups. Referring to the present-day realities, Schregle commented: 'The realities of the economic situation and the constraints of collective bargaining during times of growing uncertainty, make it necessary for trade unions to take a critical look at their role. A traditional collective bargaining approach — consisting merely of asking for "more" will no longer be sufficient because it will simply not produce the expected results. Wages are inextricably inter-related with all the elements of the economy. Trade unions in Ireland, as elsewhere, naturally need to know and fully to understand the inter-dependence of such factors as economic growth, monetary crisis, oil prices, decreasing availability of energy, inflation, employment, investment and fiscal policy, as well as the prospects of further industrialisation coupled with a balanced development of agriculture and regional development schemes.'

A SINGLE TRADE UNION CENTRE

The importance of having a single trade union centre, to which the vast majority of trade unions were affiliated, had been evident in so far as the ICTU had been able to negotiate, on behalf of the trade union movement, national wage agreements and national understandings with government and employer organisations. It also meant that the vast majority of trade unions were governed by Congress policy and by the rules of Congress with regard to the recruitment and transfer of members. The position in Ireland contrasted with other European Community countries; for example, in France there were four main confederations, in Belgium and Italy there were three main confederations and in the Netherlands there were two. Ireland differed in having a multiplicity of trade unions. In the civil service there were twelve unions, representing a wide range of grades, from messenger to principal officer.

1970-1990
1984 WORKING GROUP

In 1984 the executive council of the ICTU set up a working group on trade union organisation. The group prepared a number of papers, including a paper on the need for trade union rationalisation which was published in the 1985 ICTU annual report and was the subject of debate at the annual delegate conference of that year. The paper stated that for some time trade union membership had been growing, mainly because of the increase in membership in expanding public services. There was evidence that a decline in membership had set in and would probably continue. A stronger, better organised and more effective trade union movement was essential if workers' interests were to be protected in the changed circumstances and if the influence of the movement was to be what it ought to be.

These changing conditions in the economy, and in society generally, had serious implications for the trade union movement and would affect greatly the extent to which trade unions would be able to influence events and serve their members' interests.

The paper went on to say that unions would need to consider their position in relation to the changes that were taking place in the economy and the increased demands likely to be made on them. For many unions this must involve looking at the possibility of seeking amalgamation, transfer of engagements or some other arrangement that would ensure future viability.

Success in achieving trade union rationalisation would bring with it many benefits. It would

(a) strengthen trade union organisation, making the movement a more effective force in industrial relations
(b) extend trade union organisation to workers at present unorganised
(c) enable the movement to respond to new situations and changing circumstances
(d) make it possible to strengthen staffing levels in unions and provide better service
(e) enable the movement to provide specialist service in consultation and participation, information disclosure, health and safety, research, and so on

In Public Service

(f) reduce administrative overheads and eliminate waste and duplication
(g) enable advantage to be taken of information technology to improve communication with members
(h) improve participation by members in decision-making.

UNION RESPONSE 1971

The executive committee decided to set up a committee to examine matters contained in motions discussed at the 1970 annual general meeting. The motions read as follows:

1. The Executive Committee is urged to investigate the possibility of rationalising the structure of staff representation by reducing the number of Associations, and is requested to enter into discussions with other Associations to this end.
2. That this Association recognises the need for rationalisation of the existing structure of staff representation, and that, as an initial step, immediate action should be taken to explore the possibility of bringing about some form of unified association for all grades.

The possibility of a rationalised civil service trade union structure was examined with a view to setting out the advantages and disadvantages of such a situation. The report of the committee was adopted by the executive committee and published as an appendix to the 1970/71 annual report. The advantages were set out as follows:

(a) The existing scattered resources of the different organisations could be pooled and unified if there were a single larger organisation.
(b) There would be greater strength in a larger organisation which would, consequently, carry more weight with the official side.
(c) The quality of the executive committee and of the branch activists of the larger organisations should be higher than that of those in any of the existing organisations since there would be a larger field from which to draw such people.
(d) There was a potential for the new areas of activity in the social and recreational fields which could be tapped in a larger organisation.

1970-1990

(e) There should be less conflict between civil servants on union matters and, as a corollary, closer co-operation between civil servants would be possible.

(f) There would be more economical use of officials' time, resources, services and benefits.

(g) By virtue of the fact that there would be more officials in the new union than in any of the existing organisations, there would be greater room for specialisation in particular areas of staff affairs and also in the problems of particular branches by individual officials. This specialisation was becoming more important in view of the emphasis by management on new techniques which must be appreciated as such by the staff side as by the official side if the members were to ensure that their interests were maintained.

(h) The knowledge that all members of the staff were members of the one organisation should lend greater weight to the union-consciousness of civil servants with a consequent improvement in morale and cut-down in apathy.

(i) In view of the fact that there would be more activists in the new unions than in any one of the existing unions, there were more activities which could be undertaken.

(j) A reduction in the number of organisations would mean that less time would have to be spent in relationships between organisations and also that the executive committee of an amalgamated body could take more meaningful decisions in the sense that there would not be as much time spent in attempting to reconcile differences between organisations' points of view on particular problems. The necessity to reconcile opposing points of view at the staff panel takes up so much time that by the time a decision was made on behalf of the civil service, events had proceeded to such an extent as to render many such decisions irrelevant.

DISADVANTAGES

The disadvantages were set out as follows:

(a) Sectional interests would not be represented directly as much as they had been.

In Public Service

(b) Participation by the ordinary member in a larger structure would be more difficult unless such participation were specifically provided for.

(c) There would be a danger of the larger union becoming over-bureaucratic as it became bigger.

(d) There would be a danger of conflicts within the organisation based on difference of rank, e.g. different attitudes to staff/management relations between a higher executive officer and a clerical assistant.

(e) Dissatisfaction within a large organisation composed of previously existing sectionally oriented organisations could result in dissolution into an even greater number of small organisations.

CONCLUSION IN PRINCIPLE

The conclusion of the executive committee in principle was that rationalisation of the civil service trade union structure would produce a more efficient and workable system.

DECISION OF 1971 AGM

The following motion was proposed and adopted:

That this Annual General Meeting approves the general principles involved in the conclusion and recommendations in the report of the Executive Committee on the Civil Service Trade Union Structure and authorises the Executive Committee to proceed as outlined in the recommendations subject to any major decision on the matter being decided by a future general meeting of the Association.

1972 ANNUAL REPORT

The executive committee during the year had made approaches to other general service staff associations with a view to getting the reaction of such associations to the proposals for a rationalised civil service trade union structure. The executive committee, acting on the basis of association policy, accepted into membership the grade of placement officer in the Department of Labour, grades in the Houses of

1970-1990

the Oireachtas that formerly had their own association, and the grade of examiner of district courts in the Department of Justice.

1973 ANNUAL REPORT

During the year the association secured recognition for the grade of systems analyst.

1979

In January the following associations merged with the Civil Service Executive Union:

Comhaltas Cana — Higher Officers of Customs and Excise.
Administrative Officers' Association.
Association of Third Secretaries — Department of Foreign Affairs.

The membership of the union was also increased by virtue of a reorganisation of the court service. Under the reorganisation, the district court clerks — provincial and metropolitan — were regraded into the general service and their former organisations were dissolved.

1981

The Social Welfare Officers' Association merged with the union.

1984

The union continued to represent members in An Post and Bord Telecom.

A negotiation licence under the Trade Union Act 1941 was granted to the union by the High Court.

In Public Service

ANNUAL REPORT 1986/87

The executive committee gave detailed consideration to the position in respect of the civil service trade union structure during the year. In considering the matter, the executive committee noted that it had been the policy of the union for over fifteen years to rationalise the trade union structure in the civil service. The executive committee also noted that a number of other organisations had amalgamated with the union in that period. In addition, the union noted that the consideration which had led the union to adopt this policy — namely greater organisational strength in dealing with the employer, economies of scale and greater influence for all members — applied now with even greater force because of the problems which the fragmentation of the civil service unions caused the unions in responding collectively to the increasingly difficult circumstances with which civil service unions had to cope. In this regard, it was also noted that the climate within which the civil service unions were going to have to operate was likely to become even more hostile and that this made the matter of improving trade union structure in the civil service an increasingly urgent task. Against this background, the executive committee sought to resume discussions with the Irish Tax Officials Union and to approach the Civil and Public Service Staff Union, the Association of Higher Civil Servants and the Federated Union of Government Employees with a view to having discussions aimed at improving the structure of the civil service unions. The executive committee noted the discussions about the reorganisation of the customs and excise departmental grading structure with the Irish Customs and Excise Union and the Customs and Excise Indoor Staff Association and that the issue of union organisation would necessarily arise in that context and that the union, in such discussions, would be seeking to improve the structure of the civil service trade unions.

ANNUAL REPORT 1987/88

The following motion was adopted at the 1987 annual delegate conference:

That this Conference affirms its commitment to greater unity in the Civil Service Trade Union movement and instructs the Executive Committee to continue its efforts in this regard.

ANNUAL REPORT 1988/89

The following motion was adopted at the 1988 annual delegate conference:

This Annual Delegate Conference is of the view that the rationalisation of trade unions in the public service is necessary, and directs the incoming Executive Committee:
  (i) to engage in meaningful discussions with other Public Service Unions on the subject of trade union rationalisation,
  (ii) to report fully on those discussions to the membership by the 1989 Annual Delegate Conference at the latest.

The ICEU and the PSEU reached agreement on a merger in the form of a transfer of engagements under the Trade Union Acts. The ICEU represented about 630 members in the grades of officer of Customs and Excise and assistant officer of Customs and Excise. The merger was approved by the members of the ICEU on a vote of 353 to 121.

Discussions with other organisations mentioned had not led to any active consideration of mergers at that time.

GENERAL COUNCIL STAFF PANEL

John O'Callaghan, a member of the executive committee, was elected chairman of the panel for 1971. Maureen Donnellan was reappointed secretary. In the same year the union took up a further seat on the panel since the membership had reached 2,000. This gave the union four seats. John O'Callaghan continued as chairman until 1974.

Christopher Devine was elected chairman of the panel for 1975 at the annual general meeting. He served for a year but resigned on his appointment as general secretary of the Teachers' Union of Ireland. E.T. O'Byrne was then elected, but he retired in February 1981. John Hennigan succeeded him as chairman and he served until his death in March 1987. The panel said that his unexpected death was a great loss to the staff side and the members of the civil service trade unions generally. The panel subsequently elected Noel Desmond as chairman. He was a member of the union in Customs and Excise and had been chairman of the revenue panel for some years. In 1989 Mr Desmond left the civil service and Dave Thomas, the union's president, was elected chairman of the staff panel.

Miss Maureen Donnellan was panel secretary until 1981 when, because of illness, she was compelled to leave the post.

Thomas McKevitt was appointed secretary and he continued in this position until his appointment as deputy general secretary of the union in November 1983. Michael Foster, a former assistant general secretary, was appointed panel secretary in November 1983. He resigned on his appointment as deputy general secretary of the Union of Professional and Technical Civil Servants. In March 1984, the panel appointed Carmel Colclough as secretary. She took up duty on 9 April 1984. Miss Colclough had been deputy general secretary of the Federated Union of Government Employees.

J. D'Arcy SC acted as chairman of the Arbitration Board until his appointment as a judge in 1976. He was succeeded by R. O'Hanlon SC, who in turn was replaced by Peter D. Maguire SC, appointed chairman of the Arbitration Board in May 1981.

Mr Maguire is noted for a statement which was recorded by the panel as follows:

> It is worth recording that on 9 October he issued an important statement in relation to the embargo. In this statement Mr Maguire said that he would not have any regard to the Minister's Budget Statement of 21 July and that the availability or otherwise of public funds to meet an award was not of relevant consideration at the Arbitration Board. This commendable defence of the Arbitration process will be appreciated by the Panel.

It is noteworthy that Peter Maguire was not reappointed at the expiry of his first year and that he did not hear any cases during the final three months of that year. Hugh Geoghegan SC was appointed chairman of the board on 24 August 1982.

1970-1990
CIVIL SERVICE ORGANISATION

The tables set out below show the staffing numbers at various dates:

	1.1.71	21.7.81	31.12.84	31.3.87
Principal officer	199	340	320	333
Assistant principal officer	404	821	808	795
Administrative officer	80	132	107	80
Higher executive officer	729	1,324*	1,293*	1,435*
Executive officer	1,219	2,133	1,978	1,917
Staff officer	682	842	796	880
Clerical officer	1,691	3,023	2,714	2,845

*Placement officers and occupational guidance officers were regraded and included for 1987. They were not included in 1981 and 1984.

Other Grades represented by PSEU

	21.1.81	31.12.84	31.3.87
Social welfare officer	253	278	295
Third secretary (Foreign Affairs)	69	68	76
Auditor	26	25	25
Assistant auditor	44	35	32
Junior clerk (Dáil)	6	6	5
Senior clerk (Dáil)	6	6	4
Higher officer (Customs and Excise)	326	308	305

Statistics at 1.1.1989

Administrative officers	56
Executive officers	1,691
Higher executive officers	1,203
HEO/Systems analysts	55
Auditors	22
Assistant auditors	29
Third secretaries	64
Junior clerks	4
Senior clerks	4

The Irish Customs and Excise Union merged with the PSEU on 1 September 1989. This union represented 630 members. On 27 January 1982, the Minister for the Public Service, Liam Kavanagh, called for a meeting of the staff side. He said that he had received letters from a number of staff organisations on reports that the government was contemplating measures on staffing in the civil service. In order to respond to these letters and, in view of the fact that the Minister for Finance would be making a reference to it in his budget speech that afternoon, Mr Kavanagh had decided to invite the staff organisations to meet him so that he could inform them of the government's intention. The government, the minister said, had been faced with very difficult decisions in its preparation of the estimates and the budget in recent months. Because of the size of the public service pay bill — over 50 per cent of all current exchequer expenditure in 1982 — numbers employed in the public service were an important consideration. The government had decided to restrict the number of employees in the non-industrial civil service to the number serving on 21 July 1981. Two vacancies in every three would not be filled. The government had also decided that staff should be redeployed to meet any additional needs.

The staff side representatives, including the CSEU representative, objected strongly and related the government's decision to the campaign against the civil service by politicians and the media.

The general council staff panel raised the issue with the official side at the general council in March 1972. In the period between the meeting with the minister and the discussion with the official side, the government had changed. The official side said that the new government had not altered the policy of the previous government. The staff side objected vociferously and asked that their views be brought to the minister's attention. Following unsatisfactory discussions on the matter at general council with the official side, the staff panel sought a meeting with the new minister, Gene Fitzgerald. This meeting was held on 1 June 1982.

The staff side representatives said that they were not unmindful of the economic situation, but they were extremely concerned at the panic measures which had been announced in the budgets of 21 July 1981 and 27 January 1982. They saw these as being strongly influenced by the civil service 'bashing' that had gone on in the media almost without respite. The staff side was unanimous in its opposition to arbitrary embargoes, arguing that they sowed the seeds for future trouble. The staff side had not created the situation. There could be many views on the origin of the problem, but the staff side had to cope with the fact that the experience of the previous ten to fifteen years had shaped the attitudes and expectations of civil servants because the majority of civil servants had no earlier experience of the service. The staff side did not want confrontation with the minister on the issue, but an indication of the strength of feeling was that a number of unions already had passed motions at annual conferences calling for industrial action on the matter. The minister said that, while he had been given to understand the feelings of the staff side from the reports of the general council, he was now under no illusion about the position and that he would convey their views to the government and press for early decisions. On 30 July, the government published a statement indicating significant economy measures. Included was a statement to the effect that the embargo on the filling of posts in the public service would be retained until 31 March 1983, at least. The union's annual report for 1982/83 stated that, in all the discussions with the official side on the matter, the staff side had made clear its outright rejection of the government's approach. In addition, most other unions had taken similar positions to that of the Public Service Executive Union in advising their members not to do any more than they were doing before the embargo had been introduced.

In early 1984 the staff side and the official side exchanged letters concerning the embargo. These followed discussions under the auspices of the general council.

The following motions were adopted at the union's annual delegate conference in 1984:

> (i) In view of the arbitrary effects of the current embargo on recruitment into the public service both on Departments and on grading, this Conference instructs the incoming Executive Committee to persist in seeking the abolition of the embargo and the development of a rational basis for determining appropriate grading and staffing levels in its place.
>
> (ii) That this Annual Delegate Conference directs the incoming Executive Committee to continue to press for the removal of the embargo on the filling of vacancies in the public service with particular attention to influencing the Minister for the

In Public Service

Public Service to recommend the removal of the embargo to the government before the 1985 budget.

The executive committee decided that these motions should be considered in the context of the reaction of the branches to a circular sent to them on 15 February seeking information on the effects of the embargo. The committee reviewed the response but, at that time, only 13 of the 33 civil service branches had replied to the circular.

A further report was made to the executive committee in December 1984. At this meeting the executive committee noted that only four more branches had replied. The committee also noted that, between 21 December 1981 and 31 December 1983, 2,081 vacant posts had been left unfilled; that the government had suppressed these posts; that a further 650 posts had been left unfilled up to 30 November 1984; that it was the government's intention to continue the policy of filling only one vacancy in three up to the end of 1987; that it was expected as a result that a further 400-800 posts a year would not be filled; that it was accepted by the official side that there were sections of the civil service that needed increased staff resources, but there were no specific plans to deal with this; and that it was expected that the White Paper on changes in the civil service would cover this issue (Annual Report 1984/85).

A deputation from the union met John Boland, the Minister for the Public Service, on 27 February 1984, to discuss his statement regarding the filling of posts in the higher civil service which the union maintained had indirect implications for union members. The minister had decided to establish a top-level appointments committee to decide on appointments to assistant secretary and corresponding posts. He said that he would welcome a submission by the union on the recently published White Paper on public service reform.

The Office of the Ombudsman came into being on 1 January 1984. His remit originally was confined to the civil service. Representatives of the staff panel met the Ombudsman, Michael Mills, and officials of his office on 17 April 1984 to discuss the methods of operation of the Ombudsman in carrying out investigations of complaints by members of the public. Under amending legislation, the remit of the Ombudsman was extended to cover local authorities, health boards, Telecom Eireann and An Post. The extension took effect from 1 April 1985. In the union's annual report for 1985/86, the executive committee detailed its consideration of the issue of performance bonuses or merit pay. This resulted in the committee deciding to oppose the introduction into the civil service of any such arrangements. This view was approved by the staff panel and was conveyed to the official side. Subsequently, in September 1985, the White Paper on the public service stated that a system of merit pay would be introduced into the civil service. The official side indicated that it wished to have discussions on the issue with the staff side. A paper for discussion would be prepared, but there were no further developments.

The union's annual report recorded that, in his budget statement of 31 March 1987, the Minister for Finance, Ray MacSharry, had set out the government's policy in respect of staffing numbers and redeployment:

> With effect from today, the Government have decided on the following measures to reduce public service numbers:
> — in the Civil Service no vacancy may be filled without the consent of the Minister for Finance
> — the Minister for Finance will have authority to redeploy staff within the Civil Service as required
> — no vacancy will be filled in any other area of the Public Service funded from the Exchequer without the express approval of the Minister responsible for that area and without the consent of the Minister for Finance.

The executive committee decided to put down an emergency motion at the annual delegate conference. Among other matters the motion read: 'Calls upon the Government to withdraw from its present position which produces confrontation with Public Servants; to honour agreements freely made; to maintain commitments to independent arbitration machinery; to ensure that staffing levels are such as are needed to meet the demands of providing services and to negotiate with the unions to produce effective and workable solutions to the various problems besetting the public service in order to avoid the inevitable alternative of industrial chaos, and authorises the incoming Executive Committee to devise a strategy of industrial action

In Public Service

in the event that the government persists in pursuing policies which represent an arbitrary and unfair attack on members' rights to resolve industrial relations matters in accordance with the well established negotiating procedures.' One of the issues that concerned the union and the Irish Congress of Trade Unions was the chairmanship of the Civil Service Arbitration Board. The term of office of the chairman of the board was due to expire on 31 July 1987. The staff panel sent the following letter to the official side on 9 July:

The Civil Service General Staff Panel, at its meeting on 8 July, considered the position in respect of the Appointment of the Chairman of the Arbitration Board and the counter-statement of the Official Side in respect of the General Pay Claim. You will be aware, from the discussions which took place at the General Council on 3 June and 7 July, that the Panel has been pressing for an indication of the Government's position on the Chairmanship of the Arbitration Board bearing in mind that the current term of Office of the Chairman expires on 31 July. As you are aware, the Panel cannot see how the Conciliation and Arbitration Scheme can operate without an Arbitration Stage. The Panel, therefore, requires that the Government agrees to the appointment as a matter of urgency. In the context of the present situation where there is no assurance about the Chairmanship of the Arbitration Board, the Panel decided to record disagreement on the General Pay claim at the General Council on 3 June, and submitted the Statement of Case to the Arbitration Board on 8 June. It is now over a month since the Statement of Case was submitted but, yet, we have not received a counter-statement. You will be aware of the fact that the Official Side assured us at two meetings of the General Council that they had no interest in 'messing the Staff Side around' in the context of having an Arbitration on the claim. In the circumstances, the Panel requires a counter-statement in order to proceed with the Arbitration and expects that the Official Side will produce some immediately. I should add that the Panel's view on an early Arbitration on the General Pay Claim is determined solely by the lack of any assurance about the chairmanship of the Arbitration Board after 31 July. If we were in a situation where there would continue to be a Chairman after 31 July then, of course, as we have already indicated at the General Council, we would not be pressing for an early Arbitration but would be waiting to see the outcome of the current discussions between the Irish Congress of Trade Unions and the Government.

1970-1990

The government subsequently announced that it had agreed to the reappointment of the chairman of the Arbitration Board for the period 1 July to 31 December 1987 (Annual Report 1987/88). A further government announcement stated that it had been decided to make the following terms available to staff who left the service voluntarily and who were permanent and pensionable officers:

(a) Staff with more than forty years service:
Immediate payment of lump sum and pension based on actual service plus a severance gratuity of two weeks per year of service to age 65.

(b) Staff with less than five years service:

   (i) $\frac{1}{12}$ of salary per year of service; plus

   (ii) $\frac{3}{80}$ of salary per year of service provided service was over two years; plus

   (iii) two weeks pay per year of service.

(c) Staff with more than five years service and less than 40 years service:
Immediate payment of lump sum and annual pension plus added years of service for calculating lump sum and pension. The added years would be seven for staff with more than twenty years service. The maximum service including added years could not exceed forty years. For those with less than twenty years a pro rata figure of added years of service would apply — e.g. 3.5 years for a person with ten years service.

There would be no compulsory redundancies.

The government saw the way in which the commitment to no compulsory redundancies could be effective was a combination of natural wastage, redeployment, job-sharing, career breaks and voluntary early retirement. In the event it became clear that the application of the full package of measures mentioned in staffing streams in the civil service and exchequer-funded agencies was not capable of absorbing enough staff to meet the needs. The government decided to widen the scope of the application of the early retirement proposals to the whole public service (civil service, all exchequer-funded state agencies and health boards — the proposals already applied in the local authorities and teaching) in order to widen the field for redeployment in the public service and thereby provide an effective means of maintaining the commitment to no compulsory redundancies.

On 1 January 1988, Foras Áiseanna Saothair (FÁS) came into being. This was an amalgamation of the various manpower and training agencies.

On 1 January 1989, Coillte Teoranta came into being. This was a new state-sponsored body, set up to operate forestry on a commercial basis. Members of the union were transferred to both bodies, and the union continues to represent them.

REPORT OF PUBLIC SERVICES ORGANISATION REVIEW GROUP
(DEVLIN REPORT)

In 1970 the union recommended that the proposed Department of the Public Service should have a cabinet minister separate from the Department of Finance, but the suggestion was not then accepted. However, the government did indicate its acceptance of the Devlin recommendations for the setting up of a Department of the Public Service. It was expected that the new department would be established on 1 April 1971. The secretary-designate of the new department was Seamus O'Conail, then assistant secretary for personnel in the Department of Finance.

The staff panel informed the official side that it would require full consultation on all matters arising out of the Devlin Report. The Minister for Finance indicated that he had no objection to such consultation.

The annual report for 1973/74 noted that the staff panel was seeking representation on the Joint Consultative Council which was monitoring the follow-up action on the Devlin report. This council was representative of the Association of Higher Civil Servants, the Institute of Professional Civil Servants and the official side. The staff side's request was referred to the council and later was granted. The pilot exercises on the separation of executive and policy-making work in the Departments of Health, Local Government, Industry and Commerce and Transport and Power continued during the year. The new Department of the Public Service formally came into being during the year. The Minister for the Public Service was also the Minister for Finance. In September 1973, the union wrote to the Department of the Public Service in connection with the implementation of the Devlin recommendation providing for the establishment of a Public Service Advisory Council. The union recommended that the body should include at least representatives of the staff in the civil service. The department replied that the council was not intended to be a representative body and that, in the light of the purpose for which its setting up was recommended by Devlin and of the rather detailed recommendations on its constitution, it seemed that the bulk of its membership would have to be drawn from outside the civil service.

The report of the pilot exercise in the Department of Health was published in 1973 and the report on Transport and Power was published in December 1974.

The executive committee's sub-committee on the Devlin report continued its work during the year. The executive committee came to the following conclusions in relation to the work of the sub-committee:

(a) There was no obvious way in which a scheme of mobility in promotions across class barriers could be achieved fairly.

(b) Any other questions arising from the Devlin report should be dealt with on an ad hoc basis as they arose.

Little further was heard of the Devlin report during the period covered in this chapter.

POST OFFICE REVIEW GROUP

The setting up of the Post Office Review Group was announced in a statement issued by the Government Information Services on behalf of the Minister for Posts and Telegraphs on 8 July 1978. It read:

In their Election Manifesto the Government stressed that an efficient and dependable communications system was an essential part of the strategy for national reconstruction and undertook to examine the questions of giving autonomy to telecommunications and of

In Public Service

modernising the postal system. In accordance with that undertaking the Minister for Posts and Telegraphs has set up a group with the following terms of reference:

(1) To examine and report on the feasibility of giving to the telecommunications service such form of Autonomous organisation as is likely to be most effective in meeting current public demand and providing for future development and expansion; and to make specific proposals regarding the nature, powers and functions of the organisation recommended.

(2) To examine and report on the organisational arrangements necessary to secure the modernisation of the postal system so as to promote an efficient system nationwide.

The union made a submission to the group, strongly recommending that devolution of the function of the Post Office to an executive office be considered on the terms set out by the Public Services Organisation Review Group. However, the Review Group considered that the executive agency or executive office form might be an improvement on the existing arrangement, but also that it would fall far short of meeting the needs of the telecommunications service. The two basic recommendations of the Review Group were:

(a) to create two state-sponsored bodies to run the post and telecommunications service, and
(b) to appoint an interim board at the earliest possible date for the telecommunications service.

The government decided to accept both recommendations in principle and also decided to appoint an interim board for the postal service.

An official side memorandum of 16 July 1979 indicated very broadly the position that would obtain for the period during which the boards would function. It was made clear that the government intended that, in accordance with the Review Group's views, elected worker-directors would be appointed to the boards of the proposed statutory bodies, the directors in each case to be elected by the staff of the board concerned. Pending consultation with the staff side on the question of the arrangements that would apply for the election of worker-directors, the minister agreed to appoint worker-directors to the interim boards. T. Quinlan of the Post Office Workers' Union was appointed to the Interim Board for Posts and S. de Paor of the Irish Post Office Engineering Union was appointed to the Interim Board for Telecommunications. A further memorandum was issued by the official side of the departmental council on 21 May 1981. It dealt with the following:

(i) Options in regard to future area of employment
(ii) Safeguards as to pay and conditions
(iii) Superannuation
(iv) Security of employment
(v) Grading structures
(vi) Personnel policies
(vii) Staff representation
(viii) Recruitment procedures
(ix) Staffing of government department switchboards
(x) Negotiating structures, grievance and disciplinary procedures
(xi) Legislative framework.

The staff side considered the official side memorandum and then set out its objectives in discussions. The objectives included:

(a) Negotiations of the best possible package and report back to members

(b) To preserve civil service status

(c) To ensure that union members would retain existing work

(d) To ensure guarantees on superannuation

(e) Option on early retirement

(f) Security of tenure

(g) To ascertain proposed grading structure

(h) To safeguard expectations of promotion

(i) To ensure adequate personnel policy within new boards

(j) To negotiate on staff representations

(k) To ensure adequate negotiation structures.

On the basis of the above objectives, a meeting with the official side took place on 10 November. Following this, the official side issued a further memorandum on 9 December 1981,

In Public Service

supplying additional information and comment on the matters raised by the staff side. The 1982 annual delegate conference adopted the following resolutions:

That this Annual Delegate Conference instructs the incoming Executive Committee to ensure that members' terms of employment in any transfer to the proposed Semi-State boards for posts and telecommunications would not represent a disimprovement on their present conditions of service.

The Annual Delegate Conference unconditionally reaffirms traditional union policy that no transfer of any of our members appointed as established civil servants should take place from the Civil Service to any Semi-State employer except with the free consent of any individual involved. Conference further resolves that the full resources and strength of this Union shall be deployed in defence of this fundamental principle for Civil Servants, and that whatever measures the Executive deem appropriate to maintain our existing rights, position and status in this regard may be adopted by the Executive in full consultation with any Branches concerned.

The executive committee considered that the latter resolution clearly implied the union's policy to be that no member in the Post Office should have to transfer to the state companies and that the union was obliged to demand their retention in the civil service even if this meant transfer to other departments.

The staff and official sides met on 4 June 1982 and restated their views. The official side responded as follows:

(a) Civil Service — Secondment. This point had been made repeatedly. They would see the Post Office boards as being different from the ACOT or National Heritage Councils positions. It was intended to have all problems resolved prior to vesting day.

(b) Security of Employment. It would not be possible to give a statutory guarantee of continued employment. No other person had such a guarantee. They considered the protective legislation mentioned in an earlier memorandum as being adequate.

(c) Statutory safeguards as to pay and conditions. It would not be workable to maintain a permanent pay relationship with the civil service. In any event this would be meaningless in the case of the great majority of post office workers since there would be no comparable civil service grades.

1970-1990

(d) Superannuation. They asked the staff side to consider an option either for the civil service pension scheme or for the pension scheme of the boards.

(e) Promotion outlets. They would not regard continuation of interdepartmental competitions as being feasible.

The essence of the official side response was:

(i) that there would be no secondment
(ii) that the interest of the staff would be protected by the provision of the act and by an agreement at the departmental council.

Under the terms of the Postal and Telecommunications Services Act 1983, the staff of the Department of Posts and Telegraphs were designated to the employment of An Post, Bord Telecom Eireann or the residual ministry. The assignment notice given to members of staff read:

I am instructed to inform you that it is proposed to assign you to An Post/Bord Telecom/Residual Department on the vesting of the new State-sponsored companies under the Postal and Telecommunications Services Act, 1983. An explanatory memorandum is appended.

The explanatory memorandum covered the following subjects:

(i) Basis of staff assignments
(ii) Main provisions of the act
(iii) Grading structures
(iv) Performance of work on an agency basis
(v) Pay-related social insurance contributions
(vi) Superannuation
(vii) Negotiating machinery in the new companies
(viii) Departmental medical scheme
(ix) Staffing of government department switchboards
(x) Staff of the new companies and politics
(xi) Representation of staff in An Post and Bord Telecom Eireann.

Following consultations between the officers of the union and representatives of the branches in the Department of Posts and Telegraphs on 6 October 1983, and having regard to the motions adopted at the 1982 annual delegate conference, the executive committee sent the following letter to each member serving in the Department of Posts and Telegraphs:

In Public Service

I am directed by the Executive Committee to refer to the assignments which have been made by the Department of Posts and Telegraphs between the Postal Board, the Telecom Board and the residual ministry. The Union has a commitment arising from the 1982 Annual Conference to attempt to arrange that people who have been assigned to the State Companies who wish to remain in the Civil Service and who cannot be accommodated in the residual ministry should be allowed to transfer to other Government Departments. The Union does not underestimate the difficulties it will face in securing such an arrangement should any members want to have such arrangements made. It would require the agreement of the Department of the Public Service, other Departments, the Department of Posts and Telegraphs and, in certain circumstances, the State Companies. In the event that two way exchanges can be secured, the problems would be less severe than in circumstances where attempts had to be made to arrange one-way transfers since this would necessarily block positions which might otherwise be filled, at least in the case of promotional posts, by promotion. In addition, even if these problems can be overcome it would be necessary to have regard, particularly in the context of one-way transfers, to the seniority position of staff transferring in relation to the position of the staff in the receiving Departments. Before deciding how to approach the issue in the event that it actually is a live problem the Executive Committee, after consulting the Branches, has decided that the first thing to be established is to determine the magnitude of the problem. In this context, the Executive Committee would appreciate it if each member in the Post Office would be good enough to complete and return the enclosed questionnaire.

The result of the survey showed that a substantial number of members assigned to the employment of the companies wished the union to attempt to secure alternative positions for them in the civil service. The union sought the co-operation of the official side in conducting a trawl of civil servants in other departments to determine whether they would be prepared to transfer with staff assigned to the companies but wished to remain in the civil service. The official side refused to co-operate and would not countenance the possibility of blocking posts in the executive officer grade in other departments with executive officers assigned to the companies who wanted to stay in the civil service. In addition, the official side refused to co-operate in the possibility of using higher executive officer vacancies, which otherwise would be filled from the annual inter-departmental scheme of promotion to higher executive officer, to absorb HEOs assigned to the companies who did not wish to leave the civil service. Instead, the official side offered to have an arrangement whereby staff in the companies could continue for a period to be eligible for inter-departmental competitions. The executive committee considered the matter on 14 November 1983 and decided that these arrangements were unsatisfactory since they were far removed from the concepts outlined in the motions adopted at the 1982 conference and gave no direct outlet for staff in the Department of Posts and Telegraphs. Besides, the arrangements were almost meaningless for higher executive officers. The executive committee also decided to conduct a trawl of the rest of the members in the general service to see if volunteers willing to transfer with those assigned to the employment of the companies could be secured. In the circumstances, the committee decided to seek alternative arrangements whereby, for a number of years after 1984, a proportion of posts that otherwise would be filled from the interdepartmental competition for promotion to higher executive officer would be filled by competitions confined to executive officers and higher executive officers assigned to the board and, in return, each company would hold special competitions to fill the same number of higher executive officer posts confined to executive officers and higher executive officers in the civil service. Following detailed discussions at a sub-committee of the general council, agreement was reached on the eligibility of staff transferred to An Post and Bord Telecom Eireann for confined civil service competitions and on other issues related to the transfers.

The entire matter was considered at a meeting between the officers of the union and the branches in the department of Posts and Telegraphs on 28 November 1983. It was recognised that nothing further could be achieved unless the members took strike action to seek to enforce retention in the civil service of those assigned to the employment of the companies who did not wish to leave the service. This issue was considered at the annual general meeting of the Post and Telegraphs general branch on 2 December 1983. The branch decided overwhelmingly against industrial action. The branches in the stores and computer unit also decided against taking industrial action on the matter. The executive committee concluded that, having regard to the views of the branches directly involved, no useful purpose would be served in giving further consideration to this matter.

The 1983 annual delegate conference of the union adopted the following motion:

> That this Conference instructs the Executive Committee to make the necessary arrangements to continue to represent members of the Department of Posts and Telegraphs if they transfer to semi-state boards provided the members who are to transfer indicate by ballot their desire to be so represented; the format, method and timing of the ballot to be discussed and agreed between the relevant Branches and the Executive Committee.

A ballot was eventually conducted but, because of various problems in branches to do with the conduct and format of the ballot, the executive committee decided to arrange for discussions between the officers of the union and representatives of the branches in the Department of Posts and Telegraphs. A meeting took place on 28 November 1983. Following considerable discussions, the following proposal emerged:

(a) The CSEU will retain recognition for members transferred to the boards and any new people entering the EO, HEO and AO in the boards for a trial period.

(b) The trial period will be for not more than two years.

(c) The committees of the branches in either of the companies may, before the end of the trial period, propose to the members in either of the companies that the union should cease to hold recognition for them. A decision of the members in either of the companies on such a proposal shall be by means of a ballot of the members in either company. In order to arrange that the union should cease to hold such recognition in either company, the majority in favour of terminating union membership and recognition shall be not less than a simple majority of the entire membership employed by either company and not less than two-thirds of those voting.

1970-1990

All branches of the union in the Post Office, with the exception of the branch in the computer unit, accepted the proposals. The executive committee considered the entire situation and, bearing in mind that no outside union would be recognised for the purpose of representing members transferred to An Post and Bord Telecom Eireann, as from vesting day (1 January 1984) decided that the union should continue to represent such staff for a trial period of two years, at least.

POST-ENTRY EDUCATION AND STAFF DEVELOPMENT

The union's annual report for 1974/75 states that a large number of members had secured a refund of fees in respect of courses leading to a third-level qualification arising from the agreement of the previous year. Agreement had also been reached on the refund of fees in respect of courses leading to a Diploma in Industrial Relations. An official side discussion paper on post-entry education was published as an appendix to the annual report. Discussions commenced on this paper and among the items dealt with were second-level education, paid educational leave and ex gratia payments to civil servants holding certain university or equivalent qualifications.

The same annual report recorded that the deputy general secretary of the union (association) had been appointed to the education committee of the Institute of Public Administration. At the time, the union was not affiliated to the institute. The annual report also reviewed the work of the institute in relation to the grades represented by the union. The School of Public Administration had been established in October 1964 as a response to a number of public service personnel problems. The focus of these problems effectively determined the clientele of the school which had comprised young public officials — mainly civil service executive officers and clerical officers from local authorities. The aim was to help prepare them for administrative responsibilities. Between 1965 and 1974 some 135 civil servants attended the school; the great majority were executive officers. The institute's diploma course originated from a report on Post-Entry Education of Public Servants published in 1959. The original three-year study course aimed at pass degree level. A new four-year course was established in 1970 embracing both honours degree and general degree levels. In 1982 the institute secured degree status for the diploma course from the NCEA.

The manpower development section of the Department of the Public Service issued a discussion document on post-entry education in September 1974. This document was an update of another issued in 1969 and took account of the significant development relating to post-entry education that had taken place. The 1974 document was published as an appendix to the union's annual report of 1974/75. The 1976 annual general meeting agreed that the union should reaffiliate to the Institute of Public Administration.

The 1977/78 annual report contained the report of the working party on the co-ordination of third-level courses in public administration which was formed at the request of the education committee of the IPA with these terms of reference: to advise and report on the co-ordination of third-level courses in public administration. The union's deputy general secretary served on this working party. The report contained a summary of the existing and proposed public administration courses:

Existing Course
1. School of Public Administration — 1-year full-time
2. Diploma in Administrative Science — 4-year part-time
3. Degree in Public Administration TCD — 1-year full-time (open to IPA graduates)
4. Degree of Master of Public Administration UCD — 2-year part-time
5. Degree in Public Administration UCD — 3-year part-time; 1-year full-time
6. European Studies Public Administration, NIHE, Limerick — 4-year full-time

The 1978/79 annual report said that the arrangement would continue whereby Trinity College provided a degree course for holders of IPA diplomas. There had been a significant increase in the number of first-year enrolments for the diploma course. The primary degree course in public administration commenced in UCD in October 1978. Enrolments were on the basis of a two-year cycle. The course consisted of:

3 years part-time (evening course)
1 year full-time (day course)

General council report 749 set out the terms of an agreement between the union and the official side on a programme for staff development. An introductory pamphlet to the scheme was produced and was published as an appendix to the union annual report for 1979/80. The 1981/82 annual report contained a report of the executive committee on the scheme of staff appraisal and development. This report attempted to identify the reasons why the scheme had not been successful and to make suggestions for the future of the scheme. Notwithstanding a big effort by the official side to have the scheme launched in departments by (a) seeking commitment from their managements to the concept of staff appraisal and (b) training officers in the skills of assessing and appraising their staff, and take-up rate had been disappointingly low.

The executive committee considered that the reasons for the failure of the scheme were as follows:

(a) The scheme was voluntary.

(b) There was a lack of support for the scheme and, indeed, a less than enthusiastic attitude towards it, from management in certain departments and, in many instances, from members of the union in departments.

(c) Many of the officers who would have to appraise staff regarded this work as a tiresome and time-consuming chore.

(d) The pressure of other work and the frequency of staff changes in departments made it hard to secure the ideal combination for the appraisal of an officer under the scheme.

(e) Members might not have seen any advantage in the scheme.

The executive committee then set out proposals for the future of the scheme and recommended to members that the official side be approached to secure its agreement to the following:

(a) Formal staff appraisal should exist in all departments. In view of the inherent obligation on management to develop their staff and the benefits which should accrue to staff from

In Public Service

effective staff development measures, it was the executive committee's view that a formal system of appraisal should exist in all departments. This view had been endorsed by the Public Services Organisation Review Group and the Public Service Advisory Council.

(b) Since circumstances varied from department to department, what might suit one might not suit another although, in relation to general service grades, a considerable degree of uniformity was desirable. The basic requirements for a scheme should be agreed between the union and the official side. If a department so wished, it should be free to depart from the standard provisions, subject to the agreement of a central official side - union committee on any change of significance. Final details of its scheme should be agreed by a department at its departmental council.

(c) While appraisal should cover the development of officers for their existing grades, it should also be linked to an assessment of their suitability for promotion. The objective of each appraisal scheme should be the personal development of each officer (so as to enable him or her — at the very least — to do more satisfactorily the work of his or her existing grade) and the greater involvement of supervisors in the training and development of their staff.

(d) The scheme should be obligatory on all staff in grades covered by it. However, the appraisers should show discretion and good sense in cases where a person refused to take part in an appraisal session. No disciplinary action should be taken.

(e) The progress of individual officers should be monitored regularly, on the basis of which management should give consideration to their development, whether by way of formal training or by different work experiences.

(f) Individuals should be told in good time of deficiencies that might adversely affect their promotion prospects and should receive advice and assistance to help them overcome these deficiencies.

(g) When making promotions, managements in individual departments should have available to them sufficient information on all eligible officers to enable the best decision to be made.

(h) The appraisal should be used to assess staff during the probationary period.

1970-1990

(i) In the event that the superior officer of the person being appraised is changed between appraisal periods, then the next appraisal session should be between the person being appraised, his current superior officer and the former superior officer.

The 1982/83 annual report said that an agreement based on the union's proposals had been reached. This agreement was set out in general council report 971. It was noted that discussions on the implementation of the scheme were to be held at departmental councils and that variations in the form of the scheme could be agreed.

The 1984/85 report dealt with the difficulties experienced in securing the release of members to attend various third-level courses. It was noted that, largely because of the union's effort, all members had been released. There were also difficulties in securing repayment of fees in different departments. All such cases were being pursued. The 1985/86 report summed up events that had occurred since 1984 when the union had put comprehensive proposals to the Civil Service Training Centre for a training programme for members. Some of these proposals had been incorporated into the government's White Paper, *Serving the Country Better*, particularly the proposals to design staff development plans and also to provide induction training within three months of entry. However, the union expressed disappointment with the White Paper's proposals on education and training because it did not contain any specific commitments on the refund of fees for educational courses or on release for courses. The discussion begun in 1984 on possible improvements for third-level education was not continued in 1985 since it was clear that the official side was seeking a radical disimprovement in the arrangements. In the union's opinion, what was needed was a realistic reassessment of the refund of fees and release for courses. For 1985/86 the IPA continued with the interim arrangement for the School of Public Administration for a course of fourteen weeks, made up of two seven-week periods. The annual report noted that the future of the school was under review and that there had been proposals to discontinue it. The executive committee had written to the director of the institute expressing opposition to any such proposals on the grounds that the existence of the school provided an opportunity

In Public Service

for public servants who were unable to study part-time, to acquire knowledge of public administration and related disciplines.

The 1987 annual delegate conference of the union adopted the following resolution: 'The ADC deplores the low priority given to training in the Public Service and instructs the incoming Executive Committee to seek improvements in the situation at General Council.' This resolution was referred to the sub-committee on education, training, recruitment and development. The sub-committee, noting the continued decline in the priority given to training in the civil service, recommended to the executive committee that the whole question of the future of the Civil Service Training Centre, in the light of the redeployment of some staff from there, and training generally should be raised at general council. The matter was brought up at general council when the staff side outlined its concern at the implications of the depletion of the staffing resources of the training centre and at the fact that a number of departments did not have a departmental training officer.

In response, the official side agreed to bring pressure to bear on departments that did not have a training officer to try and ensure that this situation did not continue. In relation to the Civil Service Training Centre, the official side said that the core training functions had been maintained despite the redeployments out of the centre. The union's annual report for 1988/89, however, said that the situation regarding the provision of training in the civil service had got worse over the year. The Civil Service Training Centre had retained only the most basic functions and a number of departments continued to have no training officer. Persistent attempts by the union to have this situation redressed had no positive results.

In May 1987 discussions commenced with representatives of the Civil Service Training Centre in connection with the problems on staff development.

The union's annual report for 1988/89 expressed disappointment in its reference to the Institute of Public Administration that for the first time there had been a postponement of the School of Public Administration due to the inadequate response. This reflected the fact that departments did not send forward nominees for the school because of the prevailing staff situation. Despite union pressure, the Department of Finance refused to force the departments to release staff. The institute itself, in the light of this development, began to look at the possibility of providing other educational facilities. It was proposed to organise a part-time, two-year national certificate course that the institute hoped would attract public servants who were either not interested in pursuing the full degree course or who did not meet the educational requirement for it. At the 1989 annual delegate conference, a resolution seeking the revival of the School of Public Administration was submitted by the Department of Agriculture and Food branch. It was adopted with amendments from the Office of Public Works branch and by the Industry and Commerce branch.

CHAPTER I

1. Royal Commission on the Civil Service 1966–68, Cmd 3638.
2. Henry Parris, *Staff Relations in the Civil Service*, George Allen and Unwin, 1973, p.67.
3. G.A. Campbell, *The Civil Service in Britain*, Duckworth, 1971, p.34.
4. Parliamentary Papers 1875, Vol. XXIII.
5. B.V. Humphreys, *Clerical Unions in the Civil Service*, Blackwell, 1958.
6. *Parliamentary Papers 1888*, Vol. XXVII.
7. Humphreys, op.cit.
8. Alan Clinton, *Post Office Workers — A Trade Union and Social Study*, George Allen and Unwin, 1984, p.253.
9. Eric Wigham, *From Humble Petition to Militant Action — A History of the CPSA*, 1980.
10. Parliamentary Papers 1914, Vol. XVI.
11. Parris, op.cit., p.25.
12. Parliamentary Papers 1916, Vol. XIV.
13. W.J.Brown, *So Far*, George Allen and Unwin, 1943, pp. 83–84.
14. Lord Amulree,*Industrial Arbitration in Britain*, Oxford University Press, 1929.

CHAPTER II

1. Brennan Commission, *Final Report*, p.61.
2. Department of Finance, *Memorandum to Brennan Commission*.
3. Brennan Commission, *Final Report*, p.63.
4. Ronan Fanning, *The Irish Department of Finance 1922–58*, Institute of Public Administration, 1978.
5. *An Dion*, organ of Post Office Workers' Union, January 1930.
6. ibid., February 1930.
7. The Association of Officers of the Executive and Higher Grades, Annual Report 1930.

Notes

8. *Civil Service Journal*, May 1931.
9. *Civil Service Journal*, July 1925.
10. Letter to Post Office Workers' Union from Secretary of Civil Service Federation, 4 March 1927.
11. Department of Finance circular 6/28.
12. Brennan Commission, Interim Report.
13. *An Dion*, organ of Post Office Workers' Union, June 1932.
14. *Report of Brennan Commission*, paragraphs 158–66.
15. Minutes of Proceedings, Civil Service Representative Council First Meeting, 15 March 1926.
16. *Civil Service Journal*, September 1934.

CHAPTER III

1. *Civil Service Journal*, July 1941.
2. *Administration*, journal of the Institute of Public Administration.
3. *Civil Service Journal*, September 1936.
4. William Norton was general secretary of the Post Office Workers' Union; Archie Heron was general secretary of the Civil Service Clerical Association. Neither was a civil servant.
5. *An Peann*, journal of the Civil Service Clerical Association, July 1932.
6. *Report of Brennan Commission*, paragraph 236.
7. *Civil Service Journal*, December 1937.
8. CSEHO, Treasurer's Report 1944.
9. *Irisleabhair*, journal of Comhaltas Cana, November/December 1948.
10. Civil Service Alliance Memorandum on Consolidation Negotiations.
11. CSEHO, Annual Report 1950.
12. *An Peann*, March 1942.
13. *Civil Service Staff Officer*, journal of Staff Officers' Associations.
14. Minutes of meetings of Civil Service General Staff Panel, December 1949 – December 1950.
15. *The Bell*, Vol. XIII, No. 1, 1946.

271

16. *The Postal Worker*, May 1940.
17. *The Postal Worker*, July 1941.
18. *Civil Service Review*, January 1947.

CHAPTER IV

1. Association Annual Report 1955/56
2. Journal of the Institute of Public Administration.
3. General Council Reports 159 and 164.
4. General Council Report 342.
5. Arbitration Report 120.
6. Report of Tribunal of Enquiry into Rates of Remuneration Payable to Clerical Recruitment Grades in Public Sector of the Economy (Quinn Tribunal).
7. Irish Congress of Trade Union, Annual Report 1966, p.126.
8. General Council Reports 399 and 409.
9. Arbitration Board Report 166.
10. Minutes of General Council Staff Panel, 13 May 1954.
11. Minutes of General Council Staff Panel, 23 February 1961.
12. Minutes of General Council Staff Panel, 3 July 1961.
13. Minutes of General Council Staff Panel, 18 December 1969.
14. Judgement delivered 13 May 1963, No. 1328p.
15. *Civil Service Review*, June 1963.
16. Minutes of Special Meeting of Staff Panel, 4 June 1963.
17. *Civil Service Review*, December 1963.
18. *Civil Service Review*, June 1951.
19. First Meeting of General Council (Revised Scheme) 11 August 1952.
20. Correspondence published in *Civil Service Review*, January/February 1953.
21. *Civil Service Review*, March 1953.
22. Official organ of Post Office Workers' Union.
23. *Civil Service Review*, May 1953.
24. *Civil Service Review*, May 1953.
25. Dáil Report in *Civil Service Review*, July 1953. The motion was carried by 67 votes to 56.
26. *Dáil Debates*, Vol. 147, Cols. 1680–1723.

Notes

27. *Civil Service Review*, September 1958.
28. *Civil Service Review*, April 1959.
29. General Council Report 102.
30. General Council Report 151.
31. Report of Association, March 1958.
32. Minutes of Executive Committee Meeting, 28 September 1959.
33. Minutes of Special Meeting of Council, 3 September 1959.
34. Association Annual Report 1958.
35. Minutes of Special General Meeting, 28 July, 1958.
36. *Civil Service Review*, February 1968.

INDEX

All references to the Civil Service Executive Association and the Civil Service Executive Union have been subsumed under 'Public Service Executive Union.'

A
ACOT, 258
Adams, W. J., 45
Administration, 125-6
administrative officers, 81-3, 191, 192-3, 196-7
Administrative Officers' Association, 243
Adult Education Association, 232
Aer Lingus, 131, 165
age limits, 15
Agriculture, Department of, 80, 112, 232
Agriculture and Food, Department of, 269
Ahern, B., 102
Air Traffic Control Officers' Association, 97
Amulree, Lord, 20
AnCO, 229-30
Anthony, Richard, 54
Anti-Discrimination (Pay) Act 1974, 206, 222-8
Appropriation Bill 1936, 107
arbitration and conciliation scheme, 39-41, 81, 82, 91, 105-11, 122-3, 128-9, 163, 209. *see also* Whitley system
   attacks on, 212
   criticisms of, 199-200
   High Court action, 141-52
   and Labour Court, 132-3
   review (1951), 152-7

Index

Arbitration Board, 212, 213, 246, 252-3. *see also* McKenna award
  established, 110-11
  pay claims, 123-4, 126-7, 133-4
  proposed, 103-5, 107-9
Asquith, Herbert, 13
Assistant Clerks' Association, 12, 16-17, 23
Assurance Representatives Organisation, 77
Attendants, Association of (Dundrum Asylum), 97

B
Bank Officials Arbitration Board, 104
Barrington, Donal, 225
Barrington, T. J., 125-6, 190
Baynes, A. W., 105
Beamish, Dick, 218
Beere, Dr Thekla, 190, 218
Bell, The, 105-6
Bell, William, 101, 110, 145, 147, 157, 158, 160
Binchy, Michael, 104
Bird, M., 160
Blythe, Ernest, 41, 42
Boland, John, 250
Bord na Móna, 131, 165
Bord Telecom, 243, 259, 260, 261, 263
Breathnach, Patrick, 141, 146, 149, 157, 160, 187
Brennan Commission, 30, 31-2, 36-7, 39, 41, 48-53, 80, 106
  on bonuses, 53-7
  and executive officers, 69-71
  on non-civil servant union officials, 84-5
  and promotions, 66-7, 125
  salaries, 61-4, 88
Brown, W. J., 19
Burke, Declan, 218
Butterworth, Sir A. Kaye, 18

C
Campbell, G. A., 3
Canavan, Father, 40
career breaks, 229

Carroll, John, 223
Casey, Mr, 104
Chambers of Commerce of the Irish Free State, Association of, 49
Child Care Facilities for Working Parents, Working Party on, 228, 229
Children's Allowance Act 1944, 93
children's allowances, 93-4, 182, 228
Chubb, Basil, 104
Civil and Public Staff Union, 244
Civil Servants, Society of, 1, 18
civil service, 1-2, 28, 200. see also Irish civil service
 enquiries into, 3-10, 13-16
 examinations, 5, 15
 staff associations, 14-15
Civil Service Alliance, 17, 74, 77, 81, 87, 98-9, 102, 126-7, 155, 157, 158, 160, 166
 and arbitration, 91, 103, 107-10
 and cost-of-living bonus, 93, 112, 114-17, 120-1
 during Emergency, 75
 formed, 97-8
 and Whitley system, 22-3, 24
Civil Service Arbitration Board, 17-19, 20, 26. see also Arbitration Board
Civil Service Benevolent Fund, 36
Civil Service Clerical Association, 33, 34, 37, 39, 102, 103, 110, 121, 139-41, 154, 157-8, 160, 186
 Brennan Commission submission, 71-3
 and decentralisation, 189-90
 High Court action, 141-52
 and non-civil service officials, 83-4
 and regrading, 176-7
 secedes from Federation, 47-8
 split, 182
 and Staff Officers' Association, 98-9
Civil Service Commission, 30, 66, 69, 230-31
Civil Service Commissioners, 169
Civil Service Commissioners Act 1956, 126
Civil Service Committee (Compensation), 28
Civil Service Conciliation and Arbitration Board, 16

Index

Civil Service Court of Appeal Committee, 12
Civil Service Executive and Higher Officers' Association, *see* Executive and Higher Officers' Association
Civil Service Executive Association/Union, *see* Public Service Executive Union
Civil Service Federation, 13, 17, 22, 36, 37, 39, 74
   and arbitration scheme, 40-52
   and Brennan Commission, 49, 54-6
   and promotions, 64-5
Civil Service General Council
   staff panel, 74, 77, 101-5, 132, 139-41, 144-6, 218, 221, 245-6
Civil Service Guild, 36
Civil Service House Association, 36
Civil Service Joint Committee, 48-9
Civil Service Joint Council, 23
Civil Service Journal, 34, 45-6, 48, 81, 90-91, 117
   on arbitration, 40, 51, 106
   on non-civil servant officials, 85-6
   on union duties in official time, 80
Civil Service Library Association, 33, 97
Civil Service Organisations, Joint Committee of, 37-9
Civil Service Regulation Act, 126
Civil Service Representative Council, 45-6, 51, 56, 60
Civil Service Review, 77, 87, 91, 98, 136, 137, 138-9, 166, 173
   on arbitration, 154
   on children's allowances, 93
   cost of, 92
   on court case, 150-52
   on decentralisation, 186, 187, 188
   on equal pay, 185-6
   on promotions, 171
Civil Service Spouses and Children's Scheme, 233
Civil Service (Stabilisation of Bonus) (Amendment) Regulations 1942, 118
Civil Service (Stabilisation of Bonus) Regulations, 74-5
Civil Service Staff Officer, 100
Civil Service Staff Officers' Association, 74, 97
Civil Service Supply Stores, 36

Civil Service Training Centre, 230, 267, 268
Civil Service (Transferred Officers) Compensation Act 1929, 30, 74
Clann na Poblachta, 110
Clann na Talmhan, 110
Clarke, D. N., 140
Clerical Officers' Union, 182
Closing the Gap (White Paper), 128-9
Coillte Teoranta, 254
Colclough, Carmel, 246
Colley, George, 227
Collins, J., 103
Collins, General Michael, 42
Collins, Sir William, 18
Comhaltas Cana, 140, 211, 233
Commission of Inquiry into the Civil Service, *see* Brennan Commission
competition, open, 3-4
conciliation, *see* arbitration and conciliation
Congress of Trade Unions, 91
Connick, Patrick, 141, 146
Conroy, Judge J. C., 157
Cooke, R. N., 159
Córas Iompair Éireann (CIE), 131
Corish, Brendan, 186
Cosgrave, Liam, 159, 222
Cosgrave, Maurice, 145-7
Cosgrave, W. T., 42-3
cost-of-living bonus, 26-7, 52-8, 111-21, 163-4
 during Emergency, 74-5
Cost of Living Index Figure, Committee on the, 53
Costello, Declan, 159
Costello, John A., 77, 107, 110
Costelloe, P., 123
Coutts, Professor J. A., 104
Coyne, Father, 104
creche facilities, 215, 229-30
Crowley, P., 77
Cumann na nGaedheal, 48
Customs and Excise Indoor Staff Association, 244

Index

D
Daly, John, 208-9, 232
D'Arcy, J., 246
Davitt, Justice, 103
de Paor, S., 257
de Valera, Eamon, 49, 106
decentralisation, 131-2, 134, 186-9
　submission to PSORG, 194
Degombe, J., 225-6
Delaney, W., 101
Dempsey, A. P., 77
Dempsey, J. F., 190
Desmond, Barry, 223
Desmond, Noel, 246
Devine, C., 141, 227, 245
Devlin, Liam St J., 190
Devlin report, 122, 134-5, 189-99, 254-5, 266
　on grades, 200
　submissions to group, 190-7
Districts Board Staff, 49
Dolan, J., 157
Donnellan, Maureen, 141, 245, 246
Dooney, Malachy, 146, 157, 158, 160, 181
Doyle, J. G., 125, 135
Doyle, Noel, 212-14
Dublin Trades Union Council, 232
Duffy, Justice Gavan, 116

E
Eason, J. C. M., 103
Education, Department of, 68, 134, 166, 187, 194
Electricity Supply Board (ESB), 129, 131, 165
Emergency, The, 74-5, 88-90, 93, 108-9
Emergency Powers Act 1939, 74, 119
Emergency Powers Orders, 57, 75, 112
Employer-Labour Conference, 219
Employment Equality Agency, 231
Employment Exchange Managers' Association, 33
equal pay, 182-6, 203, 204-5, 206, 218-19, 222-8
Equal Pay, Interim Report of Commission on, 219

equality legislation, 212, 215, 218-31
   seminars on, 230
ESB Manual Workers' Arbitration Board, 104
ESB Salaried Staff Association, 163
Established Attendants' Association, The, 33
establishments division, 15-16
Estate Duty Office, 139
European Community (EC), 200, 204, 224, 225-6
   union organisation, 238
Evening Herald, 188-9
Evers, J. S., 101
exchequer protection clause, 124
Executive and Higher Officers' Association, 82, 87, 122-3, 164. *see also* Public Service Executive Union
   affiliation with ICTU, 134, 138, 165-6
   annual reports, 79, 88-9, 91, 93, 96-7, 122-4, 125-9, 130-31, 134, 137-9, 170-71, 181-2, 187, 198-202
   and arbitration, 122-4
   and Civil Service Alliance, 97-8
   and decentralisation, 186-9
   and equal pay, 182-6
   and equality, 218-22
   and grades reorganisation, 175-82
   and High Court action, 141-52
   membership controversy, 94-5
   name changes, 198
   number of members, 36, 96, 135, 232
   organisation, 79-81, 135-9, 232
   and pay freeze, 131-4
   post of secretary, 84-7
   and promotions, 89-90, 127-8, 166-71
   submissions to PSORG, 190-7
   treasurers' reports, 92, 135
executive officers
   role of, 68-71
Executive Officers' Association *see* Executive and Higher Officers' Association
External Affairs, Department of, 96

F

Faherty, Eoin, 214-17
Farrell, W. J., 102, 103, 139-41, 146, 157, 160
FÁS, 254
Fawsett Association, 11, 33
Federated Union of Employers (FUE), 126, 129-30
Federated Union of Government Employees, 244, 246
Federated Workers' Union of Ireland (FWUI), 229
Feeney, Brenda, 229
Female Clerks, Female Typists and Intermediate Clerks, Association of, 17
Fianna Fáil, 41, 48, 49, 54, 82, 110
  and arbitration, 91, 107
  'cuts committee', 52-3
  and equality legislation, 227
Finance, Department of, 29, 79, 81-2, 102-3, 138, 182, 215, 233, 254, 269
  and arbitration scheme, 40, 42-52, 107-9, 124-5, 149
  and bonus schemes, 112-21
  and Brennan Commission, 31-2
  and decentralisation, 134, 187, 194
  and Department of the Public Service, 198-9
  grades, 68, 70, 83, 139, 193
  and grades reorganisation, 141, 175-82
  and McKenna award, 157, 158, 162
  and non-civil servant union officials, 83-7
  and promotions, 67, 89-90, 169
  and PRSI, 217-18
  recognition of associations, 99-100
  and salary scales, 59-60, 126
  and staffing, 248
Finance Bill 1939, 112
Fine Gael, 82, 91, 110, 162
  and equality legislation, 222-7
First Division Civil Servants, Association of, 18
Fitzgerald, Gene, 248
Fitzgerald, L. M., 146, 157, 190
Fitzpatrick, Brian, 232, 233
Foras Áiseanna Saothair (FÁS), 254
Foreign Affairs, Department of, 137, 243
Foster, Michael, 232, 246

In Public Service

Friendly Societies, Registrar of, 234
Fulton Commission, 1
Fulton report, 199

G
Gaffey, Peter, 190
Gaffey, Seamus, 146
Gannon, S., 157
general elections
    1932, 48
    1937, 81
    1938, 107
    1943, 91
    1977, 226-7
Geoghegan, Hugh, 246
George V, King, 17
Geraghty, Thomas, 232
Gillespie, Richard, 200-02
Gladstone, W. E., 3
Gosling, Harry, 18
Government Employees' Federation, 101, 110, 155, 160
Government Minor Grades' Association, 37
Griffin, Matt, 223
Guinness and Co., 165

H
Halliday, R. N., 160
Hannigan, William, 232, 235
Hanon, Robin, 229
Harrington, Denis, 146
Haughey, Charles, 189
Head Postmasters Association, The, 33
Headen, Dympna, 135-7
Health, Department of, 254, 255
Hennigan, John, 245
Heron, Archie, 47, 82, 83
Hickey, Des, 199-200
Higher Civil Servants, Association of, 74, 96, 101, 121,
    244, 254
    and equal pay, 218

282

Index

and IPA, 171
Higher Officers of Customs and Excise, 243
Hobhouse, Postmaster, 17
Hollingsworth, Samuel, 141, 146
Holt Committee, 12
Horan, P., 101
Horgan, J. C., 135, 139, 155-6, 157, 160, 181
hours of work, 16-17, 26
  during Emergency, 75-6, 93
  five-day week, 130, 174
Hughes, T. J., 37-8, 82
Humphreys, W. A., 11-12, 19-20

I
Igoe, T. K., 101
income tax, 123, 206, 207, 211
Industrial Relations, Commission on, 209
Industrial Relations, Diploma in, 263
Industrial Relations Acts, 132-3
Industry and Commerce, Department of, 68, 80, 81-2, 126-7, 254, 269
Ingram, J., 103-4
Inland Revenue Associations, 12
Inland Revenue Service, UK, 66
Inland Revenue Stamping Department Association, 33
Inspectors of Taxes, Association of, 33, 101
insurance schemes, 131, 134, 206, 217-18, 233
Intermediate Education Established Clerks' Association, 33
International Labour Organisation (ILO), 237
Irish Bank Officials Association, 77
Irish Civil Aviation Radio Officers Union, 97
Irish civil service, 127
  clerical structure, 71-3
  cost of, 210
  grades, 174-82, 192-3, 200
  numbers employed, 31-2, 78-9, 94, 122, 210-11, 214-15, 216-17, 247
  organisation, 247-54
  recruitment embargo, 210-11, 212, 213, 214-15, 216-17, 248-50

reform proposed, 212
and social welfare, 76-8
temporary recruitment, 30
transferred officers, 29-30, 59-60
Irish Congress of Trade Unions (ICTU), 134, 138, 164-6, 201, 204-5, 206, 210, 217, 231, 232, 252
and equality legislation, 219, 222-5, 227-8
and pay freeze, 131, 132-3
and taxation, 211
and union rationalisation, 236-40
Irish Customs and Excise Union, 218, 232, 244, 245, 247
Irish Government Workers' Union (Minor Grades), 54
Irish Labour History Society, 232
Irish language, 212-13
Irish Local Government Officials' Union, 117
Irish National Teachers' Organisation (INTO), 77, 163, 223
Irish Post Office Clerks, Association of, 18-19, 33
Irish Post Office Controlling Officers' Association, The, 33
Irish Post Office Engineering Union, 101, 110, 139-40, 155, 157, 158, 160, 181, 257
and Arbitration Board, 104
Irish Postal Union, 33
Irish Postal Workers' Union, 33
Irish Professional Civil Servants' Association, 101
Irish Shipping, 165
Irish Tax Officials Union, 244
Irish Waterguard Customs and Excise Federation, The, 33

J
job-sharing, 214, 229
Johnson, Thomas, 32, 42-3
Johnson Committee, 54, 56-7
Joint Whitley Councils, 22-3
Jones, Pauline, 229
Junior Officers, Association of, 33
Justice, Department of, 68, 79

K
Kane, D. A., 36
Kavanagh, Liam, 247-8

Index

Keane, Joe, 218
Kelly, J., 80, 113
Kenny, Justice, 142-3, 146-52
Keyes, M. G., 101
King, Frederick C., 105, 157

L

Labour, Department of, 228, 229-30, 233, 242
Labour, Royal Commission on, 11
Labour Court, 132-3, 199, 209
Labour Gazette, 27
Labour Party, 48, 54, 82, 131, 162
  and arbitration, 91
  inter-party government, 110
Land Commission, 35, 36
Lands, Department of, 134, 187-8, 194
language teaching, 90
Larkin, James, 237
Law Union and Rock Insurance Co. Ltd, 131
Leahy, Professor P., 190
Lemass, Seán, 126, 129, 163
Leydon, John, 82
Linehan, M. P., 77, 163
Linehan, Thomas P., 78-9
Liston, T. K., 157
Local Government, Department of, 254
Local Government and Public Health, Department of, 68
Local Government Auditors, Association of, 101
Lonergan, Michael A., 102, 111
Lowe, Robert, 3
lower division clerks, 6-9
Lucht Meteoríochta na hEireann, Cumann, 97
Lynch, Jack, 131

M

Mac AnBhaird, Seán, 110
McCann, P., 101
McDonald, Martin, 218, 232
MacDonald, Ramsay, 17-18
MacDonnell Commission, 2, 13-16, 17

McElhinney, P. J., 34
McElligott, J. J., 112-16, 158
MacEntee, Seán, 75, 152, 154, 157, 159, 161
McGamhna, S., 157, 158
McGilligan, Patrick, 110, 162
McGinley, Nabla, 202-5
McKenna, General D., 157, 158
McKenna award, 157-63
McKevitt, Dr, 104
McKevitt, Thomas, 231, 246
McMahon, T., 140
McPartlin, M. J., 101
MacSharry, Ray, 251
Magner, Michael, 135, 137, 138-9, 194
Maguire, Peter D., 246
Maher, John, 103
Maher, Thomas, 194, 198-9
Mannion, L., 160
marriage, 182-3, 204, 212
   discrimination ends, 219-22
   readmission of widows, 126
   salary differentiation, 61, 119
Martin, J., 101
Maternity Protection Act, 228
Maxwell, James, 12
Meade, D., 82
Meade, Michael, 110
Medical Union, 165
Meehan, Sylvia, 223
Micks, Mr, 104
Mills, Michael, 250
Ministers and Secretaries Act 1924, 30-31
Molloy, B., 82
Moore, Justice Kingsmill, 104
Morrissey, D. A., 102, 110, 158
Mortimer, Eddie, 202
Mortished, R. J. P., 104
Mulcahy, General Richard, 110
Murphy, D. F., 77, 141, 164
Murphy, Daniel, 135, 139, 141, 165-6, 223, 231

Index

Murphy, E. J., 140, 146
Murphy, N., 173
Murphy, Paul, 229
Murray, Paddy, 139
Murtagh, Martin, 147-8

N
Nally, Harry, 141, 187, 188
National Council for Educational Awards (NCEA), 264
National Health Insurance Commission Office, 29
National Health Service, UK, 77
National Heritage Council, 258
National Labour Party, 110
National Manpower Service, 203
National Recovery, Programme for, 215, 217
National Understanding 1980, 233
national wage agreements, 126-7, 198, 201-2, 204-5, 209-10, 222
National Wage Recommendation, 133
National Whitley Council, 1, 22-3, 24, 26-7, 42
Nevin, Donal, 223, 227
Nolan, K. J., 134, 194
Northcote-Trevelyn report, 1, 2, 3-4
Norton, William, 48, 78, 82, 83, 158
 and arbitration, 40, 45, 46
 and McKenna award, 159, 160, 162
 Tánaiste, 110

O
Ó Braonain, P. S., 102
O'Brien, James P., 205-6
Ó Brolchain, M., 158
O'Byrne, E. T., 245
O'Callaghan, John, 245
Ó Cleirigh, D. N., 157
Ó Coigligh, S. B., 135
O'Colman, D., 87
Ó Conail, Sean, 209-11, 235
Ó Conaill, D., 84, 99
Ó Conaill, Seamus, 146, 157, 158, 175-6, 254

Ó Conchubhair, D., 87
O'Connell, T. J., 48
O'Doherty, May, 139, 173-4, 178
  and equal pay incident, 182-6
Ó Donnchadra, S., 110
Ó Donnchu, Con, 211-12
O'Donnell, Seán, 173
O'Donovan, J. J., 104
O'Driscoll, D. J., 127
O'Driscoll, M. J., 135
Ó Dubhthaigh, C. S., 102
Offences Against the State Act 1939, 106
Officers of Customs and Excise, Association of, 39
Officers of Employment Branch, Association of, 97
Officers of Executive and Higher Grades, Association of, 3, 23, 33-7, 39, 44, 67-71, 112
  Brennan Commission submission, 58, 61, 64-6
  name change, 79
  subscriptions, 34
Officers of Outdoor Branch, Association of (Social Welfare), 97
Officers of Taxes, Association of, 33, 39, 49
O'Hanlon, R., 246
Ó hEidirsceoil, Seán, 87, 89
O'Higgins, K., 101
Oireachtas, Houses of the, 74, 96-7, 242-3
  pay tribunal, 131-2
O'Keeffe, J., 80
O'Kelly, John J., 101
O'Leary, J. J., 103
Ombudsman, Office of the, 250-51
O'Morain, Michael, 188-9
Ó Muinneacain, Seán, 115
Ó Muirgheasa, Liam, 102, 103, 139, 153, 157, 158, 159-60
O'Muiri, P., 124
O'Quigley, J. B., 77, 87, 101-2, 110, 135, 136, 139, 158, 164
Ordnance Survey Staff Association, 33, 97
Osborne, Mark, 105-6
O'Shea, Patrick, 146
Ó Suilleabhain, Tomas, 110

Index

O'Sullivan, Colm, 114-15, 146, 157
O'Sullivan, D., 104
O'Sullivan, H., 125
O'Sullivan, T., 101, 158
Owens, Evelyn, 223

P

paternity leave, 228, 229
patronage system, 1
Patten, P. F., 80
Pay-Related Social Insurance (PRSI), 217-18
Pay Research Unit, 207
PAYE, 211
Peard, W. A. K. H., 77
pension schemes, 131, 134, 217-18
People's College, The, 232
petition privilege, 2
Playfair, Sir Lyon, 4
Playfair Commission, 2, 4-6, 14, 15
Post, An, 234, 243, 251, 259, 260, 261, 263
Post Office, 17, 27, 29
  accountants' branch, 35-6
  strike, 33
Post Office Accounts Branch, 29
Post Office Clerical Association, 157
Post Office Controlling Officers' Association, 97, 141
Post Office Review Group, 255-63
Post Office Savings Bank, 11, 12
Post Office Workers' Union, 33, 37-8, 54, 78, 83, 87, 101, 110, 140, 145, 154-5, 157, 158, 160, 257
  and Arbitration Board, 103
  and arbitration scheme, 40, 43, 44-8
  and cost-of-living bonus, 112, 116-18, 121
  pay claims, 111, 182-6
Postal and Telecommunication Services Act, 1983, 259
Postal Clerks' Association, 33
Postal Inspectors' Association, 97
Postal Worker, The, 105, 110-11, 117-18
  on McKenna award, 160-61
Postmasters' Association, 97

In Public Service

Postmens' Federation, 33
Posts and Telegraphs, Department of, 49, 234
    Post Office Review Group, 255-63
President, Department of the, 68
Price, T. R., 82
Prison Officers' Association, 97
Probst Efficiency Rating Report, 65-6
Professional and Service Associations, Irish Conference of, 77, 98, 126-7, 129, 163-4
Professional and Technical Civil Servants, Union of, 246
Professional Civil Servants, British Institution of, 37
Professional Civil Servants, Institute of, 33, 38, 49, 101, 110, 157, 158, 160, 166, 254
    and arbitration scheme, 43, 44-8
    and decentralisation, 188, 189
    promotions, 8, 25-6, 60-61, 65-9, 190-91, 207-8, 212
    during Emergency, 89-90, 93
    equalisation scheme, 127-8
    HEOs, 125-6, 130, 166-71
    submission to PSORG, 196-7
Provisional United Trades Union Organisation, 126-7
PSORG, *see* Devlin report
public administration, 94, 263-5, 267-9
Public Administration, Institute of, 171-4, 230, 263-4, 267-9
public relations, 192
Public Service, Department of the, 198-9, 203, 212, 254-5, 264
    and equality, 223, 225, 227-31
    and staffing, 247-8
Public Service, White Paper on, 251
Public Service Advisory Council, 255, 266
Public Service Executive Union, 198, 200-02, 254-5
    annual delegate conferences, 206-18
    and equality, 222-31
    honorary life membership, 235
    image of, 202-3
    membership, 208, 211-12, 218, 233
    mergers with, 218, 232, 243, 245, 247
    office premises, 214, 233, 235

Index

organisation, 231-5
and Post Office Review Group, 258-63
and promotions, 205-8
and recruitment embargo, 248-50
sub-committees, 206, 229
and trade union rationalisation, 240-45
Public Services Organisation Review Group (PSORG), *see*
  Devlin report
Public Works, Office of, 30, 269

Q
Quinlan, T., 257
Quinn, Ruairi, 223, 229

R
Railway Clerks' Association, 77
recruitment, 30, 190
  administrative officers, 128
  submission to PSORG, 194-6
redundancy, 128, 253
Reorganisation Committee, General, 24-5
Reorganisation Committee, Report of, 2
retirement
  compulsory, 204
  early, 216-17, 253-4
Revenue Commissioners, Office of the, 30, 49, 68, 135, 137, 141
Revenue Group of Departmental Associations, 102, 140, 141, 155, 157, 160
Ridley Commission, 2, 7-10, 11, 14
Robinson, J. J., 103
Robinson, Mary, 223
Roe, Judge, 104
Russell, M. P., 80, 82, 112
Ryan, Dr James, 187
Ryan, Richie, 222-6

S
salary scales, 5, 9, 18-19, 25-6, 35, 95-6, 111-21, 133-4, 191, 202, 205-6, 208-9, 214

alterations in, 58-64, 126-7
bonus payments, 74-5. *see also* cost-of-living bonus
'cuts committee', 52-3
equal pay, 182-6
and marriage, 87-8, 119
McKenna award, 157-63
Supercut, 26-7, 53-4, 101
wage freeze, 129-30, 131-2
Schregle, Joannes
Schregle report, 237-8
Seanad Eireann, 164, 223
Seanad Electoral Act, 164
second division clerks, 11-12
Second Division Clerks, Association of, 2, 3, 10, 11, 17, 23
Senate, *see* Seanad Eireann
Serving the Country Better (White Paper), 267
sexual harassment, 231
sick pay, 76
Smithwick, M., 34
Smyth, Joseph, 206-8
social welfare, 206
and civil servants, 76-8
PRSI, 217-18
Social Welfare, Department of, 128
Social Welfare Act 1953, 78
Social Welfare Officers Association, 243
Social Welfare Programme, 203
Social Welfare Supervisors' Association, 97
Spelman Foundation, New York, 66
Spence, Miss H. F., 80
Stabilisation Order, 118
staff associations, 2-3
Staff Clerks and Other Civil Servants, Association of, 18
Staff Officers' Association, 99-100, 139, 181
Stanley, Michael, 135, 176-7
Status of Women, Commission on the, 218, 222
Stokes, Colin, 229
Stratton, S. R., 137
strikes, 10-11, 33, 106, 213
Sullivan, H., 135, 140, 157, 173

Index

Superannuation Act 1834, 134
Superannuation Act 1909, 82
Supplies and Services (Temporary Provisions) Bill 1945, 119
Swallowe, M. F., 102
Sweeney, Garry, 231, 232, 235
Sweetman, Gerard, 157, 163

T
Teachers' Union of Ireland (TUI), 227, 245
Telecom Eireann, 234, 251
Telephone Contract Officers' Association, The, 33
Temporary Clerks' Association, 97, 100
Third Secretaries, Association of, 243
Thomas, Dave, 217-18, 246
Thompson, Lt Gen Sir Geoffrey, 190
Tomlin Commission, UK, 69
trade disputes, 233-4
Trade Disputes Act 1906, 233
Trade Union Acts, 2, 10, 134-5, 233, 236, 243
trade unions, 10, 203-4
  within civil service, 33-9
  functions of, 200-01
  rationalisation, 212, 213, 215, 235-45
  recognition of, 234
  right of membership, 215
Trade Unions, Congress of, 91
Trades Union Council, 91
training, 25, 192, 213, 215-16, 230
  staff development, 263-9
transferred officers, *see under* Irish civil service
Transferred Officers (Compensation) Act 1929, 120
Transferred Officers Protection Association, 121
transfers, 5-6, 75-6
Transport and Power, Department of, 135, 166, 254, 255
Transport Workers' Federation, 18
Trinity College, Dublin (TCD), 94, 264
tuberculosis, 76, 93
Tucker, C. J. 194
Tunney, C. J., 157
Twohig, Sheila, 183

U
United Nations Covenant, 191
University College Dublin (UCD), 264-5

W
Wages Standstill Order, 118-19
Welby, Sir R. E., 7
Whitaker, T. K., 158
Whitley, J. H., 20, 22
Whitley Councils, 14, 19-23, 40, 41-3, 60-61, 105-6
   road to, 16-19
Wigg-Cochrane case, 29-30
women civil servants, 25, 31, 68, 212, 215. *see also* equal
     pay; equality legislation
   association for, 49
   as clerks, 12, 18-20, 26, 71-2
   maternity leave, 228
   salary scales, 18-19, 61
   superannuation, 81-2
   training course, 215-16
   under-representation, 212, 214
   widows, 126
Women Civil Servants' Advisory Board, 183-4, 185
Woods, F. J., 130, 131-2, 137
World War I, 13-14, 19-20, 26, 30, 40
World War II. see Emergency, The
Wylie, W. E., 28, 104